THE BIG DEAL

THE BIG DEAL

Hollywood's Million-Dollar
Spec Script Market

THOM TAYLOR

WILLIAM MORROW AND COMPANY, INC.

NEW YORK

Library of Congress Cataloging-in-Publication Data

Taylor, Thom, 1962–
    The big deal : Hollywood's million-dollar spec script market /
Thom Taylor.
        p.   cm.
    Includes index.
    ISBN 0-688-16171-5 (alk. paper)
    1. Motion picture authorship.   I. Title.
PN1996.T32   1999
808.2'3—dc21   98-48054
                                                                    CIP

Printed in the United States of America

First Edition

1   2   3   4   5   6   7   8   9   10

BOOK DESIGN BY JO ANNE METSCH

www.williammorrow.com

To my father,
for his courage and his faith

Acknowledgments

ANY EFFORT TO chronicle the process of filmmaking—the most collaborative of the arts—relies on the wisdom, acumen, and experience of its participants, many of whom kindly offered interviews for this book. There are a number who lent help to the writing of *The Big Deal* in extraordinary ways.

Special thanks go to Stephanie Argy, Tim Ballou, Ben Bellinson, Lisa Chambers, Anne Cole, Nichola Ellis at Bumble Ward & Associates, Alex Epstein, Glenda Ganis, Christian Garton, Jeff Gordon and Writer's Boot Camp, Andrew Judge, Mark Litwak, Noah Lukeman, Tom Quinn, Gregory Solman, Shari Wendt, Kris Williams, Craig Williamson, Rochelle Winters at Smoke & Mirrors, Travis Wright, and David Wyatt.

I am also indebted to the late Brandon Tartikoff for his early support of my manuscript; to Clark Moffat for putting up with my middle-of-the-night phone calls; to my friend and mentor Laurence Becsey (an agent strong in all the "Three *A*s" you will find at the end of chapter 7); to the joyful Eric Brown for his endless hours of interview transcription; and to my editor at William Morrow, Katharine Cluverius, for her valuable and laborious guidance in shaping this work for publication.

The "cast of characters" in the chapters profiling each individual spec script sale are identified by their roles at the time of a particular script's sale. A more comprehensive biography of their current career status is listed in the Appendix.

Ultimately, this book depended on the contributions of those who had the power to say yes in a business all too accustomed to deferring to the negative. It is with your largesse that this work was ever attempted and completed.

—THOM TAYLOR

Contents

Introduction

WHOEVER HAS MADE an effort to create a motion picture—and that includes anybody who has succeeded—will contend that the process is a Sisyphian task of constantly pushing a granite boulder until it overcomes the movie mountain's crest.

Then it can't be stopped.

The course of getting a script to screen is an enigmatic exercise that requires assembling a large number of talented individuals with sometimes differing agendas while working within often constraining budgets. Once going, it can be as difficult to contain as a tornado, with clashing egos—often observed by a distracting media and pushy paparazzi—serving as a reminder that collaboration and compromise are vital to the end result.

Hollywood's image of stretch limousines, with dazzling stars at elegant premieres, is maintained by manila envelopes, stand-by messengers, high-speed xeroxing, and waiting by the telephone. And at any movie's core lies its screenplay, one of Hollywood's most precious commodities.

With a different dynamic at play, the selling of a screenwriter's dream is an altogether distinct process from making a movie. For those involved in the script-selling game, the passion to sell, and not necessarily the vision to create, becomes a paramount desire. In other words, the deal is the sex, and the movie is the cigarette.

The following pages take you on a journey into Hollywood's script-buying game. Its playing field includes a cast of studio executives whose reliance on purchasing, rather than generating, original material has elevated the value of the "spec script" (written on speculation that a studio will purchase the script) to unprecedented sums.

The Big Deal: Hollywood's Million-Dollar Spec Screenplay Market looks at how the players operate in a *Melrose Place* movie world of back-stabbing and fickle hearts. Through a number of examples, *The Big Deal* illustrates how the entertainment industry works, and why it came to be the way it is today. Several key turns in the Hollywood business cycle affect the movies that we as an audience pay for. The audience response again changes the movies that Hollywood chooses to make. This book connects many of its disjointed dots.

The Big Deal delves into the backstories of several spec screenplays that played a part in changing the environment for future purchases. It evolved from an article that screenwriter Patrick Sheane Duncan, who made $4.5 milion in spec sales over a two-year span from such screenplays as *Mr. Holland's Opus* and *Courage Under Fire*, proposed I write for his magazine, and it involves interviews with many of Hollywood's top decision makers.

Rather than attempt to create a "how-to" book of an ultimately inexplicable process, I gathered the insights of the industry's players to construct a "how-it-is" behind-the-scenes analysis of the often perverse, occasionally hilarious, and always high-stakes game that today's studios play.

Perhaps no other industry relies so much on impetuous decisions that can result in such radically different outcomes, as well as having such dramatic impact on the lives and livelihoods of all involved, including the films' viewers. Motion pictures move us, as a culture, with a power to shape our thinking and being. Filmmaking is an art form that simultaneously reflects and propels pop culture.

When a studio purchases a screenplay, it can pluck a writer out of obscurity and thrust him or her into the limelight. It's often said that "success has many fathers, and failure is but an orphan," yet something can be learned from the lineage of every story. Included herein are firsthand observations from participants involved in the spec market's "contact sport," as well as those who shape the scripts and make the writers' dreams become realities.

The Big Deal examines how fear drives today's moviemaking process, and provides a candid look at the lucrative screenwriting trade from the buyer's perspective. Five chapters fully detail the journeys of very distinct screenplays, which were each sold and developed in very different ways. The spec scripts *While You Were Sleeping, Seven, In the Line of Fire, Last Action Hero,* and *Waterworld* are each part of Hollywood legend but could just as well have been any other screenplay that came over the Hollywood transom. Their backstories provide examples of the real-life dramas that go on daily in the land of creating make-believe.

It is important to point out that all movies are made of many puzzle pieces fitting together. A decision for one company to "pass" on a script that becomes a hit for another may have been, in fact, the correct business decision. After all, had a different buyer purchased a given script, the picture would have been made differently or, in many of the cases, not made at all. Such projects could have easily wound up "in development," therefore never seeing the screen.

Beginning when "the million-dollar script" first became a Hollywood buzzword, this book features the war stories, the fun-filled anecdotes, the indelible scandals, and many tales of overnight success—invariably preceded by years of preparation and anticipation—while examining the mystifying process behind the movie's curtain. The journey of each spec sale shows the play-by-play process of its construction.

After all, every script sold has another story behind it.

—THOM TAYLOR
Los Angeles, 1999

THE BIG DEAL

The Lure of the Million-Dollar Script

WHERE IS THE WIZARD IN TODAY'S HOLLYWOOD?
AND HOW DOES HE CREATE THE WONDERFUL ILLUSIONS
THAT HE DOES?

A genius is one who shoots at something that no one else can see, and hits it.

—UNKNOWN

SNOW BLANKETED THE tarmac at New York's JFK airport while all hell broke loose back in Burbank, California. Stuck incommunicado on an obstructed runway, Bruce Berman grew increasingly aggravated while he shifted in his first-class seat aboard United Airlines's Flight 7. Berman, then Warner Bros. president of production, utilized his phone in the way Hollywood's top executives do, as if it were an implement in the war of deal making before one's enemy gets the chance to bear arms.

On this snowbound February Friday, Berman, the key Warner executive capable of granting the $1 million bid on a script, could not be reached. Berman was returning from the other coast after attending a memorial for Steve Ross, a legendary media executive who had originally made his fortune in the funeral business. But it was as the architect of the Time, Inc. and Warner Communications merger that Hollywood would memorialize the silver-haired mogul.

While Berman stared at the snow pounding outside his window, the security procedures prevented him from leaving the airplane to check on the studio; what if he were a bomb-planting terrorist? Nor could the Warner production chief use his cell phone on the tarmac; frequencies might get jammed. Nor could he operate the plane's phone until he was air-bound. Nothing to do but wait as more snow continued to pour.

Meanwhile, phone lines at the William Morris Agency in Beverly Hills were buzzing on overdrive as agent Alan Gasmer fielded call after call. A natural-born salesman, Gasmer knew he had a hot script burning through town, causing a long-standing rivalry to emerge between Burbank's brethren studios, Walt Disney and Warner Bros. Adrenaline levels rise throughout town with a spec script's sale, an often frenetic process of pushing and pulling, which can culminate in seven-figure deals once the dance ends.

At the center of this particular bidding war were 128 pieces of paper, a character-oriented historical adventure about the father of modern stage magic, Frenchman Robert Houdin (after whom America's Houdini named himself). Envisioning it as another *Raiders of the Lost Ark,* Disney hungered to acquire the property, and with interest potentially brewing from Universal, Steven Spielberg's Amblin Entertainment, TriStar, and other buyers, Warner Bros. faced a high probability of being left out of the game. The screenplay's writers, the husband and wife team of Lee and Janet Scott Batchler, pulled over at various pay phones every fifteen minutes along their way to a three-day writers' group seaside outing.

Gasmer used his inability to reach his new clients to the bidding war's advantage. "Okay, how about this." Anxious studio executives would toss in offers for a script that quickly attracted Sean Connery to star and Spielberg's long-time producer, Frank Marshall, to direct. "And tell your clients to stay on the phone."

"I'm going to have to wait until my clients call in," Gasmer happily and honestly replied. "I can't reach them." The Batchlers' frequent stops at pay phones extended what would normally be a four-hour drive up the California coast to nine.

Jay Stern, a former New York location manager who had landed an executive position at Disney's Hollywood Pictures, latched on to the Batchlers' script like a pit bull. Before the days when every story editor in town feverishly tracked scripts about to enter the market, Stern had directly heard about this large-scale action-adventure from Alan Gasmer over lunch the previous week at the Beverly Hills' industry hot spot, The Grill. "Sounds great. Please, I want to get this," Stern beseeched, his appetite whetted. "That's one I would really, really like to get my hands on."

The screenplay first arrived in Stern's Disney office in Burbank late Tuesday afternoon. After returning to his West L.A. home at around 11 P.M., Jay watched the news. Planning to read the first forty pages before catching his sleep, Stern couldn't stop until he was finished. By page 128, Stern was anxious to acquire the property, strategizing his following morning's game plan. As is the industry's standard practice, a Disney reader also covered the script overnight to provide a shorthand analysis Stern could submit to his bosses, then Hollywood Pictures president Ricardo Mestres and studio chieftain Jeffrey Katzenberg.

Before the next day's commute to work, Stern picked up his phone to dial Gasmer and also left messages with Interscope and Cinergi; scripts were on their way by messenger. Because of the project's epic nature and megabudget scope, Disney—then in an austerity phase—would enlist one of these studio-aligned production companies to split the costs.

At 9 A.M. every Wednesday morning, Hollywood Pictures executives gathered for a weekly bagel-and-fruit-filled story meeting in an airy boardroom of the Team Disney building. "This is a big movie, this is definitely going to sell, and probably for a lot of money," Stern announced to Katzenberg and his subordinates, all mouse ears. "A master magician goes to Algeria to debunk the sorcerers; it's an original idea, and it's well executed. I think it's distinctive and has great potential."

Mestres began reading the script that morning and agreed with Jay's assessment. Rarely would a studio find an action picture with the character relationships this one offered: a love triangle between the famous magician, his coquettish wife, and the fearless American in the French Foreign Legion who romances her. Castable with a capital *C*.

By then Tom Lassally, a prominent executive at Warner Bros., was just as hot on the material. Ricardo Mestres over-nighted the script overseas to Andrew Vajna, Cinergi's illustrious Hungarian owner, while Stern did his best to find out Warner's take on the material. It would determine what William Morris wanted from the deal.

"I'm looking for a million," Gasmer told the interested parties by Friday as the script's simmer turned to a boil. And Stern began to sweat.

"TriStar was supposedly circling," Stern recalls. "What TriStar did was get it to Wolfgang Petersen [the studio-based German director of *Das Boot,* who would later direct Clint Eastwood in *In the Line of Fire*]. One of the things that studios do is slip it right away to directors or stars. That's *always* been done. I don't know if they got an answer from Wolfgang, but it was Friday afternoon and I knew that Bruce Berman was unreachable. I actually heard that he was stuck on the tarmac. I was concerned that as soon as Lassally reached Berman and had the conversation, they would just put a million dollars on the table."

The heat generated by Burbank's burning inferno seemed to quell that nasty East Coast snowstorm. And as Berman cleared for take-off, Disney's Mestres and Cinergi's Vajna agreed to split fifty-fifty on the development costs. Snapping up the project, along with a "blind-script" commitment that the Batchlers would later write, Disney and Cinergi plunked down the money.

The screenplay's title: *Smoke and Mirrors.*

By the time Warner Bros.' Berman could check on the status, the screenplay had sold. Hollywood Pictures' Mestres promptly showed *Smoke and Mirrors* to Frank Marshall, Mike Ovitz's former UCLA fraternity brother, who dabbled in magic himself and directed the studio's hits *Arachnophobia* and *Alive.* Although Marshall had recently signed an overall producing and directing deal with Paramount, he wanted to bring *Smoke and Mirrors* to the screen.

Meanwhile, Cinergi chieftain Andy Vajna gave the script to his friend, Sean Connery. The former James Bond agreed to take the role of Houdin, the famous magician wooed by his government to Africa to join the French Foreign Legion in defeating a powerful sorcerer of false magic. Stern's acquisition of the hot property helped earn him a promotion to vice president.

Lee and Janet Scott Batchler, who originally met at an all-night Dungeons & Dragons party at their Bel-Air church, had a lot to celebrate. They enjoyed a wonderful three-day weekend on California's central coast, treating their writers' group to dinner. Broke at the time, they had to borrow the money, but their friends didn't doubt they were good for it.

But the *Smoke and Mirrors* title proved to be a premonition. The script was rewritten and now languishes in what's commonly known as "development hell," a fate suffered by over 85 percent of studio-purchased spec scripts. While the project achieved the almost unheard-of "go movie" status within only three weeks of its purchase, with a then $60 million-plus budget (which would run over $100 million today), ensuing mounting costs from preproduction trips to Morocco and Tunisia, as well as expensive rewrites to sharpen the characters' voices, led to the project's collapse. Connery desired more work on the script, and Paramount topper Sherry Lansing wanted Frank Marshall back at her studio (where he would later direct *Congo*). Momentum lost, and now with millions of dollars in studio expenditures against it, the ashen script may always remain an illusion.

Eager as ever to work with the writers, Warner Bros. hired the Batchlers to script *Batman Forever,* the latest installment in what the Warner executives referred to as "their biggest corporate asset." Bruce Berman approached the amiable couple at the *Batman Forever* Westwood premiere, recalling the *Smoke and Mirrors* screenplay that had brought them together.

"That should have been our movie." Berman smiled under the klieg lights. "I would have made it."

Feeding on Frenzy

HOW THE SPEC BUYING PROCESS EMERGED, AND WHY THE BOTTOM-LINE FOCUS OF TODAY'S HOLLYWOOD DOMINATES ITS DECISIONS

It's not who you know. It's who knows you.
—THE GENUINE SECRET TO HOLLYWOOD SUCCESS

DURING HOLLYWOOD'S EARLY stages, the movie moguls were kings of their day whose decisions guided the entertainment that their studios brought to the masses. The moguls wielded immense and feared power, ruling over their domain with often autocratic control. Yet filmmaking has always been a collaborative process comparable to assembling an army for war, so the moguls' chosen producers would handpick their soldiers from the studio's stable of writers, directors, and actors.

Many things changed in Hollywood when "the studio roster system" dissolved, primarily attributed to Olivia de Havilland's successful legal challenge to her Warner Bros. contract in 1945. From that point on, creative personnel began to freelance their talents. The 1948 Paramount decision, a landmark case requiring studios to divest their theater operations, as well as the advent of television, tore away at the studios' oligopolistic reign and contributed to their weakened role.

In today's studio environment, a writer's material must wind its way through a massive labyrinth of noise and confusion, a collective industry primal scream that can often drown out the screenwriter's voice. But an original spec screenplay remains the easiest entry into Hollywood's game and can lead to gratifying bidding wars and huge paydays.

However inadvertently, the 1988 Writers Guild of America (WGA) strike prompted Hollywood's current fascination with spec material. The writers who normally took studio assignments were not getting work during the strike and thus returned from picket lines to toil on their specs. Technically, writers were not even supposed to write on spec. But who plays a slave to the rules?

Five and a half months later, when the strike ended, just as the studios' pipelines were drying up, the agents waited a discreet period before slowly flooding the studios with fresh material. A "spec boom" erupted, offering an unprecedented entry for writers into the studios' previously guarded gates. Feeding on the studios' desperation, the agents drove up the price of script sales, and a new system of business resulted. The security of Hollywood's bygone era no longer remains, but has been replaced by the insecurities of a new studio system that feeds off the screenwriters' original material.

"In the last several years, you hear of many writers getting a million dollars. That's a recent phenomenon," says showbiz veteran Stu Robinson, a partner at Paradigm Literary & Talent Agency, whose career included brokering such deals as *Slap Shot* and *E.T.: The Extra-Terrestrial*. "It's the way it *should* have been since day one. But now a spec sale for a million dollars doesn't have people falling on the floor and hitting their heads. It's almost routine."

One need only glance at *Daily Variety* or *The Hollywood Reporter* to be constantly reminded that there is proverbial gold in Hollywood's hills. When *Lethal Weapon* scribe Shane Black's *The Last Boy Scout* sold in 1990 for $1.75 million, pundits thought the bubble had burst. Within a few years, Black more than doubled his previous sale with *The Long Kiss Goodnight* in a closely watched bidding spectacle. When potential buyers gathered in a boardroom at International Creative Management to ask what Black wanted, his agent David Greenblatt slid a piece of paper across the table with nothing on it but "4." New Line Cinema added the six zeroes to purchase Black's spec script.

The ground underlying Hollywood studios raised Richter scales even higher when *Basic Instinct* writer Joe Eszterhas penned but a five-page outline for *One Night Stand* to New Line Cinema for $2.5

million up front, with another $1.5 million on production (Eszterhas subsequently removed his name from the final credits). Throw in pitches—stories told verbally—such as the $1 million paid to *Back to the Future* author Bob Gale for the comedy-fantasy *In Control;* the $3 million offered Will Davies for his *Fool on the Hill* comedy treatment; the $2.25 million given to relative newcomer M. Night Shyamalan for his spec script *The Sixth Sense,* given a production green light on its purchase; and the $8.5 million two-picture deal that unproduced writers Brandon Camp and Mike Thompson received for their *Steinbeck's Point of View* spec script, and the studio floors continue to shake.

By touting their big deals, Hollywood decision makers have effectively given agents justification to up the ante when going out with new scripts. "It's self-perpetuating in that the more we read about these big spec sales, the more agents want to deliver that," says Barri Evins, president at Debra Hill Productions. "More clients want it. Writers want it delivered for them." Those in the industry respond to big sale flurries by continually making an effort to top them. After all, the big deals are sexy.

"Part of it is that in the 1980s, a tremendous amount of pitches were sold, and studios did not know how to develop them into successful projects and viable movies," Evins contends. "Now it's not as easy to set up a pitch, because the studios found it didn't really pay off for them. At least with a spec, we see what we've got here. We have a whole script." Such scripts possess an immediate value in the marketplace, and the search for a "hot spec" prevails as one of Hollywood's more inextricable occupations.

In today's technology-based society, where consumers are bombarded with media in all its forms, continued advances affect the market feeders directly, with computers, Internet providers, and fax machines linking the whole "information well" of ideas. Perhaps that is the primary reason why spec scripts can now sell in a few hours when it used to take a few days, and it often has a sorry effect on how the proposed pictures are penned.

"A spec for sale is not written as a movie," says producer and former development executive Nicholas Hassitt. "It's written to be read on the page, to really capture a reader. It's a different style of writing. It's more visual.

"Those are just lottery tickets," Hassitt continues. "Luck of the draw. That's not a career in writing. It's started several and ended several.

There are a lot of people who sold spec scripts a couple years ago who are no longer working in the business."

Any skilled producer beats the bushes to obtain a hot spec, which can ignite fiery sales for massive sums of cold cash. Like gold, silver, or pork belly futures, scripts are optioned, purchased, traded, and abandoned on the market for somebody else to acquire ("put into turnaround" in studio parlance).

Roughly speaking, a spec script's value correlates to how few people have seen it. Fewer eyes mean fewer passes. Similar to the aboriginal notion of a photograph taking a bit of one's soul away whenever snapped, a spec script loses its virginal quality when potential buyers are able to actually read it and form a consensus. The brokers of spec scripts thus elevate their value by hyping the unseen pages, since creating a taste before a script hits the market can lead to feeding frenzies.

Naturally, there were specs before the WGA strike, but it was ten times tougher to sell them back then than today, according to Ron Shusett, cowriter of *Alien* and *Above the Law*. "In those days, you had to get a studio deal, an overall deal. You, and the studio, would option a novel. Or you would bounce twenty ideas off of them, and one of them would say, 'Okay, go write that.' So you were under contract. But you didn't break in so easily. It was very hard to get anybody interested in a spec script."

In the years before the WGA strike, the screenwriter generally had to find a sponsor at the studio to have any script even considered. When Dan O'Bannon, hot off the University of Southern California student film *Dark Star* (which O'Bannon made with the subsequent director of *Halloween,* John Carpenter), and Ron Shusett first met, they worked on the scripts for *Total Recall* and *Alien* at the same time, yet the pictures were made ten years apart.

Without an agent, Shusett and O'Bannon went to a mutual friend who had some contacts at 20th Century–Fox. A production company headed by Gordon Carroll, producer of *Cool Hand Luke;* Walter Hill, who had directed *Hard Times;* and *The Parallax View* screenwriter David Giler had a development deal and proper access to the studio. "And *they* took *Alien* to Fox, and they made the deal," Shusett says. "They just walked right in and Fox optioned it immediately. And the studio started shooting it a year and a half later."

In time, spec sales became more commonplace. David S. Ward's *The Sting,* Chris Matheson and Ed Solomon's *Bill & Ted's Excellent Adven-*

ture, and Shane Black's *Lethal Weapon* were all notable spec sales prior to the 1988 WGA strike. But it was William Goldman's $400,000 sale in 1968 of *Butch Cassidy and the Sundance Kid,* a project that was originally submitted to actors Paul Newman and Steve McQueen, that first brought such tremendous attention to scriptwriting, although Goldman had been a known novelist and screenwriter at the time.

Romancing the Stone's sale made a huge stir in 1979 when a then unknown writer's spec script nabbed $250,000. While scripting *Romancing the Stone,* Diane Thomas, a genial blonde from Michigan, waitressed at Malibu's Coral Beach Cantina and returned to her one-room apartment each night to complete her spec over a nine-month period. Through a friend, she submitted the finished script to agent Norman Kurland, who sent out ten copies to potential Hollywood buyers. Less than a week later, it sold to actor Michael Douglas and Columbia Pictures for a sizable sum that also earned Thomas instant recognition in Hollywood and elsewhere.

Michael Douglas felt that since Thomas was a novice, it actually helped make her work more attractive. "It just had a spontaneity about the writing," a 1985 *Los Angeles Times* interview quoted Douglas as saying. "She was not cautious. The script had a wonderful spirit about it. There was a total lack of fear about the writing." The film's development involved a five-year uphill battle during which the script changed hands from Columbia Pictures to 20th Century–Fox. Douglas finally starred with Kathleen Turner in the 1984 film, directed by Robert Zemeckis. As Diane Thomas said at the time, "Hollywood loves an overnight success. But as everyone knows, it's never overnight."

At age thirty-nine, just a year after Hollywood released her motion picture, Thomas died in a car accident on the rain-slicked Pacific Coast Highway near her Topanga Canyon home. She handed the keys of her new Porsche Carrera to her twenty-seven-year-old boyfriend after they had both been out drinking with another friend. Spinning out of control, Thomas's boyfriend plowed into a power pole at eighty miles per hour, instantly killing her and the other passenger.

A self-proclaimed "hopeless romantic" who was working on Steven Spielberg's 1989 feature *Always* at the time of her death, Diane Thomas left behind a hopeful legacy for sanguine screenwriters to follow their dreams.

CREATING THE ILLUSION

It was literary agents Evartz "Ziggy" Ziegler and Mel Bloom who are most acknowledged as the progenitors of today's spec auctioning process. "Mel Bloom and I got the notion of auctioning scripts after the sale of *Butch Cassidy and the Sundance Kid*," recalls Stu Miller, a literary agent partnered with Bloom in the early 1970s. When the Bloom-Miller Agency announced to the town that they had a spec script, the studios would get a look at it on Friday. On Monday morning, the agency would be open for bidding, thus marking the ostensible birth of the studios' famous "weekend read."

"I've been amused to see what's become of the spec process today," says Miller, who helped Paul Brickman (writer of *Risky Business*) launch his career by auctioning his spec titled *Bloody Harlem*. The script, incidentally, didn't sell, but brought Brickman notice for the quality of his writing. "Much of what gets sold now ranges from terrible to mediocre. I'm not comfortable with the hype that accompanies so many of the submissions, that the buyers may not know what they're getting."

Partnered with Hal Ross, who covered the TV side of their agency, Evartz Ziegler sold *Butch Cassidy and the Sundance Kid* as the modern industry's first notable spec sale, due to its $400,000 price tag. William Goldman stumbled upon the true-life story in the late 1950s and wrote the original script over a Christmas break from teaching at Princeton in 1967.

"That was, as I recall, a situation where a lot of people bid, and Ziggy put that price on it and everybody met it," Ross reminisces in his Brentwood office. "It was the author's decision of who it went to." Under Richard Zanuck's leadership, 20th Century–Fox produced the 1969 box office smash.

"We had a lot of great writers and were representing a lot of publishers," Ross recalls. "I just remember the business being so different when we first started—the relationship with people who were agents and so forth. Irving "Swifty" Lazar was a major agent when we first went into the business, and our offices were in the same building. I remember he was going on vacation. He was visiting a major writer in Switzerland, and I was partnered with Zig."

"Do you mind covering me for the next three or four weeks?" Swifty Lazar then asked.

"No, of course not," Ziggy replied.

"We covered clients for [him] while Swifty went on vacation." Ross breaks into a chuckle. "Can you picture that happening today?"

Not a chance. Today's competitive script market resembles more of a modern-day gladiatorial event, and the Hollywood game's players fight ruthlessly to secure precious material, sometimes courting its authors with false promises.

"Ziegler had a very interesting kind of business," says Mike Medavoy, Chairman of Phoenix Pictures and at the time of the *Butch Cassidy* sale an agent at the powerhouse agency CMA. "His business was basically just writers; he didn't handle actors. Often what happened then was that a piece of material would come in and the big agencies would package it. It wasn't just the material going around, it was the combination of material plus Steve McQueen or Robert Redford or Paul Newman.

"In the early to mid-1970s—'71 through '74—the spec market really started to speed up," says Medavoy, who represented such talents as Steven Spielberg, George Lucas, Francis Ford Coppola, John Milius, and Jane Fonda. "Every other week there was another script out there trying to be sold. But the numbers weren't anywhere near what they are now. I mean, $400,000 for a John Milius script was a lot of money.

"The truth of the matter is that good material determines good movies," Medavoy continues. "The question is: Are they really buying good material, or are people just being basically pushed into it . . . because they think somebody else is interested in it? But people have their own tastes to determine whether something's of value or not. And there's a premium to be paid for a movie that gets made. The problem is, if it doesn't get made."

Hollywood loves to wave its golden carrots to the world. It is, after all, a glamour business and the possibilities of "swinging with the rich" at Beverly Hills parties, as well as having financial security for life, attract most people. The "million-dollar screenplay," a buzzword to rival "high concept" in the hallways of studios and agencies, has become moviemaking's loose equivalent of the California lottery.

"The interesting thing you will find is the minuscule percentage of spec scripts that actually command the kind of dollars and sales that are publicized," says Jonathan Sanger, the producer of *The Elephant Man* and *Without Limits*. "You probably have a better chance of winning the lottery than selling spec scripts for millions of dollars. . . . So this isn't about the way to find great material, I don't think."

Sanger's estimation bears repeating: The WGA reported that between 1985 and 1994 screenwriting accounted for 393 millionaires, while the California lottery provided 1,333 individuals with that golden bank account. Certainly, more people play the lottery than write spec scripts, but the gamble of making the big deal creates a false illusion for hopeful screenwriters. "I think the reasons for a spec sale," says Sanger, "are that it hasn't been seen by a lot of people, that it comes out at the right moment, has some buzz, and people are bidding before they even know what they're bidding for."

"Every time we talk to a new writer we tell them, 'It's not about hitting the lottery. It's not about selling your script for a million dollars. It's what happens afterward,' " says William Morris agent Rob Carlson, who joined forces with Alan Gasmer to sell numerous spec scripts. "Writers come to us and say they want to spec something out, 'What do you think?' We'll say, 'Here's what you should do,' and try to point them. We think more like a studio and have a slate.

"Our business is all about instinct for what we do," Carlson says. "We've sold scripts that have been here a year. We've sold scripts twice. We've sold thirty pages. We've sold treatments. We're vested in it. If it's people who are represented here, we're behind it. It doesn't matter if it sells or not. . . . It may not happen on the first one, but if you're aggressive and work hard at it, it will happen. That's why you write a lot, experiment, and find your niche."

Gasmer adds, "The problem is that most agents don't operate this way. Most agents just shove it out there, they don't read it, they don't say to the writer: 'You know what? Your character doesn't arc.' Or 'This character's got to come in five pages earlier.' " The changes in the market have required agents to operate more like the studios used to. And although specs are sold in completed forms, they still endure a frustrating and complicated studio development process, in which they might go from half-baked to fully baked or to burnt. That is where the studio and filmmakers involved make all the difference. It's rare for any screenplay sold today to appear onscreen in a manner resembling its original form, if it appears at all.

"People who aren't in the business or who are marginally in the business, or who are wannabes, don't really understand how our career came off a movie that never got made," says Janet Scott Batchler of *Smoke and Mirrors.* "But everybody read it."

Husband Lee elaborates, "That's how we got *Batman.*"

FROM ASSIGNMENTS TO SPECS

Prior to the 1990s, a screenplay considered well written, even if, like Paul Brickman's *Bloody Harlem,* it didn't sell, could often get the writer assignments. Oliver Stone's widely praised screenplay for *Platoon* earned him almost a decade of assignments before he could bring that script to screen. The haunting tone of *Platoon* made Stone an obvious candidate for his first assignment, 1978's *Midnight Express,* bringing him an Academy Award for that year's Best Adapted Screenplay. Nowadays, to the chagrin of many screenwriters, someone might land a high rank on studio assignment lists simply from the bandwagon buzz his or her huge sale creates.

During the 1988 WGA strike, the studios faced the dual problem of not being able to develop properties or initiate any new ones. They could, however, purchase spec screenplays written *prior* to the strike that hadn't sold. Thus, studio executives scrambled to purchase near-ready script projects, and high-concept screenplays such as *Duke & Fluffy,* about a cat and dog who turn into human beings, sold for six-figure sums. Executives wandered the hallways, cursing writers and mumbling the casting choices of Arnold Schwarzenegger and Michelle Pfeiffer as the lovable pair of animals. Needless to say, *Duke & Fluffy* never got its green light.

Following the strike, a number of million-dollar screenplays sold, titles ranging from *Texas Lead and Gold* to *The Cheese Stands Alone* to *Hell Bent and Back* to *The Ticking Man.* Every seller tried to outdo each other with a gimmick, and the latter script's submissions included a ticking clock to entice a bidding war. Often the million-dollar moniker was media embellishment; the deals would be backloaded (paid upon commencement of filming) or included the blind-script commitments like the Batchlers made with *Smoke and Mirrors.* Nonetheless, the term "million-dollar script" suddenly had more people both inside and outside moviemaking circles paying attention to specs.

"The spec market is another aspect of how power has shifted from the studios to the agents, which is crazy for the studios," says the bearded Leonard Goldberg, a former Fox president who later produced *Sleeping with the Enemy* and *The Distinguished Gentleman.* "The studios have become these distribution apparatuses. They don't seem to rely on internal development as much as the product driven by a spec script, hyped by very smart agents, who get a bidding war going. In many cases, the script's not even read by anyone who's bidding two million dollars for it. Now the material holds them hostage."

The onset of the spec boom left some profound repercussions. "The spec script business was initially very unrealistic," says Interscope's Scott Kroopf. "It made you feel there was all this action going on. Then you would see these scripts." Studio executives scrambled for whatever material was available, "and someone would acquire it. You'd read the script and go, 'Oh . . . my . . . God,' " summarizing the astonished reactions that many would have to the mediocre material that could attract the big deal.

The musical chairs of studio appointments in the wake of Michael Eisner and Jeffrey Katzenberg's departure from Paramount to Disney on October 1, 1984, also altered the corporate culture; and the ensuing spec boom "changed the face of development a lot, and the economics of the business have really changed," says Kroopf. Whenever a new regime replaced its predecessors, it was a common practice to make a clean sweep of the studio's projects, throwing out the babies with the bath water.

Because such top-level management change meant that a lot of existing projects were abandoned, "you start looking for material that you reckon is closer to being ready to shoot," says Interscope's Kroopf, whose company paid $1.4 million for Patrick Duncan's spec script *Mr. Holland's Opus,* a "low-concept" project made on a modest budget that reaped a fortune (topping $90 million in its lengthy domestic theatrical run).

"When the spec market originally got going," says Kroopf, "people would buy spec scripts if they thought the idea was good, and they would eventually rewrite the writing. A lot of spec scripts are written by lesser-known writers, because that's a way lesser-known writers can get their foot in the door."

Many continue walking through with stellar success. "I think people are starting to trust scripts again as being potentially literate in and of themselves," says Shane Black, whose mid-eighties spec sale of *Lethal Weapon,* when he was fresh out of UCLA's drama program, put him at the start of a new wave of media attention. "People in the studio positions are willing to say, 'Well, we could buy this novel or look at this spec script. Maybe the script has something intelligent to say.'

"I'm not sure, because I don't read the trades really, but my sense is that there are fewer scripts being sold because they can say, 'Oh, it's great, it's *Predator* meets *Die Hard*—it's an *Alien* trapped in a sky-scraper!'" Black continues. "There are people who used to just sit around and do that, because that can be my key to money in Holly-wood. A, B, how do we combine that? It became a joke." Thus, today's Hollywood relies on specs of a less formulaic quality, although the desire for "event" movies remains a studio's goal.

In the mid to late eighties, "the studios wanted those big high-concept action movies," says Jeremy Zimmer, a partner and head of the motion picture department at United Talent Agency. "*Die Hard* became this kind of a movie that, because it was going to be so ex-pensive and because the idea had to be so taut, you could build a whole movie on an idea and an actor. So the script could be this lo-comotive for this huge, at the time, $40 or $50 million enterprise. Now-adays that's nothing."

In his first starring role, former *Moonlighting* star Bruce Willis earned $5 million for the original *Die Hard*. "If Bruce Willis got $5 million, everybody said, 'Okay, we want to do big action movies and we need a concept to hang it on.' I think Joel Silver and his way of producing had a lot to do with it, Joel and (*Waterworld* producer) Larry Gordon's appetite for 'Gimme a good idea,'" Zimmer continues. "Also Katzen-berg, although he wasn't a buyer, was idea ravenous. The spec script market was for the most part an idea market."

The spec market also has to do with stars, Zimmer explains. "All of a sudden you have a big star who is available, and you don't have time to develop a bunch of scripts. You want to take a big shot on a star, and if you bet a million dollars on a script, a star is going to pay atten-tion and read it right away. That's a gold cup."

Interscope's Scott Kroopf concurs. "There was a whole mania of high-concept movies, largely driven by when all those Paramount guys went over to Disney. They brought a lot of their TV training into the film business, and with it, really good ideas that were very effective at the time. The plan was really strategically brilliant at the time, but then the market changed. Talent got more expensive, and it became a mar-ketplace glutted with product. Now the distinction isn't concept any more. The distinction of 'Who's in it?' is more prevalent now, or 'Has this movie been given credibility by the press?' "

Yet underlying any star-driven motion picture is its screenplay, and attaching a star naturally protects the executive. "It's still perceived to be a star-driven business, even though it's proven time and again that whether you have a star or not makes very little difference in terms of whether you have a hit movie," says John Truby, who teaches a popular course on story structure. "If you look at the most popular movies of all time, many of them had *no stars* in them at the time. *Star Wars,* for example."

Likewise, the blockbusters *E.T.: The Extra-Terrestrial, Independence Day, Jurassic Park,* and *Titanic* did not rely on star power. "They still haven't learned their lesson from *Speed* or *Die Hard,*" says screenwriter Patrick Duncan of motion pictures that garnered stratospheric status for Bruce Willis, Keanu Reeves, and Sandra Bullock. "The action movie makes the star, not the other way around."

When the screenwriter embarks on the long and often lonesome journey through Hollywood's land of Oz, it's to sell a dream. And the Lions and Tin Men and Scarecrows one meets along the way better share and love that dream, because it takes a lot of heart, brains, and courage to reach the final destination. When you pull back the curtains, you find that the Wizard isn't a humbug filled with hot air, as Dorothy Gale discovered; it's really you. The once-closed studio system has burst open, and a new world has emerged in which writers are capable of earning millions.

Hollywood's Food Chain: Little Fish Meets Big Fish

In today's "studio system," the process of going from script to screen relies on building a profile at each of the several stages. "You know those cartoons where you have the smallest fish getting eaten by the next bigger one in the food chain? That's exactly what this town is about," says Clark Moffat, a former agent who turned to producing. "Basically, you have the genesis of an idea: a light bulb goes on in somebody's head, a real-life event happens, somebody writes a book or a play, an idea happens. The small fish.

"Then, what you have to do is turn around and sell it through representation: a manager, an agent, what have you," Moffat continues. "They have to sell *themselves*. If they're not good at selling themselves, the material has to sell itself. Then the agent is the buyer, because the agent's looking for clients." The bigger fish.

"The agent turns around and sells it to probably a development executive of some stripe. Depending on which level the agent deals with, it could be an executive VP or a head of a production company. That person reads it, likes it, and calls the agent: 'I'm gonna give it to my boss.' They sell it to the producer." An even bigger fish.

"The producer turns around, sells it to the studio executives. The studio executives huddle together in the Monday morning meeting and decide: 'Are we going to buy it or not?' " Moffat continues. "They flip a coin: 'You owe me because we did that stupid horror movie that you wanted to do,' or 'We really need another Adam Sandler movie because we don't have one after *Water Boy*." And they do their little politics, and for whatever reasons they decide which ones they're going to buy." Let's say the bigger fish bites.

"Then it's in development," says Moffat, describing the pretty large fish swimming at the studio level. "Then you have to sell it to the green-light guy, the president, or the chairman. He's the one who says yea or nay. He has to make that fateful decision, which is an *ominous* decision—I don't envy it—of why you choose one movie over another.

"But that guy, in fear of his job, has to sell it to the stockholders, and at the same time he has to sell it with his own marketing people. They have to sell it to the public. So he has the hardest job, because he has to sell it to the powers that be. 'Is it going to generate enough money to turn a profit?' Stock dividends, or whatever. He has to sell it to the public, which is blood in the sand. Basically that's what Hollywood is: a huge food chain, and it culminates with that guy who has to take that final bite."

In this sense, the audience is the final arbiter. The studios shift their judgments based on audiences' recent response to market offerings while many instinctual and individual decisions must be made along the way.

Writer-producer Ron Shusett (*Total Recall*) adds to the analogy, "But in that sifting-out process, they eliminate a lot of the creativity of the good scripts. Those [stars and directors] who would go for them never read the scripts. You can rarely get them to *read* them, unless you have a contact with them, or you've made a successful movie with them, or your agent's powerful enough to convince them."

Shusett recalls a story Peter Weir, acclaimed director of *Witness* and *The Truman Show,* once told about the development process: "It's frustrating, you sit around and you have these story conferences with the studios, but they go by 'reason' because that seems logical. 'Well, why would this guy rob a bank, and the safe? Why did he steal the money in the safe? His friend was worth millions and he might have loaned it to him.' So Weir would say, 'Because borrowing money isn't *dramatic.* What's great is that he breaks into his friend's office in the middle of the night and betrays his friend by robbing him . . .' and the executives go, 'Well, I don't know. That makes him unlikable, and he's the hero.' 'Then maybe he does something to make up for it in the third act, and it's daring, and it's marginal, you know, it's mixed, it's what the audiences *like,* it makes the hero a complex character.'

"But you can't explain that with logic, only with gut feeling, and with so many executives, that's not their end of it," Shusett concludes. "Yet they *make* it their end of it, they have to, to decide what to do. So I'd say, that's what's wrong with Hollywood. And the people who *are* creative don't *want* to run the studios."

The Sleeper Surprise

A BIRTHDAY PACKAGE AWAITED THE SALE OF *WHILE YOU WERE
SLEEPING* (ORIGINALLY TITLED *COMA GUY*),
a screenplay by Fredric Lebow & Daniel G. Sullivan

Purchased by Caravan Pictures and Hollywood Pictures
MPAA Rating: PG
Director: Jon Turteltaub

*A comedy of errors about a subway toll taker named Lucy
who lusts after a dashing lawyer, Peter Callaghan. When
Lucy saves Peter's life on the subway tracks, he falls into a
coma and the Callaghan family mistakes Lucy for Peter's
fiancée. In turn, Lucy falls in love with Peter's brother,
Jack.*

CAST OF CHARACTERS

Arthur Sarkissian, producer
Jim Crabbe, William Morris agent
Dan Halsted, VP at Hollywood Pictures
David Phillips, Crabbe's colleague at William Morris
Jonathan Glickman, Caravan development exec
Roger Birnbaum, Glickman's boss at Caravan
Joe Roth, chairman of Caravan Pictures

RIDDLED WITH ANXIETY, Dan Sullivan waited outside a frenetic hospital room on one frightening January day. After forty or so uncomfortable hours witnessing his wife Patti's labor pains intensify, Dan
assisted Patti into their blue Nissan Sentra and drove straight to Cedars

Sinai Hospital. Perhaps their baby-to-be refused to make his appearance until the timing was right, but the emerging child had already given its parents a fair share of frustration. After all, Dan had been unemployed for the last year and a half and didn't know how he would provide for his growing family.

"It was a really stressful delivery," the father recalls, as doctors prepared for a cesarean-section delivery. "They had a fetal distress. His heart was in jeopardy. . . . Seven doctors were in there, and they still couldn't get him out. They had the oxygen mask on Patti, and she didn't know what the hell was going on. I didn't know what was going on. I just knew it was bad."

The hospital staff began rushing in with trays. "They had these giant forceps that looked like hedge clippers. They were just yanking on the kid. Oh God, it was awful, just awful." Sullivan stood by helplessly as the newborn's guardian angel suddenly entered the room.

"This big, heavy nurse was walking by," Sullivan remembers.

"Get outta the way! Get outta the way!" she hollered, charging in.

"This big black woman just jumped on Patti's stomach twice, and the baby popped out like a cork. She was intimidating, man. She was *big*. And still I don't even know who she was," Dan wonders. "We never saw her before. We never saw her after. She just came in for that moment and literally popped the kid out. Here we had all these Harvard doctors who couldn't get the baby out."

As Dan Sullivan breathed a heavy sigh of relief, unbeknownst to him, he had just sold a feature film script for what would become the year's number one romantic comedy, *While You Were Sleeping*. Sullivan's generally jovial screenwriting partner received one of Dan's first calls made from the hospital. Fred Lebow congratulated his buddy on two milestones—the latter being one only few fathers, or bachelors for that matter, ever surpass.

"Pick up the trades tomorrow," Fred's somber voice crackled over the phone line. "We're on the cover." Their script sold for enough money to send Danny's boy to the Ivy League school of his choosing.

Today, Sullivan proudly displays bassinet photos of his son cradled next to the *Daily Variety* headline. And while January 13, 1994, marked Dan's great day for new beginnings, his partner Lebow was not quite so overjoyed. Just two days before, Fred's father had died.

"I was still in shivers," Lebow recalls of the moment he got the call with news of their scriptwriting deal. "For me, I feel a lot of bitterness, because it all came too late. And I can't share it with him."

Their path to screenwriting success was paved with potholes. "We were beaten," Sullivan concedes. "We were still going to write, and we knew *While You Were Sleeping* was a real good story. The pitches, we knew, were very, very funny. We knew we had a really strong story. But I didn't think in a million years it would sell. I would have bet my life on it that it wouldn't, actually. How do you figure falling in love with a guy in a coma is commercial? I don't think anybody knows what that is."

"YOU GUYS GOT A DEAL"

Dan Sullivan and Fred Lebow met some thirteen years before their big deal when taking Ian Hunter's screenwriting class together at New York University's film school in spring 1980. They each wrote feature scripts evaluated by professors. "Our department sent scripts separately to two producers at Warner Bros. by the names of Jeff Mueller and Andy Licht." Partnered in Licht-Mueller Productions, Andy and Jeff both read Sullivan and Lebow's submissions.

"Hey, we like you guys," Andy Licht smiled.

"Would you like to collaborate on something?" his partner Jeff asked.

"We'll do anything we can do to get into the business," Lebow beamed. The two writers came up with a pitch for a live-action *Flintstones* in 1982 as the first project they intended to sell to Hollywood.

"We were going to have Rodney Dangerfield as Fred," Sullivan recalls.

"It never happened," Lebow promptly interjects.

"The funny part is that we'd just gotten out of school," Sullivan explains. "We went in on a Tuesday and pitched them our idea for the live-action *Flintstones*. Andy and Jeff said our meeting's with Mark Canton [then a young exec at Warner] who liked it. We went into the next meeting with Bob Shapiro."

"Okay, I love it. You guys got a deal," responded Shapiro, then production president of Warner Bros.

"What's everyone complaining about? What's so hard about this? We were just out of film school. We met with the president of Warner

Brothers And he said, 'You got a deal,' " Sullivan reminisces on another of his life's bright moments. "We went through this whole process of getting the rights and it never happened. The film fell apart, and we didn't get another break until 1989."

"We got a deal, a *Flintstones* deal. It still might happen!" the curly-haired Lebow hopefully told everybody for the next seven years of waiting for their big deal to finally arrive. They knew their luck was wearing thin, yet that self-doubt would eventually bear the seed of what turned into *While You Were Sleeping*.

"When they actually made *The Flintstones* movie [at Universal Pictures in 1993] with thirty-something writers, we couldn't get a pitch," Sullivan now chuckles. "It was our best pitch. We were begging to get in."

But Hollywood's fortress held its guard. During one day of desperate introspection, something sprung to Lebow's open mind.

"I couldn't get a date if the girl was brain dead," the humble Long Islander frowned. Feeling for his friend yet amused by his sense of humor, Dan thought aloud, "How about we make a movie about a man who treats a girl who's fallen into a coma, then falls in love with her?"

As somewhat of a comical update on the classic *Sleeping Beauty* fairytale, Dan and Fred came up with a story called *Love in New Jersey* and began to pitch it around Hollywood. This was in 1989, the ostensible genesis of their eventual spec script. Although Fred did manage to get a few dates along the way, for the next five years Lebow and Sullivan climbed a steep, circuitous path to get to their destination. Occasionally, the two writers had to work from both coasts, during the times Dan took a job to make ends meet at his folks' drive-in restaurant in Hampden, Massachusetts.

Before their remarkable spec sale, the story went through several incarnations. "We came up with a really broad pitch idea about a guy who falls in love with a woman in a coma," Sullivan recalls. Once the man gathered the courage to talk to his vision of beauty, she gets run over by a newspaper truck and falls into a coma. "She then comes out of the coma and almost instantly tries to steal his money. He's a salesman from New Jersey, and she's basically trying to take this guy."

The writers pitched it everywhere they could in town, and every place turned it down. "We even knew it was bad," Sullivan admits.

"But what was interesting is that most of the big beats [from *While You Were Sleeping*] were in that original *Love in New Jersey*. . . . It was about a fish salesman (instead of the brother) who ends up falling in love with a very plain nurse.

"The woman in the coma who he was in love with was a Nordic beauty, and all he saw was how beautiful she was," Lebow steps in. "Now when she woke up, he realized she was a bitch. And the nurse was always very plain. But always very sweet."

"While the big beats were there," Sullivan continues, "we didn't know the movie was there. We hadn't found the key yet, but we had something that was out there. And everybody trashed it, as well they should have. We didn't really resurrect it until a producer by the name of Scott Rosenfelt approached us." The trio had worked on a couple of Fox TV movies by then.

"What about that idea you had about the guy who falls in love with a woman in a coma?" Rosenfelt asked the two writers. One fan was enough to again stir Dan and Fred's juices.

"We then started going out, pitching it again," says Sullivan, "but instead this time it was a con man who fell in love with a woman in a coma." Despite the change, Sullivan and Lebow still weren't getting very good responses from the pitch. One esteemed female 20th Century–Fox executive told the pair they were "creepy" for coming up with such a sleazy tale.

"It was very predatory that this guy's sitting next to a woman like a wolf," Sullivan says with a troubling grin. "We just plowed on until we met with Meg Ryan's company."

"Why would Meg Ryan want to do this?" her development exec shrieked. "She's in a coma the entire movie." The two packed their bags and regrouped.

"Let's switch it," Dan and Fred decided. From now on, they would pitch the story of a man who's in a coma, succinctly calling it *Coma Guy*.

The new formula clicked. "That was really the big change because once you've made it a woman desiring the victim, the predatory aspect was gone. It became a nice, soft story, rather than an aggressive story," Sullivan says. "I think that was the key to the whole success . . . then everything else developed over the pitches. . . . We then realized that we were trying to make the love story, but there was nothing going on. There was this guy lying in a coma. And this girl's in love with him. But then what do you do?

"Well, somebody's gotta come into this," Sullivan answers. "Either a brother or a best friend. We felt the brother raises the stakes and makes it a little more intense. It actually seems like a logical thing now. . . . The [*Coma Guy*] gets to wake up and you have an actual romantic triangle with one of the people unconscious."

Nonetheless, Sullivan and Lebow weren't able to set up *Coma Guy* as a pitch. There had to be another way to bring their idea to the screen.

"The world loves a good love story," says Jim Crabbe, the William Morris agent who first got a look at Dan and Fred's story once it became a spec script. "The reason there's so few is that a good love story requires an obstacle to love. In this day and age, already being married is no longer an obstacle. Feuding families are no longer an obstacle. Anything can be overcome. Therefore, the secret is to come up with something—a believable obstacle—and that's what they did." The 1989 film, *When Harry Met Sally,* for instance, was an exceptional love story in which the characters' abstract obstacle was their friendship.

"In recent years," Crabbe continues, "there were two other good examples: *Sleepless in Seattle,* where the two had never met—that was the obstacle. And *Ghost,* where the love interest was dead, and he had to communicate through this other woman, through this third party. Other than that, try to name a good love story. You can't."

In order for the script to wind its way to the William Morris Agency, Lebow got another idea: to call a producer he used to work for named Arthur Sarkissian. "Fred and Dan I've known since 1984," Sarkissian fondly recalls. "I've had three projects developed by Fred. I met Dan through Fred, and then they wrote *Snowflakes* [a Bruce Willis project]. That was in 1987, I believe. I made the deal with them on a napkin at the Beverly Wilshire." Fred Lebow was originally introduced to Arthur Sarkissian by Carol Yumkas of William Morris; Sarkissian optioned one of Fred's first scripts, titled *Echo of Valour,* but was unable to set it up.

By January 1990, however, Universal Pictures optioned Sullivan and Lebow's *Snowflakes.* The story involved a man whose wife is ill and dies at the beginning; the hero is given the chance to go back in time and prevent his wife's death, but in doing so, must give up the possibility of ever meeting her. Their clever screenplay earned the writing tandem enough attention in Hollywood to land a deal to write two TV movies for Fox, neither of which was produced. With more doors opening for them, however, in 1992 the writers pitched *Coma Guy* everywhere, but still couldn't attract a buyer.

"We were gonna write a book called *Four Thousand Pitches and No Deal*," Lebow dryly quips. "We had been pitching, on and off, for thirteen years. Everybody in Hollywood always says, 'Oh yeah, I was really close,' and 'We had a deal and it fell apart.' But we always got to that point. Then we realized that *everybody* says that, and we must really sound like shmendricks."

"Even though we knew we had the story, nobody gave us a deal," Sullivan confirms. "Everybody passed on it again. At the end of that, we decided to go write it on spec."

FROM PITCH TO PAPER

What Lebow and Sullivan couldn't sell as a pitch turned into a fiery fastball once Arthur Sarkissian stepped to the plate. "If someone says nobody's seen it, 95 percent of the time you just take that with a grain of salt," says Sarkissian. "As far as I'm concerned as a producer, if it's been seen a hundred thousand times, I don't care, if it's what I like. A perfect example is *While You Were Sleeping*. It's the same story they pitched everywhere, and nothing happened for five years.

"The thing about Fred and Danny that I like is that they're pretty much outspoken," the Iranian producer continues. "They weren't beating around the bush. They didn't tell me, 'We have something brand new that nobody's heard.' They know they can't pull that kind of crap."

"We've been everywhere two or three times," Sullivan and Lebow admitted.

"It's so funny," Sarkissian replied. "There's nothing left."

Sarkissian thought about their tale. "You know that it's a great story. And I *know* you can write it, because I know how you write."

As owner of a successful men's clothing boutique in London, Sarkissian relocated to Los Angeles to produce the 1987 Rutger Hauer movie *Wanted: Dead or Alive,* based on the Steve McQueen television show. Arthur decided he liked the *Coma Guy* pitch enough to front the writing tandem $10,000 to write the script on spec, on which he would have a one-year option.

Sarkissian took Dan and Fred on a final pitch before the writers put *Coma Guy* onto paper. "I did take them to New Line with the pitch fully fleshed out, a forty-five-minute pitch. And again, turned down."

New Line's consensus: "It's too old-fashioned, it's too soft."

"I could never understand what that meant, and I still don't to this day," Sarkissian wonders. "Either I love a story or I don't. When somebody says to me, 'It's too old-fashioned,' I just can't get it. So then they wrote it for me when there was nowhere else to go."

"They were very good with it," Sarkissian recalls. "They delivered the script about a month after I hired them, and I had something that I really believed in. Suddenly, because one place wanted it, you know that everybody else wanted it, too."

Sullivan and Lebow gave the script to their producer in November 1993 after a series of breakfast meetings at Il Fornaio restaurant, always a popular Beverly Hills meeting spot for the industry's movers and shakers. The writers did another pass with minor changes. "I knew there was some more work to be done on the Jack character," says Sarkissian of the role Bill Pullman ended up playing. "But I was very confident."

Sarkissian submitted the spec to his agent, Jim Crabbe. While Crabbe thought the script was terrific, he wanted to attach another client, Steve Barron, as a producer. With Barron, a former music video wizard and director of *Teenage Mutant Ninja Turtles,* the goal was to set up the project at Polygram (the entertainment company then owned by Dutch electronics giant, Phillips, N.V.), where Barron had a tight relationship.

"Arthur was not that established as a feature film producer," Crabbe points out, "and lots of times it makes sense to get an element attached, so somebody—a name entity—is involved and will get buyers to look at it in a slightly different way." Crabbe's thinking proved correct, though not right away. After two weeks of waiting, Polygram wasn't ready to commit to the terms Sarkissian wanted.

"Look, you know what?" Arthur told his agent. "Let's go out wide."

Crabbe agreed, but following conventional wisdom, didn't want to submit the project until the beginning of the new year, since many executives aren't likely to read new scripts in December.

Crabbe called Sarkissian after New Year's, 1993. "Arthur, I'm going out wide to Hollywood Pictures, to Castle Rock. I'm giving it to Amblin, and I'm going to give it to Warner Brothers."

"Fair enough," Sarkissian replied, knowing Crabbe well as both a friend and his only agent at the time. Crabbe, who epitomizes the deal maker that the William Morris Agency has been known for, also showed Dan and Fred's spec script to a younger colleague named David Phillips, a high-energy representative of young Hollywood, spurred on by quick information and the chance to launch writers into lucrative lifestyles.

"Who would go see a movie called *Coma Guy*?" David laughed, thumbing past the title page. But mentor Crabbe assured his younger colleague that it was the best script that he had read in a long time. Phillips closed his door and read the script straight through. Since Phillips had just signed *Sleepless in Seattle* scribe Jeffrey Arch, the town's trackers were pursuing the agent for another romantic comedy. He had just gotten off the phone with his friend Jonathan Glickman, who told him that Joe Roth's new company, Caravan (which had an output deal at Disney), wanted a romantic comedy along the lines of *Sleepless in Seattle*.

"Dave," the bespectacled Glickman asked, "since you handle writers, whattya got?" Phillips messengered *Coma Guy* over to the Santa Monica offices Roth had set up with his former 20th Century–Fox colleague, Roger Birnbaum.

A Boston native, who attended UCLA's MBA program before fighting his way out of the ICM mailroom, Dave Phillips was now a William Morris agent eager to make his mark. Meanwhile, Crabbe phoned Dan Halsted, a vice president at Walt Disney's Hollywood Pictures. Crabbe had previously sold Halsted *The Hand That Rocks the Cradle* and *Tombstone* (both spec scripts) so they shared a track record of spec success.

"Jim told me there was a big script coming out," Halsted remembers. "As you often do, you give it to a junior executive to read first." Himself a former agent in the halcyon days of Bauer-Benedek (later merged into the United Talent Agency), Halsted handed the script to an intern, Vivien Mejia, who read it by lunch. "She really deserves a lot of the credit. She was the first person at Disney to read and flag it."

Vivien told her boss the story, "and it was pretty much the script that was on the screen." Halsted found something special in the tale of a love-struck girl with a mistaken identity. "I read it during lunch and it hit me. I can't explain why or how, but I said to everyone that day, 'I love this. I would go see this movie on Friday night when it opened.'

"I remember when I read the script . . . and thought, 'This is me, this is my story. This is like *everybody's* story, because everybody feels lonely.' That's what hit me," Halsted recalls. "We all sort of hope that there's someone out there for us."

Casting ideas began kicking around. Rosie O'Donnell displayed proven comedic ability, vital for the part of Lucy. However, Marisa Tomei had played a similar girl-next-door type in successful romantic comedies. But Demi Moore, an A-list actress, provided the star bankability to guarantee the script would reach the screen.

"My boss, Ricardo Mestres, who was then the president of Hollywood Pictures, was out of town on vacation and not really reachable," says Halsted of a situation that was both a blessing and a curse. "You can't really buy anything with him out of town. At the same time, you can go right to [then Disney chieftain Jeffrey] Katzenberg."

At Caravan, Glickman got hold of the *Coma Guy* script at about 7 P.M. "I had received enough of the heat from Jim Crabbe and Dave Phillips that I knew to read it immediately. I also wasn't at Caravan that long, so I was easily swayable by such heat. . . . They told me it was for sure gonna go."

Since Caravan didn't have a romantic comedy, *Coma Guy* was a perfect match. "We also had a deal with Julia Roberts, and it seemed like this could fill a gap for a Julia project," Glickman figured. "Although [it] did seem similar in tone to *Pretty Woman,* it did make sense [that *Coma Guy*] would be a good idea.

"The second thing for me personally, it was obviously a well-written script. It's very funny," Glickman adds. "It was an interesting and unique idea, and it went beyond just the concept. There were some great things . . . in that first draft that you could see as future 'movie moments.' The other thing—just as a premise—my favorite type of romantic comedy is when somebody has to appear to be somebody else to their romantic interest. Whether it's *Tootsie* or *Dave,* it's a premise that you can kind of rest a movie on." In addition to *Coma Guy,* Glickman read another script that night that sold the next day, strengthening his resolve not to lose out on this one. He got on the horn to his boss, Roger Birnbaum.

"You gotta read this," Glickman exclaimed. "There's a good idea in here and it would be good for Julia." Roger Birnbaum also read the screenplay while Glickman tossed in his sleep.

TWO PLUS TWO MAKE A SALE

The next morning arrived as Birnbaum passed Jon. "Yeah, I like it," which is all Roger needed to say to make Glickman's day.

"We both had a concern about it," Glickman recalls. "It was set in New York, and there was kind of a *Moonstruck* vibe. A lot of movies that were made in the same vein as *Moonstruck* had bombed since then. That was the only slight concern, but it was [eventually] developed in a way that took it away from that vibe."

While Glickman didn't want to lose this script, neither did Halsted. As Crabbe was to discover, others in town felt likewise. "A number of places expressed serious interest," says Crabbe. "What it really came down to was Roger Birnbaum and Danny Halsted pushing and shoving to get Hollywood Pictures to make an offer before anybody else would really step up.

"One other offer on the table was substantially lower," Crabbe continues. "There were two other places that I heard were going to make offers, which hadn't. Caravan and Hollywood made a very generous offer where Fred and Dan received the maximum amount that they could under their existing option with Arthur.

"Caravan was relatively new at the time and had been very aggressive about trying to get projects," the agent explains. "With them passionately wanting to do it, it was virtually a guarantee of it getting made. If Roger and Joe and Jon said, 'We promise we're gonna make this,' that's good enough for me.

"One of the studios made a low-ball offer and was notorious for only making movies with big stars," says Crabbe, who heard on the QT from one of that studio's underlings that the executive making the offer hadn't actually read the script, but was simply aware of the enthusiasm around town. "There were not that many ladies who were big enough stars in their book to carry this. It didn't seem to make as much sense as doing it with Caravan and Hollywood Pictures."

At the time, Caravan operated somewhat like a separate studio under the Disney logo, like Touchstone or Hollywood. Disney as a whole encouraged agencies to submit projects simultaneously to Hollywood,

Touchstone, Caravan, Miramax, and Walt Disney Pictures. "They were all free to compete with one another for material," says former banker Crabbe, who worked in distribution at the Mouse Factory before embarking on a then seventeen-year career as a William Morris agent. "For whatever reasons Disney had, when Danny Halsted wanted it, and Jon and Joe and Roger wanted it, the decision was made that the two entities would do it together."

Dan Halsted recalls when the bidding spectacle began. "It was submitted to me with two producers, Steve Barron, who I knew a little bit, and Arthur Sarkissian, who I didn't know at all. The first thing I tried to do was to carve out some niche for the studio.

"Look, remember when we had dinner," Halsted called up Steve Barron to entice him. "I really want this script."

"Before my bosses even knew about the script, I was already making overtures that we were going to buy it. That's what you do often. You tell the agents and producers, 'I want this. We're interested in it,' " adds Halsted.

Jim Crabbe could read the signals. "Ideally, what you want to do is get things that are sort of at a feverish pitch, so people will pay as much as possible for these things and yet in the end, not piss anybody off too much; because you want to continue to do business with everybody in the future.

"There are ways to do it," adds Crabbe, who earned his agent stripes after working for legendary Morris agent Stan Kamen. "There are calls that you can make along the way at certain times to certain people, so that in the end they don't feel like they were treated unfairly. I think for the most part, we managed to do it in a way that nobody did." Interest in the script now bubbled over the same story Lebow and Sullivan had pitched around town for several years without success.

"I tried to get hold of Ricardo Mestres, and Ricardo wasn't around," Halsted remembers. "After reading the script at lunch, I gave Jeffrey Katzenberg a synopsis and faxed it to Ricardo. I told Jeffrey how much I liked it and thought it was a movie. He said that Disney would buy it if I could get it in the $100,000 to $200,000 range. I knew that amount was never going to take that script off the market." So Halsted had to prevent it from selling elsewhere.

"Sometimes the agents will shop your interest, saying 'Halsted's interested at Hollywood Pictures.' But often what happens is that you log your interest so that they won't sell it without telling you. They'll give you a chance to bid on it in case somebody else comes in with a preemptive bid."

By eleven o'clock on the morning of January 12, Crabbe called Arthur Sarkissian to say he could make a deal at Hollywood Pictures. "I kind of left it to him," says Sarkissian. "He was the agent to make the calls. He was the one selling the script."

At the time, Disney didn't pony up much money for specs. "We were the deal-breaking company, with Jeffrey Katzenberg's memo," Halsted recalls the former Disney president's historic twenty-eight-page directive to make lower-budget projects. Given this directive, Disney execs had trouble making deals at the time. "And we weren't going to overpay for a spec script. In fact, much of my job was devoted to working on our own original ideas, and not chasing spec screenplays." Odds were that the really hot specs wouldn't be submitted to him anyway. "They'd be submitted directly to the president [Mestres] or to Jeffrey Katzenberg, because the agents wanted a movie commitment. The chain of command was leaner at other production companies" than at Disney.

By now, Halsted had learned through the grapevine that Caravan had read *Coma Guy,* and that Jon Glickman really liked it. In a totally mercenary move, Halsted rang up Glickman to propose an unusual plan.

"All right, Jon," Halsted suggested. "Why don't we try to get it together? I'll chip in what Jeffrey's giving me, and you chip in what your bosses are offering." Glickman got the go-ahead, and with that collaboration, Hollywood Pictures and Caravan would jointly own the project.

Meanwhile Dan Sullivan was having trouble sleeping.

PUTTING THE PIECES TOGETHER

At Cedars Sinai Hospital, at 4:45 P.M. on January 13, Dan and Patti Sullivan became the proud parents of a nine-pound, five-ounce baby boy they named Thomas Patrick Sullivan. Meanwhile, across town, Arthur Sarkissian packed his final bag en route to the Sundance Film Festival in Park City, Utah. At about 6:00 P.M. his phone rang. It was his agent, Jim Crabbe.

"They're going to make it, but they also feel that Joe Roth and Roger

Birnbaum would come in with Caravan," Crabbe propositioned. "Would you mind?"

"No, I don't mind," Sarkissian replied. "As long as I'm producing the picture." Sarkissian didn't feel he had to retain "produced by" credit as long as he was completely and totally involved with the movie. "You make the deal. I like Joe and Roger. If that's their wish, fine."

Halsted also saw his wish fulfilled. "We made a really good deal, actually an unbelievable deal for the studio. We bought it for very little money, relatively speaking, $300,000 to $400,000. We later learned that there were so many more interested buyers out there."

Still, the two entities that shared in the purchase had many details to work out. "The relationship between Caravan and Hollywood Pictures was in its infancy at the time," Halsted says. "I don't think we would have been able to buy it alone. And I don't think Caravan would have either. It was at the time that Caravan was really defining itself." The two entities had not really defined their precedence with each other: Who spends the money during production, and who spends the marketing money. "It was a case study for the internal lawyers and bureaucrats at Disney, since it was all essentially Disney dollars. It also defined the creative relationship between Hollywood and Caravan."

Yet the process of going into production was a whole new story.

Caravan's chairman, Joe Roth, had just returned from Japan and Hong Kong after the purchase. "I remember when he got back after we had bought it," Glickman recalls.

"So you brought in that script?" Roth asked Glickman.

"Yeah," Glickman responded, fearing the chairman might hate the thing.

Roth paused, then said, "Cute."

"I was totally taken off the hook at that moment," Glickman recalls. "Because we have a very high rate of production to purchases, are we just buying this for development? Or do we see a light at the end of the tunnel, and are we gonna make it?" Production companies often buy material to fill their coffers, or as a sign to the town to attract more material, but Glickman had the vision to see this script reach the screen.

"As soon as we bought the script, we gave it to a couple pieces of talent, immediately, to see if they were interested in us developing it for them. That was Julia Roberts, and I think Marisa Tomei. Both of whom passed."

Coma Guy remained on Caravan's fast track, although not every-body knew for sure if it would become a motion picture. Because nobody knows whether a movie will succeed, it wasn't until the pic-ture tested well in preview screenings that everybody and his cousin would begin taking credit. Although they shared in the script's own-ership, Caravan didn't want studio interference while they packaged the talent.

Dan and Fred began with rewrites. Of course, the first thing was their project's name. "Drop the title, guys," said Caravan execs on the first note. "Let's get rid of it." No other titles came readily to mind.

Sullivan always loved the *Coma Guy* title, and many of the folks to whom they had pitched the story over the years still refer to it. "We kept thinking and thinking. We called a bunch of our friends and said, 'You guys have any ideas?' That's when Mike Himmelstein—he's writ-ten a lot of music for The Temptations and Johnny Winter—he came up with *While You Were Sleeping.*"

"I liked *Token Love,*" says Lebow.

"Actually, that was the tone of the movie," says Sullivan, recalling the final scene in which Bill Pullman's character drops an engagement ring in place of a subway token. "That was our first suggestion. That closing scene always worked in the pitch. We knew it was going to work. That was fun to see how you always knew that worked in the pitch, and then to see it actually come on in the screening and it worked in the movie. 'Oh, wow, that worked all along.' They never changed that beat."

Well, maybe, as the two writers would later learn.

Another change was their location. Once Caravan acquired the script, they sent it out to what's known as a "line producer" to oversee the physical production. Charlie Schlissel got a stack of five Caravan scripts getting ready to go and chose *Coma Guy.*

The movie's location, Chicago, was selected after a five-city scout. "There certainly was the idea that we didn't want to make it an 'inside New York' movie. We felt that New York had been seen so many times," says Jon Glickman. New York was then hosting *Batman For-ever* and *Die Hard 3,* big-scale shows, which had taken away potential crew members.

"But mainly, if you're spending a third of the movie in a hospital, and a third of the movie in a subway station," says Charlie Schlissel, "New York felt just too internal, and not right tone-wise, for a character in a light romantic comedy." On the other hand, Chicago's stations are elevated, opening them up.

The production team considered shooting Toronto for New York, to save on its budget, but ultimately figured they were simply better off filming in Chicago. "Although it's funny," Glickman recalls. "[Dan and Fred had] never been to Chicago before, so they did every single location as Michigan Avenue."

Every picture that previously filmed Chicago's transit system was forced to shoot at night or on one sad-looking "El" track on the outskirts of town. Yet for four weekends in a row, *While You Were Sleeping* made history as the first production to take over a downtown loop station, due to great cooperation from the Chicago mayor's office and the film commission.

"We were in a hotel on Michigan Avenue," recalls Lebow of their first expedition to the Windy City. "The only street we knew was Michigan Avenue."

"That's why you had Lucy's landlord, Joe Jr., who was obviously from Brooklyn, living in Chicago," Sullivan continues, chuckling at the thought. "When we arrived in Chicago, we said to the doorman, 'Hey man, what's that water at the end of the block?' "

"Oh, that's Lake Michigan," the doorman replied.

MOVING FORWARD IN CHICAGO

"After you make the sale, make sure to try to do as good a job as you can on the rewrite," Sullivan advises. "Be involved with your movie. Because the sale's like the end of the beginning. Sometimes they sell it and you never see your script again. They do whatever they do. So in our case, I think we worked hard in making sure that we kept trying to make the script better. Important to be able to stay aboard. Otherwise, you can get thrown overboard, and you're in big trouble. That was our first concern, but you never have time to think about it. We sold it, and we were in meetings, and then you get your notes, and we were working on it. So we never had a chance to stop and think. We were always just working."

Caravan wanted to keep the momentum going, and the production started within nine months, rather quickly by Hollywood standards. Glickman recalls when it got its green light and its crazy thirteen-week prep phase. "Even though the script wasn't *perfect* at that point, it was actually an excellent rewrite. Because [Dan and Fred] were so experienced as screenwriters in this business before they came here, their rewrite was probably the best rewrite I've ever read by anybody. The ability to rewrite yourself is a huge talent that you have to have, even if it's rewriting without getting anybody's notes, because that shows a willingness to look at things from different perspectives."

Now with a script on track, picking a director becomes the most crucial decision in shaping any final product. Hollywood Pictures had already been pursuing Jon Turteltaub for a modern-day script akin to *Guess Who's Coming to Dinner.* But Turteltaub was more attracted to *Coma Guy.* Hiring Jon meant Hollywood Pictures had great faith in the project, since he had directed Disney's most profitable live-action movies in each of the two previous years: *Three Ninjas* in 1992 and *Cool Runnings* in 1993.

After his agent, David Lonner, negotiated his deal, Turteltaub went to New York originally to scout, then to cast. Turteltaub and producer Susan Stremple walked down to Schlissel's hotel room. "What are you doing tonight?" they asked. Schlissel, a friend of Sandra Bullock's for several years, said he was going to see the opening of her new movie *Speed.*

"Sandra Bullock?" Jon responded. "We keep trying to meet with her and we keep pushing it off." Schlissel suggested they come along to the movie.

At the screening, Turteltaub tugged on Stremple's arm while turning around to see the crowd's reaction. "God, she's great, the audience loves her! They're really in love with her." Bullock first got hold of the *Coma Guy* script while on the set of *Speed,* yet felt she did not have a chance in hell of getting the part. Quickly rising talents Bullock and Bill Pullman, both clients at United Talent Agency, were not then considered star caliber and elevated their careers by taking the lead roles in *While You Were Sleeping.*

This was Sandra's first movie she had to carry and Bill Pullman's first role as a leading man after generally being cast as a loser (the chump who got dumped by Meg Ryan in *Sleepless in Seattle,* Nicole Kidman in *Malice,* Jodie Foster in *Sommersby,* and Linda Fiorentino in *The Last Seduction*). Yet after *While You Were Sleeping's* success, Pullman would go on to portray the U.S. president and savior of the world in *Independence Day.*

"I understood and knew Lucy; I understood the comedy. But I had no power to get anything made and thought no one would want to go see me [in a lead role]," Bullock said in a *Dramalogue* interview. And until *Speed* came out, most people in Hollywood might have felt the same. In the meantime, the script had also gone out to Demi Moore.

When Turteltaub returned to L.A., Demi Moore by now decided she wanted to do the movie. One potential glitch: She was acting in *The Scarlet Letter* and not readily available. So while Caravan was waiting, *While You Were Sleeping* was put to sleep, literally shut down. Dan and Fred's dream once more came to a standstill.

It was Thursday afternoon in June 1994 when producer Charlie Schlissel got the news, so he hopped aboard an airplane to Borneo for some recreational scuba diving. Once he got to the town of Kota Kinabalu, he checked his message machine: nine heated messages from Ned Dowd, head of production at Caravan.

"Get back here! Demi asked for too much money and Sandra Bullock's making the movie," the telephone blasted. "We're moving forward. You gotta get back here now!" Because of the two weeks they lost, the picture was now pushing into Christmas, a nightmare for any production.

"When we got Sandra Bullock, we were really interested in getting a major actor to play Jack so that we could take the burden off Sandra," says Caravan's Glickman. "This was going to be the first picture she was going to carry." This was a chore, since many male stars don't feel comfortable playing second fiddle to a female lead.

As two guys who had been integral to the whole project's evolution, Dan Sullivan, then watching his baby Tom sprout, and Fred Lebow, then mourning the loss of his father, discovered another big change. They were fired.

PREPPING WITHOUT A SCRIPT

As *Buffy the Vampire Slayer* creator Joss Whedon once said of the Hollywood system, "They switch directors because something is very wrong. They switch writers because it's Tuesday."

"I think they felt they needed another approach," says producer Arthur Sarkissian. "They again had this 'it's too old-fashioned' thing. That was the whole issue, which I fought. I'm all for developing Jack's character a little further because he needed it. But you've got to do that anyway. So my whole feeling was, we cannot take these two guys away from something they have written and give it to somebody else who's used to doing twenty rewrites in a month. Because I feel when you're dealing with people who have fallen in this rewrite world of writing script after script, they lose touch. There's no way to avoid losing touch.

"The whole thing with this movie that I wanted to get made so badly is that it's fresh," Arthur continues. "These guys are unpretentious, they're not Hollywood. They're very soulful."

Sarkissian shared the feelings of others involved who didn't want a part of the rewrite. "The script that came in was a total disaster as far as I was concerned. . . . It was exactly what I didn't want to make. It was *exactly* the kind of movie I hated.

"I remember telling Jon Glickman, 'Look, if you guys move on this, as far as I'm concerned, I'll pull my script out,'" Sarkissian recalls. "What *really* bothered me more than anything else was the original was a terrific script, wonderfully written and very unpretentious, which is so important. It wasn't like somebody sat down and went, 'Okay, we need a scene here with a dog, one with a cat, a line here to make people laugh.'

"There were such lame lines in the rewrite that by about page thirty, I said to myself, 'This is just another Hollywoodized story.' The heart is gone. That wonderful scene at the end, when Jack goes up and gives her the ring, it was all out. . . . It had nothing to do with what I developed. And I said, 'No wonder things don't get made.' Somebody just thinks, 'Okay, we can make it a little better.' And by saying, 'We can make it a little better' you can go completely wrong. The whole innocence was gone, and it just turned into a cliché.'"

Says Jonathan Glickman, "The character that Bill Pullman played, Jack, was sort of lightly written in Dan and Fred's draft. We really pushed them to give it more weight and substance. . . . We realized that we had to invest more in this character, and that's part of the reason why Dan and Fred were taken off the project. They didn't see it at that moment, until we invented an entire storyline with Jack and saw him in the furniture business."

With the decision to bring in another writer, Fred and Dan didn't really know what was going on. "They told us they were going to do a little tweaking with one of their characters," Lebow recalls. "And then the script came in; it wasn't our script. It was a totally different tone. It was a different genre."

Glickman, who in his pre-show biz career worked for the Democratic National Committee, did know a bit about politics. And anybody who was part of *While You Were Sleeping*'s evolution was amazed by his ability to hold this project together. "Some of the cast said yes to the rewrite and some of the cast said no, based on the previous script," Glickman says. "It sort of took a lot of diplomacy in getting this script ready in time to make the movie." Sarkissian brought up his gripes with Caravan and Hollywood.

"Thank God, Jon Glickman backed me up on it," Arthur says. "And so did Roger. I brought the boys back and it was put back to what it was." When Sullivan and Lebow secured their 1990 deal to write those two Fox TV movies, they had spent a lot of time on the lot (where Joe Roth was then chairman of the studio), so Roth was also aware of their long haul.

"Fred and Dan were two humble guys who were knocked off the project at first, and they brought in a new writer," says David Phillips, who left the Morris agency in 1996 to produce for Davis Entertainment. "But then they went back to Dan and Fred. Jim Crabbe and I kept telling them, 'Stay on the project, stay on the project,' because one of the keys you want is to get sole writing credit. In the very end, Fred and Dan got sole credit."

"These guys are two very talented writers," says Sarkissian. "Nobody wanted to take a shot at them. Nobody. They'd rather pay somebody a million dollars to write something than pay Fred and Dan a little money for something that has ended up being one of the most profitable pictures of 1995. What does that tell you? 'I'd rather not take a chance on an unknown than take a chance on somebody known.' But that doesn't mean the known person can always deliver."

So things again moved forward with the original writers, and would have moved even faster if not for another roadblock: a $10 million lawsuit in June filed by TriStar Pictures. Glickman wondered if this would ultimately abort what could by now be considered his baby. TriStar, a division of Sony Studios, had already spent $2.5 million developing Cornell Woolrich's 1948 story, *I Married a Dead Man* (made in 1950 by Paramount), which TriStar would release the year after *While You Were Sleeping* under the title *Mrs. Winterbourne*. TriStar claimed the writers copied the theme, plot, characters, and story elements licensed to TriStar "while at the same time intentionally altering collateral elements thereof in an attempt to evade detection of their infringing conduct."

Sullivan and Lebow, who had never read the Cornell Woolrich book or seen the Barbara Stanwyck movie *No Man of Her Own* on which it was based, were stunned. It became a very painful period for all involved; some Hollywood insiders surmised that TriStar's posture may have been the result of residual animosity over Disney's previous year release of *The Three Musketeers* at the time TriStar had their own public domain project in development. In the case of *While You Were Sleeping,* the parties settled quietly out of court.

"The lawsuit delayed the writers from turning in the draft for about a month and a half, which was lost time," says Glickman. In fact, the lawsuit hadn't been formally resolved until the production started up during the first week of October.

"I think nowadays any time a studio movie gets made, there's somebody out there claiming it's their idea," says William Morris agent Jim Crabbe. "If it were fine with [the studios] for me to comment, I'd be happy to, because I have very definite and strong feelings about it. But these two companies have reached a settlement, and part of it was for no one to comment."

Because of the change of writers, producer Charlie Schlissel had been prepping the movie without a script. With only two weeks before the start date, Jon Glickman spent much of his time at Chicago's Drake Hotel arbitrating between the director and Dan and Fred, who didn't want to make script changes. Stuck in the middle, Glickman ultimately got the best out of all parties and avoided an impasse. Bill Pullman came on only three weeks prior to shooting and had a number of character issues, and Dan and Fred integrated the furniture business storyline of Pullman's Jack character into the voice of the original script.

"Right before the movie got made, we did a read-through based on a script that was a combination of the last draft Fred and Dan wrote and the new draft, and it just wasn't 100 percent there yet," Glickman explains of the "table reading" involving all of the actors sitting around a large room. "It was probably the worst read-through I've ever been to in my life. I think a lot of the actors were uncomfortable. And we were able to pull it through, but then I got very nervous.

"I knew we were probably going to make the movie," the executive continues, "although I was very nervous at that point." The polishing meant many down-to-the-wire, late-night writing sessions. "We did a lot more rewrites based on the read-through. And the read-through was very helpful, but it was just too close to production to really calm anybody down. I remember Dan, Fred, Jon Turteltaub, and I were working with the actors during the days and nights [while Turteltaub and Schlissel] had preproduction things to take care of, finding locations and all.

"We would work from basically noon until four or five in the morning," Glickman recalls. "I would sometimes fall asleep before Dan and Fred were done. I would wake up with pages left on the couch, on my arm, and I would take a look at them. Generally they were great, just perfect.

"But sometimes Dan and Fred would be sort of punch-drunk in the middle of the night, and they would write some nutty things," he laughs. "They'd be sleeping for a few hours, and I'd read these pages and go, 'Oh my God, what're we gonna do about this thing?' It was definitely an intense experience, *but* some of the best moments of the movie came during that last week of writing, no doubt about that. I do think the originality of voice in a screenplay will translate to screen, and I think Dan and Fred's voice is all over *While You Were Sleeping.*"

On the night before shooting, Charlie Schlissel likes to throw a kick-off party for his whole crew to get past the stresses of the thirteen-week prep. It allows the team to start fresh that first day of shooting, to clear the slate. The location was the Chicago club, Drink, and included the actors as well.

Most actors had been there for the table read a couple of days earlier, except Monica Keena, who played the little girl Mary. She arrived just after working on *Promise Kept: The Oksana Baiul Story.* Jon Turteltaub and Susan Stremple made their entrance, relieved that they had worked out all the aggravating character problems for this complex ensemble piece. Then Monica arrived at the party.

"Hi, I'm really happy you're here," said Turteltaub. "It's great to have you on this movie."

"I'm really happy to be here," little Monica responded. "But I have some notes about my character I'd like to talk to you about." Jon's face dropped.

Before the director popped a blood vessel, Schlissel grinned ear-to-ear as he walked Jon and Susan to the bar and ordered up double margaritas. Then Charlie kindly guided Monica in the other direction, saying, "Monica, let's go talk. . . ."

SHOOTING, TESTING, AND OPENING

On Saturday, October 8, along the banks of the Chicago River (near Michigan Avenue), Jon Turteltaub called "action" for take one of the hot-dog vendor's scene. The story of a shy, lonely girl named Lucy, who lives with her cat, works in a token booth for the Chicago Transit Authority, and lusts after a handsome lawyer named Peter Callaghan (played by Peter Gallagher, who fortunately didn't mind being in a coma most of the movie) was now being put onto film.

Not only did the buyers get the script at a good price, Dan Halsted secured the added cachet of two additional options for Lebow and Sullivan to write projects for the studio at prenegotiated prices of around $150,000. But the studio had limited time to find two other projects for Dan and Fred to write.

Once Disney test-screened the movie in the Los Angeles suburb of Agoura Hills (where an astounding 98 percent responded in the precious top two boxes—those highly recommended), suddenly every single person at Caravan and Hollywood wanted to work with Sullivan and Lebow. Now Jim Crabbe could secure new deals for them at two and three times the level Hollywood Pictures had once locked up.

"We had a blind option, which we learned means the studio doesn't *have* to pay in that time period," Sullivan says of the period before the movie test screened so exceptionally. "But if they do like what you have, you're locked in at a certain price. We weren't really getting a lot of job offers—some, but not for a lot of money. As soon as *While You Were Sleeping* screened well, everything changed, even before the movie came out. Then whatever idea you had became more valuable. But the great thing with Caravan was, I think that in the very beginning they believed in us."

On Tuesday, April 11, 1995, this seventeen-million-dollar production held its media premiere at Westwood's Avco Cinema. Critics found the movie enchanting, like a warm-hearted Capraesque comedy. *The New York Times*'s Janet Maslin proclaimed, "The year may be young, but the first hit of the summer is here. . . . As written by Daniel G. Sullivan and Frederic Lebow with echoes of well-worn screwball love stories,

While You Were Sleeping touches familiar comic bases with efferves-
cent style."

Ten days later, the movie opened wide, taking first place at the box
office with $9.5 million (knocking out previous champ, *Bad Boys*), and
its audience kept growing. A "story about love at second sight," as
Disney's ads illuminated, it grossed $35 million within its first three
weeks as women across the country grabbed their boyfriends to see
one of the best date movies in history. In May, the Film Information
Council voted its "Excellence in Film Marketing Award" for April to
Disney's distribution arm for *While You Were Sleeping*. Members said
they were impressed with the effectiveness of communicating a complicated storyline through sixty-second television commercials. *While
You Were Sleeping* ultimately grossed $206 million worldwide in all of
its markets. Dan and Fred emerged after years of struggle to become
highly desired screenwriters.

Jim Crabbe felt that despite the roadblocks the movie came together
rather magically. "They had Jon Glickman, who was *really* there every
day. And Danny Halsted and Roger Birnbaum were all very supportive.
Dan and Fred came back to finish the writing and it turned out fine.
You have to have somebody in a position of power fighting on your
behalf, which they did."

WHILE THEY WERE WAITING

It had been a long haul for Dan and Fred, although their journey was
well worth the effort. "When we were pitching *Coma Guy,* we had
some of the worst pitches," Sullivan recalls. "We had a woman who
watched a *Ren and Stimpy* cartoon the entire pitch."

"Worse than that," Lebow cuts in. "I got lost in the middle of a *Coma
Guy* pitch one time. I turned to Danny and said, 'So then what happens?' "

"I don't know, I lost you a half hour ago!" Sullivan laughed.

On another pitch, they were so beaten down they left a treatment
at A&M Productions in which they screwed up the characters' names
and had left in a bunch of pencil marks. "This is before we had computers," Sullivan confesses. "We had named the woman in the coma
Laura in one half of it, and Athena in the second half. And then we
tried to get it back!" (A&M Productions, incidentally, was the company

developing *Mrs. Winterbourne* for TriStar, but didn't inform Sullivan or Lebow of this.)

All along the way, the toughest question the writers faced was when to give up on their dream and return home. When Lebow first arrived in Los Angeles in 1982, he worked for B-movie meister Roger Corman. "I would have been ecstatic if he had made my movie," Fred reminisces. "God, if he makes *Grand Prix 2000*, I could tell everybody I got a sequel to *Death Race 2000*. The scripts were just terrible, and I felt really bad.

"The whole thing with Corman is budget. He looked at script length, and I had hired someone to professionally type it," Lebow recalls. "She wanted to make more money, so instead of doing ninety-five pages she did one hundred thirty-three shorter pages. Corman flipped out when he got the script, saying, 'I'm not going to make this movie.' He was yelling because I told him it would be maybe ninety-eight or ninety-nine pages. It came out at one hundred thirty-three pages, and I wanted to strangle this woman. I got fired after I turned it in.

"I had no other skills, and I had nothing else to do with my life," says Lebow, reflecting on the doubts he faced during the years he and Sullivan waited. "Otherwise I would have quit a long time ago. No matter what we wrote, even if we put it in script form, I would have bet it wouldn't have sold. No matter how good it was. . . . I had always talked about going to law school, just anything. That's something that I always wanted to do since I was in college. But I did terribly on the LSATs. I was a political science major back then," before attending NYU's film school.

"We painted ourselves into a corner," Sullivan says. "We'd gone this far, and we were in our mid-thirties when it sold. And until then it was like, 'We don't know how to do anything. What are we going to do?' It's not like we could be a plumber. We don't know how to do that."

Caravan's Glickman attributes *While You Were Sleeping*'s success to two key factors. "First of all, casting, such as with *Sleepless in Seattle,* which is completely driven by the chemistry between two people. You always see that in any sort of romance. For every *Casablanca*, there's a movie that does very well that doesn't have such a good story, but there's so much chemistry between the two leads, you're involved in it for the rest of the movie. I also think that if you have a novel idea, an interesting hook is something that'll make a romantic comedy seem less than ordinary. It was the whole coma thing.

"The movie was compared a lot to *Pretty Woman* in that it took very dark premises and sugar-coated them," Glickman continues. "To a certain extent, that's why they worked. Because the premises were intriguing enough, and not too soft, you could go on a ride with this movie." Going for a lighter tone, rather than a real psychological one, made the journey an easier and more accessible one in which the audience could indulge.

As a result of their sleeper surprise, the writers garnered a multi-picture deal at Caravan. Among the projects Sullivan and Lebow subsequently developed are *Stanley's Cup* for *Hot Shots!* director Jim Abrahams; an adaptation of Jules Verne's novel *The Killing Time,* about a coward who can't kill himself and thus hires an assassin but changes his mind once he suddenly falls in love; as well as a screenplay about a kid who believes he's contacted an alien on the Internet, based on an idea by basketball coach Pat Riley.

"Caravan was great to work with because they let us write," says proud papa Dan Sullivan. "They basically gave us their notes and said, 'You're the writers, go write.' They didn't bother us. . . . It wasn't like you hear of all those horror stories about dotting *i*'s and crossing *t*'s. These guys were pretty cool. They said, 'That's your job, we expect you to do your job.' We said, 'Thanks, that's all we want.' " The company changed its name in late 1998 to Spyglass Entertainment, which Birnbaum runs with Gary Barber.

As the initial shepherd of *While You Were Sleeping,* Arthur Sarkissian (who next went to New Line Cinema to set up a remake of Akiro Kurosawa's *Yojimbo,* titled *Last Man Standing,* set during the depression, and starring Bruce Willis; it opened at number one in September 1996; he also set up 1998's blockbuster *Rush Hour,* again with Caravan) attributes much of *While You Were Sleeping*'s success to its lack of pretension. "I couldn't be more pleased about the job Jon Turteltaub did. He's very good. Bill Pullman, Sandra Bullock, they're all great. I'm very proud of it, of course.

"These were new people in the movie and you believed it," Sarkissian continues. "You believed this girl being somebody who worked in a toll booth because you hadn't seen her wearing a $20 million dress the month before. It was the freshness of it, between Fred and Dan, that made it different. And that's what made *me* go after it so strongly. It came out of their heart. That's why it worked."

Now that Sullivan and Lebow are embraced by Hollywood, they

have returned to their respective towns in western Massachusetts and Long Island, New York. "We had real diverse things going on when the script sold," says Lebow. "Danny had his baby, and my dad passed away two days before. . . . My mom's [around], thank God, and she can enjoy it. She gets a kick out of [the attention], watching *Entertainment Tonight*. The other day she was watching *Regis & Kathie Lee* and Kathie Lee was talking about the movie. That's, like, my mom's favorite show, and she goes, 'They're talking about my son!'

"My Dad had no idea he was dying. He had been down that road too many times," Lebow recalls, sorrow lingering in his speech. "He was at his lowest, lowest ebb. Two days later, his life would have changed. . . . I see these people who treat me like *gold* now, who years ago treated me like garbage. And I kind of blame them for not letting me into the club seven years ago, when I could have shared it, and enjoyed it, with my father."

Sullivan reflects on every Hollywood screenwriter's dilemma. "What if we had quit before we went through all the pitches and said, 'You know something, screw it'? It would have never happened for us. You don't know when to quit, but on the other hand, you don't want to be fifty or sixty years old and saying, 'You know, I've got a little pitch for you.' "

"It's a sequel to *The Flintstones*!" Lebow chimes in. "Find somebody who's interested!"

At a subsequent meeting with Amblin Entertainment, Dan and Fred were finally able to pitch their original *Flintstones* idea to the producers of the 1994 Universal Studios' production.

"How come you guys didn't pitch this to us before?" the producers asked after hearing the story.

"We'd been trying to do it for sixteen years," Lebow responded, "and they wouldn't let us in the door!"

Learning the Screenwriting Craft

"If you're devoting the time to write a screenplay, understand what it takes, understand what is expected, understand the marketplace, who the buyers are, and what they're looking for," says Avenue Pictures' Cary Brokaw.

When meeting young writers Brokaw provides them with a collection of screenplays. "The obvious ones are *Chinatown,* and things like that. One of my favorite scripts is Steve Tesich's *Breaking Away,* which I worked on marketing at Fox. I say to writers, 'Take your idea and script and put it on hold for a while, and here, read this. Look how magnificently it's structured. How beautifully each character is defined, how it works, how its tone is consistent; and take it apart.'

"It's like building a car," Brokaw continues. "Look and study one that works and understand how the components work with each other. Look at examples of other movies. Not that originality and invention aren't essential, but you need the originality and invention on top of the craft of writing a good story in screenplay form. I find that too often people don't understand the many objectives that a good screenplay must achieve."

Interscope's Scott Kroopf finds that he's often pitched a one-liner that's intriguing, but then reads the script to find its execution derivative and predictable; it makes little sense in today's market to buy the spec for just the idea. "As a studio executive, you're much better off buying a character that you love—maybe he's a commercial character—but you want that character to have a voice. You don't want to go, 'Oh, now I have to get someone else to rewrite it.' Because people in Hollywood don't really get that much rope.

"As a writer who comes into town, you really want to be able to keep writing," says Kroopf. "You don't want to . . . fall into the Hollywood bullshit trap. The worst thing you find is when some guy sells a spec script, makes some money, starts to do the meeting circuit as being the 'hot guy' in town, and he forgets how to write. I think most writers would say this: 'If you're really a writer, you better write every day.' You better be looking for an idea every day, or something that keeps you going. Because the business part of Hollywood really is for businessmen."

Yet the spec writer must also keep an eye on the business essentials. "Most first-time, second-time, third-time, and tenth-time writers have difficulty suppressing themselves and their screenplays and the stories *they* find interesting, as opposed to the stories they think are interesting *and* they think the entire moviegoing public—and therefore the studios—would be interested in," says writer Kurt Wimmer. "That's learning how to be incredibly ruth-

less with yourself before sitting down to write something and going down a checklist. Writers are very apt to lie to themselves and
say it doesn't matter if this is not castable, if Mel Gibson would
not want to do this role. . . . But you should see that every one of
those realms of commerciality are covered."

"If you write a big action piece that showcases a great character
for Harrison Ford to play, you stand a better shot of selling it,"
says agent David Phillips of Innovative Artists. "Studios look for
these projects to feed an international marketplace that thrives
on such films. The key is in writing something that looks commercial first, before you write *Gandhi*. Case closed. It's the fastest
way in."

In desiring that path in, however, writers may overlook what
the buyers appreciate most: a voice, a point of view, something
to distinguish the script's personal identity. "I think it's pretty
much been corrupted by the get-rich-quick point of view," says
director Tony Bill. "Writers are writing what they think people
want. I hear all the time, in the last five or six years when I would
lecture to classes, the first question they'd ever ask is, 'What are
people looking for?' Well, who cares what people are looking for,
unless you're a shoe salesman? That's a shoe salesman mentality:
'How can we create something that will sell for the people who
are buying.' Which is exactly backward.

"It's even backward if you take the sort of scientific approach
and analytic approach," Bill concludes. "I'm betting that if you
took a coldly analytic approach to the history of hit movies, you'd
find that the majority derive from the writer writing something that
was either ignorant of, or antithetical to, the marketplace."

For a writer to spec out a script takes a special combination of
forethought and passion for the material. "Working out what I can
do with a spec script is 80 percent of it," says *Daylight* and *Dante's
Peak* writer Leslie Bohem. "They don't pay you as much for a
development deal as a spec, their theory being it's more of a gamble. In one, you're putting your money on a number in roulette,
and in the other, you're taking the whole board. . . . To me, the
spec is much easier.

"I've been really fortunate in both million-dollar sales [of my
specs]. I did get on well with both of the directors," Bohem continues. "On the other hand, they could get the most temperamen-

tal person in the world and it could turn into hell. . . . If you're pissing and moaning about that sort of stuff, in the immortal words of Super-Chicken, 'You knew the job was dangerous when you took it.' You're a fool if you don't recognize that. That's the system."

Maintaining the Vision

*The voyage of discovery is not in seeking new landscapes
but in having new eyes.*

—MARCEL PROUST

*Whenever I am asked what kind of writing is the most
lucrative, I have to say, a ransom note.*

—LEGENDARY LITERARY AGENT H. N. SWANSON,
SPRINKLED WITH RUBY DUST

BY ITS TURBULENT nature, with executive seat shuffling and sudden
rises and falls, today's Hollywood breeds insecurities. This is, in part,
the reason why its players develop such oversized egos. The basis of
a studio executive's career ultimately depends on a fickle audience.
One's achievement relies on pointing out past successes and distancing
oneself from the previous failures, a process that in many ways the
executive really knows is out of his or her control. The "Teflon" executives are the ones who tend to stick around longest, and when they
have one huge success, the failures fade from memory.

During the studio system, when a producer figured that such books
as *The Wizard of Oz* or *Gone With the Wind* might make magnificent

motion pictures, he would kiss the hand of his mogul for the necessary anointing. The moguls loved their power and exercised it with judicious concern for maximizing the company's profits, thereby keeping shareholders happy. The studios operated like factories, churning out as much product as their audiences could handle. For instance, *The Wizard of Oz* (employing ten separate screenwriters and four directors) was but one of forty-one pictures that Metro-Goldwyn-Mayer released in 1939, a relatively light year for Hollywood's then premiere studio.

The rights to L. Frank Baum's fantasy tale, *The Wizard of Oz*, belonged to Samuel Goldwyn, who acquired them in 1932 for $40,000. Legend has it that Goldwyn originally purchased the rights after reading only six pages (in other words, most things in Hollywood don't really change) of an elaborate children's edition playwright Sidney Howard bought for him as a gift. In 1937, semiliterate MGM mogul Louis B. Mayer, who hired a lady to read stories to him, paid his former partner Sam Goldwyn $75,000 for the rights, beating out 20th Century–Fox, who envisioned it as a Shirley Temple movie.

Goldwyn was quite happy, history tells us, with the quick $35,000 profit he made. The Wizard role, written for W. C. Fields (who turned it down), went to a lesser name. Unable to lure Temple away from her Fox contract, MGM cast a young singer on the rise, Judy Garland, to portray the part of Dorothy.

It took over twenty years for *The Wizard of Oz* to earn back its money. As was more often the case than now, the project was designed as a prestige picture, not a moneymaker, although the studio would have loved to see it match the stellar box office returns of Walt Disney's sensational *Snow White and the Seven Dwarfs* released the previous year. Yet over time, *The Wizard of Oz* made a hefty profit and became a Hollywood classic.

THE STUDIO SYSTEM: THEN AND NOW

"It's not that the old dons weren't concerned about money. They certainly absolutely were," says John McTiernan, director of *Die Hard* and the remake of *The Thomas Crown Affair*. "But they were also to some extent gamblers and showmen, and they had their egos out there about being showmen. [In today's system] when you have an absentee corporate owner, there is more of a desire to build the big 'ride' films. They're not really movies at all. They're conceived as giant corporate entertainment projects. And they leave people who like to believe they got involved in movies because they loved them—because there was a passion—feeling hungry and unsatisfied."

Many filmmakers are discouraged by today's corporate structure that depersonalizes the moviemaking process. "Unless you're free to make mistakes [and] indulge your tastes, then you're thinking, 'How can I protect my job?' And if you're worrying about protecting your job, then nothing moves," says Tony Bill, the former actor who went on to direct and produce such movies as *Untamed Heart* and *My Bodyguard.* "The studios are now set up so everybody has a job. Even the head of the studio has 'a job.' The head of the studio can be fired.

"That was not the case before, in general," Bill explains, referring to the days of Jack Warner, who with his siblings owned Warner Bros., and Adolph Zukor, who remained nominal chairman of Paramount until his death at the age of 103. "Heads of studios were not fired. They certainly weren't fired for making a couple of loser movies. Now they're fired for mysterious reasons. So the studios are now faceless and basically without personality, which I also suggest scripts should not be. . . . The studios are so schizophrenic in their personality, their multi-personalities, that you can't say that they have *a* personality. There are a few, maybe the established ones. . . . But people who are making decisions are all subject to review. And that's unfortunate."

The change has occurred, however, and it will never return to the old days so long as filmmakers and stars can make such big deals. "Across the board—producers, agents, writers, directors, actors, studio executives, managers—very few people want to go on the line and say, 'I'm the reason this movie got made,' " says Chris Moore, the young coproducer of *Good Will Hunting.* "When you had Louie Mayer and Samuel Goldwyn and all those other guys, *that's* what they *loved.* They vibed off that: 'Yes, I'm telling the *world* that this movie should get made and *they're* going to like it!'

"When they made *Gone With the Wind,* everybody might think they're a nut case, but it becomes this gigantic success," Moore says. "And the guy goes home thinking, 'I'm a genius.' Now when the Universal executives go home after *Jurassic Park* makes [$900 million], do you think they say, 'Wow, I'm a genius; I am a smart man'? No. They go home and say, 'Thank God Steven Spielberg works at *my* company.'

They don't have the kind of drive of the old studio heads anymore. It's not about that. It's about keeping their jobs."

Today's movie factories have many more competitors: home video, paid cable services, Internet providers, CD-ROM games, etc. So making money, perhaps at the expense of making good movies, is their chief concern. "When you're a vice president at a studio and walk into your weekly creative meeting, and you really, really like the script," says Ross Hammer, a development executive turned producer, "the first thing a studio head will ask you is, '*Why?* How much is this going to make? Who's gonna watch this movie? And is this going to give me a $100 million hit?'

"You better be able to answer '*Yes*, and here's why . . .' to all of those questions, or else you're going to get laughed out of the meeting," says Hammer. "Very seldom will you be in a creative meeting at a studio and have somebody say, 'This just totally, totally moved me. It was incredible. It was really passionate . . .' unless that's followed by '*And* we can get Clint Eastwood and Meryl Streep to play the leads.' "

ON THE RIGHT TRACK

The spec script can be a locomotive in the whole process, yet to get attention, the spec needs to stand out from the rest. Oftentimes, it depends on the status of the agent submitting it. "Selling a script is really about heat," says George Huang, who was inspired by *El Mariachi* phenom Robert Rodriguez to quit assisting studio power brokers in order to write and direct his own motion picture, *Swimming with Sharks*. "God forbid you're the one who misses out on it. You may not have even read it, but you'll start bidding on it because you don't want to be out of the game."

Whenever a studio makes a sizable spec purchase, it inevitably sets off a shock wave of second-guessing by competing executives of whether the purchase was a savvy buy. "The buzz doesn't equal 'Great script, let's buy it,' and obviously a lot depends on the buzz that's created by scripts, and who's submitting it," says studio union reader Janet Goldstein. "You can write the best script in the world, but if it isn't submitted by somebody impressive, it's generally not going to be taken seriously if it's slipped in with a lot of other submissions."

Readers are the first chain in the process of bringing a script to screen, and they work on either union or non-union basis. Entry into the union is coveted and rare, usually after years of toiling for little or no pay. Also called "story analysts," readers provide a synopsis and critique of any submitted screenplay, something akin to a high school book report that breaks down the script's literary merit.

"You can train somebody to understand story structure and analyze the story, but how do you train somebody to know what will be a fun story to tell, and a fun story to *watch?*" says Ross Hammer. "A good movie has to be both. It has to be an interesting, fun, and emotional story that engages the audience *in addition* to something that is fun to watch. You can't survive without both in this business, and I think readers are only half of that. They can tell you technically what works and what doesn't about a story, but how often do you have a reader telling you how this is going to play? They can't do that."

"Well, nobody can," answers Goldstein. "Think of how many films people had *no* expectations for, like *Star Wars,* which wound up being multimillion-dollar successes. Or the films that seem to have all the right elements, which totally bombed, like *Rhinestone Cowboy.* I mean, I wouldn't have thought those were the right elements, but obviously some people did.

"I don't think anybody can predict 100 percent that any script is going to be a success, because there are so many factors," Goldstein continues. "Starting with the script, there's no telling if it would be rewritten badly, for instance. If you do attach a major star, and part of the contract is to have a rewrite—even if it's just for that character—it could take the script in a totally different direction that's inappropriate to the story, and suddenly the script is not working. Then problems just snowball from there.

"Then you've got the director. The art direction could be inappropriate. There could be one crucial element that just sinks the whole project," says Goldstein. "My feeling is, if you could predict what would be a hit, you'd never be out of work. . . . Everybody thinks they know, but you don't, really, until it's up there on the screen. Until that first weekend is over and you count up the numbers, you don't know how it's going to play."

Any reader's goal is to find a diamond in the rough and provide a rave review when nobody had any expectations. "Executives read it, love it, it gets bought," Goldstein concludes. "That's like every reader's dream: to find something that's *not* a hot spec, that *is* something really great, to find one little gem in all those piles that nobody else has found."

Another phenomenon that arose with Hollywood's spec boom is individuals known as "trackers." Often with titles of story editor, creative executive, or director of development, their job is to "keep track" of the writing community. "The development person is relatively new," says Peter Scott, a former development executive who manages writers. In the past, "a writer was under contract with the studio, and that studio would send them a script and say, 'Fix this, or that.' The writers themselves were the development people."

The studios benefited from hiring staffs of writers, paying them what seemed a handsome amount, to rewrite other people's work. "[When] the agencies recognized that fact, they said, 'No, no, don't go under contract. Let us make a deal for you each time. We will capitalize maybe as much as $500,000 on each deal,'" Scott continues. "Many writers would say it's the classic case of a writer who sold out, who sold his soul to Hollywood."

With the spec boom, the development process has evolved even further into internal, and external, development. "The internal development person is like that writer who was under contract: They sit in a room, they do notes, they fix scripts, they develop ideas, they cut articles out of magazines and work on new ideas that maybe they will pitch to writers or to the studios to get made into movies. The external person is 'the tracker,' the person who is a little bit more like a studio executive," Scott says.

"Professionally, trackers are into the relationship game," Scott continues. "They know a lot of people, and their job is to know when every writer is finishing their script, *every* writer. They want to know that Paul Attanasio (*Donnie Brasco, Quiz Show*) is just about to finish a script, and that Paul Attanasio has a relationship with Robert Redford who will get to see the script first. But if Robert Redford passes on it, [the tracker's company] wants the script and wants to be in business with Paul Attanasio.

"So it's the tracker's job to know when every writer is finishing something: what they're writing, what it's about, what's the title, who's the agent representing it, and exactly how it is going out—a little mini-strategy with each script on how *we* are going to get it *first*, or as soon as possible. Each production company is in competition with every other production company to get there first. We're called trackers," Scott says, "because we're tracking all that information."

The hierarchy within a production company determines the specific tracking responsibilities. "There are people who do nothing but track, which means they have a large network of friends they talk to frequently, at multiple times a day to find out what is going on, what's going out, what are they getting, what did they see, what did they think, what have they heard?" says Barri Evins, president of Debra Hill Productions. "I track with one person, and the focus of her job is to do that. That's enough for me." Every tracker inevitably feeds off of another's information trail.

"It's like venereal disease, she's tracking with a whole lot of people," Evins laughs. "I don't have to, because I'm a higher-level executive than she is. I'm frequently talking directly to agents to clarify details and things for her. She's trading information with other people who are more on her level, so at least she has more information, but I have very specific information."

Trackers know that a script designated to go out to only a few key producers has a perceived special value. "If they find out it's only going to Joel Silver, Mace Neufeld, and Jim Cameron, they're thinking, 'Wow, this must be something special.' It creates the illusion of heat," says producer Ross Hammer. "So much of selling scripts is about heat!

"All of the D-People (development people) tracking scripts know weeks and weeks beforehand that a spec is coming out, and approximately when. But if you start some sort of rumor that it's going to only three people, and they each have only four hours to respond to the material, and *especially* if it's coming out from a high-profile agent, suddenly this gives the impression that this is an incredible find," says Hammer.

"It might be a piece of crap. But they play up that heat, and then they compound it by calling other people during that four hours, saying, 'So and so really loves it. I'll slip it to you guys but nobody can know it; and you gotta move within an hour if you want to make anything happen with this.' It's a whole game. A lot of specs are sold that way—just based on heat—not the material."

Trackers routinely gather to trade their tips, often at secretive places so as not to be overheard. Once the spec script market heated up, their busy schedules conflicted, so they would convene in online computer chat rooms where they could see onscreen all who were present.

When an unfamiliar screen name entered, the conversation quickly steered away from industry gab. At the session's end, trackers could download and print their data. Nowadays, they have special Web pages that require passwords to get the latest scoop, which in the words of one producer "makes an evil process more evil."

One time, agent Jeremy Zimmer grew so frustrated by a particular executive's leakage of information that one of his fellow UTA agents called the guy to say, "Look, there's a brand new spec that Zimmer brought up in today's meeting, and it's called *Boomerang*. But you gotta swear to secrecy. Don't tell anybody, okay?" That day, Zimmer received six phone calls from various executives requesting a sneak peek at *Boomerang*. He happily called the initial blabbermouth to inform him he was busted: *Boomerang* never even existed.

While the spec market has opened up the playing field for new writers, it has subsequently allowed agencies to be selective in the screenplays they disseminate, thereby strengthening their role vis-à-vis the studios. Trackers came about as a result of that spec world, because there never really has been an open market for a spec script.

"The interesting thing to look at is this: Are agencies inhibiting free trade as a result of only giving it to such and such individual?" says producer Peter Scott. "The agencies say, 'We're gonna give this spec to you, you, and you to look at it first, and we are going to decide who we want to give it to.' That, to me, is a closed market, and they are basically monopolizing their talent and distributing it to certain individuals.

"A tracker's job is to call them up and ask, 'Please let me see this script first. I think it's right for my company because we already have an idea that's like it that's not working and we'd really like to be in this arena.' Or, 'I was an adopted child, and I know this script is about an adopted child, and I just feel it's a movie that I would get.' They might say, 'So what? *We* want to give it to so-and-so, the most powerful producer on the lot, and we know who that is.' Thereby, it inhibits us from even having an opportunity to look at it." Thus, a very skilled tracker is capable of changing an agent's mind, but generally only with a pocketbook, or quid pro quo, to back it up. "The tracker's job is to come up with all these reasons why we would be better than them, so the best trackers have good reason, and they get to see the material," Scott says.

Often, a tracker will find out who a spec's going to and call his friend at that company to say, "Slip it to me. I just want to know what it's about. Even though it's given to you for your consideration, I want to read it simultaneously. If you don't buy it, we'll be able to call the agent and say, 'You know what? We really want to make this movie, we love it, or, we really like the idea' and pretend like we haven't read it. Or you can read it and know if it's not right for us, and not even bother to tell the agent at that point.' The skilled tracker might get it from a secondary source. The agencies are not an open market or an open auction anymore. It's a closed auction.

"The tracker's job is to get a first look at everything," Scott says. "You can see how relationships matter, especially in that world. The interesting thing about it is, instead of focusing your energies toward making great movies, coming up with ideas, and just working the relationships you know will have positive results, you could potentially spend all your time finding out this information, and then get *none* of it in."

WHY THE STUDIOS EXIST

Studios are the nuclei that the movie business is built around, and production companies are the electrons that encircle them. Production companies are designed to attract, and generate, screenplays to bring in to the studio's coffers. Brokers of spec scripts, whether they be agents or individual producers hoping to align with production companies, must convey an image that their movie will take a big bite out of the box office.

Of the bottom-line mentality that rules the game, "I would say 90 percent of the screenplays are purchased based on financial concerns, and a breakdown of what [the studio's market analysts] think it's going to bring the studio," says producer Ross Hammer. "It really starts at the financial end. I would like to say there's a heavy emotional connection to the material. But in my experience, unfortunately that's one of the things that's lacking."

Hammer hits on what's perhaps the clearest distinction between the new Hollywood and the golden days of the studio system. Back when Hollywood had little competition for entertainment, studios were about the only entities that offered a diversion from reality's doldrums.

Then came television, and at first studios were afraid of it. A slice of the studio pie was disappearing before the studios got wise and incorporated television under their banners.

"Studios exist to make money," adds Hammer, formerly a development executive for a Disney producer, Universal, and Addis-Wechsler. "If they don't make a lot of money producing movies, there's no reason for them to exist, because they don't offer anything else. They offer entertainment, but you don't need studios to make entertainment. You don't need studios to make movies. The reason they exist is to make money."

While today's studios exist as sort of investment banks to protect their corporate enterprise, what type of studio movies does that leave the audience with? "In the 1960s and the early seventies, there was a competition in the creative community to make the 'great film,' " says producer George Litto, who during that period as a William Morris agent helped package such films as Robert Altman's *M*A*S*H* and John Schlesinger's *Midnight Cowboy*. "The great film wasn't necessarily the film that grossed the most money."

Studios found huge commercial success on such movies as *The Poseidon Adventure* (the top grosser of 1973), *Airport* (the 1970 champ), or *The Towering Inferno* (number two at the box office after *Jaws* in 1975). But they also took chances with "special" films like *Lilies of the Field,* made for a few hundred thousand dollars. Actor Sidney Poitier took a share of the huge profits in what resulted in a distinguished picture. "That environment, that attitude, doesn't exist anymore," explains Litto, who left agenting to produce such movies as Robert Altman's *Thieves Like Us* and Brian De Palma's *Blow Out.*

"I'm not saying people aren't trying to make great films right now, but everything is more fixated on the marketing potential," Litto continues. "Hollywood has become the new Gold Rush, the boomtown, drilling oil wells, hitting gushers. We went from the sixties, which was the social conscience era, to the seventies, and then in the eighties it became the 'me' generation—me, me, me. That all has something to do with it, the disenchantment of the Vietnam War in the sixties and seventies had something to do with it, probably. And society changed."

With the societal transitions came developments in Hollywood's business environment. "The previous executives cared about the 'art,' and nowadays it seems to be more about the 'numbers,' " says George

Huang, who studied the business of entertainment at USC before embarking on a filmmaking career.

"This is particularly true in the late eighties; the executives were all business graduates. They hadn't *watched* movies," says Huang. "On the other hand, they had these Harvard MBAs. Somehow, Hollywood sort of became the refuge for all the Wall Street fallouts, because Wall Street was the business everyone was going into when it was at its boom. When the market crashed, everyone came to Hollywood.

"The most frustrating experiences I had as an assistant were talking to an executive," Huang recalls. "I would say, 'It's like *Romancing the Stone,*' and my boss would reply, '*Well,* I never saw that.' Then I would say, 'And this one's like *The Terminator.*' And he would counter, 'I didn't see that movie.'

"You know, these aren't extraordinary films or anything. These are, like, big hits!" thought Huang, as if rehearsing lines he'd later use in *Swimming with Sharks,* the movie he wrote and directed about a studio exec taken hostage and then tortured by his harassed assistant. "I would think, 'You didn't see *Romancing the Stone,* and you didn't see *The Terminator;* why am I taking orders from you?' It's the most frustrating thing in the world," Huang laughs.

Producers aligned with studios have an immediate inroad to the coffers of their studio, but must play a political game to assure their access. Deals for producers generally are on a first-look basis, meaning that if a producer brings in a script and the studio passes, he or she is free to search elsewhere to set up the movie. Sometimes a studio only offers exclusive deals, which lock down the producer. A "housekeeping" deal is simply a way a studio provides a home, and there's often an implicit obligation that the producer will submit material to that studio, although the producer isn't obligated to do so.

More potential buyers entering the game make the current era a heyday for screenwriters, and even major studios have divided themselves up into separate divisions to allow even more potential buyers. "It's a pretty good market because there are many more buyers competing because of the fragmentation of the studios—the way they have tried to differentiate their market by creating these divisions that are aimed at certain niches of the marketplace. Now every studio has become three or four studios, such as Fox Searchlight, Fox 2000, the Family Division, and the main section, Fox Proper," says Fox 2000 executive Christopher Vogler. "We really have four operations running here at Fox, and four potential buyers for any piece of material, and that's happened everywhere.

"I believe that was a Disney creation, under an old principle, really, which was Walt Disney's idea long ago, to kill the competition with product. Just get a lot of product out there," says Vogler about the company he formerly worked for, which itself subdivided under the Eisner-Katzenberg era to create Touchstone and Hollywood Pictures, in addition to its long-standing Walt Disney Pictures. "That's what's going on here at Fox. There's an attempt to fill up the pipeline and to create a library for the larger purposes than just the theatrical release and also to fill a lot of the TV outlets and videos, and so that has made more possible buyers."

"The studios became more of a business. The blockbuster mentality came in after *Jaws* and *Star Wars*," says Bob Kosberg, producer of *Twelve Monkeys* and *Man's Best Friend*. "Everybody saw the pot of gold that ideas and scripts represent. Everyone always wanted to sell material, because you hoped you would get your movie made. But *now* the studios and the buyers not only want to find something good to get a movie made, everyone's constantly talking about finding that 'next big thing.'

"Because the money out there is so gigantic, the studios are these gigantic machines that are prospecting and searching and are all desperate. The competitiveness has increased, and the feeding frenzy for ideas, books, and scripts has increased," says Kosberg. "The doors are open to anybody who has relationships, because no one knows when you walk in the door whether or not you might be the guy with the next one.

"Once you do walk in a door—to any studio, certainly—there are all these production companies on the lot that are fighting each other," Kosberg explains. "All the studio executives are fighting politically to find the project they can bring in that will make them a star. For the outside creative person, I find, it's a better environment" than in the past. In Hollywood, money buys freedom, at least insofar as a temporary vacation from the labyrinth.

The Hollywood game has often been called "high school with money," a place where studios operate on big campuses and their executives constantly bring home piles of weekend homework. "We're one big high school, and we all talk about each other, gossip about each other, date each other, and, you know, make fun of each other," says Agency for the Performing Arts agent Justen Dardis. "It's like Sundance could be our prom. It's *exactly* like high school. It's very closed, and we all have blinders on."

REMOVING BLINDERS FOR A FRESH PERSPECTIVE

After settling in Los Angeles in the 1940s, Igor Stravinsky cleverly noted that "the only way to avoid Hollywood is to live there." In his landmark book, *Adventures in the Screen Trade,* William Goldman described Los Angeles as "a very difficult and potentially dangerous place to work in, and I think anyone seriously contemplating a career as a screenwriter ought to move there as soon as it's humanly or financially possible."

Nowadays fewer filmmakers choose to. Robert Rodriguez has remained in Austin, Texas, ever since his breakthrough with *El Mariachi,* and even after going Hollywood, John Waters remains in Baltimore. Santa Barbara, San Francisco, and Seattle now host a number of Hollywood directors and writers. On that other coast, the city that never sleeps provides a home for William Goldman and many other screenwriters.

Working out of New York provides Miramax's Jack Lechner with a different vantage point on the spec game. "In terms of specs, there are people writing independent films and trying to get them developed with New York independent film companies, like us, or any of the independent production companies like HBO [NYC Productions], where I was previously. Or there are people focused on Los Angeles, who write what they think are commercial screenplays and try to get them to Hollywood through either a New York agent or an L.A. agent, or whoever they know."

Independent filmmaking doesn't rely on the same dynamic of studio purchases, so the New York indies are more like the Hollywood writers of the past, writing screenplays they're hoping to make into films, Lechner continues, "which I think is very different from the idea in L.A. of someone trying to hit the jackpot with a screenplay."

Hollywood's spec market has effectively strengthened the writer's role in relation to the rest of the filmmaking team. According to *Lethal Weapon* screenwriter Shane Black, specs opened the opportunity for writers to stay involved rather than remain removed from the studio machine, and whereby writers can "develop capabilities and skills if they're just *watching* what's going on. That makes them more a part of the process.

"That's what's going to make for good filmmaking," says Black. "Politics to me is the ability to express your ideas in as influential a way as possible, based on what you believe to be the best movie, *not* knowing what job someone holds, or wanting that job for yourself." Black considers himself fortunate to have gotten into the spec script game when the waves were just beginning to swell.

"I remember walking into [*Lethal Weapon* producer] Joel Silver's office and he'd just be sleeping in the middle of the day," Black recalls. "He'd be lounging, reading a book or something, and I'd say, 'Hey, Joel, you know, what d'ya think of this?' He would say, 'Na, nahhh . . . I don't think so.' 'Well, all right, let me try it again,' and I would come back five minutes later.

"In subsequent years, I would have to take a meeting with him, walking really fast beside him on the way to another meeting, speaking as quickly as I could," says Black. "It was just an amazing difference to feel the energy of getting in on the ground floor with someone who's just kind of breaking on their own."

Black first got into Hollywood's doors with his spec *Shadow Company,* about a group of Vietnam soldiers. Then he tossed his partial draft of *Lethal Weapon* into the garbage when a poet friend criticized his potboiler writing style. "I pulled it out of the trash about a week later, which says more about my lifestyle and how often I throw out the trash than about the script," says Black. "I even auctioned that original script off, with lettuce stains on it and coffee grounds, at some little charity. But there was a joy in finishing that script and knowing it *wouldn't* sell. Then I got the call that it had just attracted all this attention, and I was flabbergasted." The price on Black's specs has gone up ever since.

Although a known writer's stellar track record at churning out spec material can have studio execs thirsting for a peek at his next script, new writers are now sought after more than ever. "When I started in the business, when a script did not come from an established writer, or a novel or a play, it was rejected out of hand," says Tony Bill, who produced *Taxi Driver* and *Going in Style,* and is known especially for working with first-timers from his career's start.

"An original script was kind of a black mark," says Bill, recalling the changes since his introduction to the business. "That's come 180 de-grees now. If there's a script that's written by somebody you've never heard of, then everybody's falling all over themselves trying to get a look at it or buy it." Studios have learned from mistakes, yet can still fall prey to overly hyped high-concept material while overlooking many quality screenplays. "And the scripts that have been treated like they're worth nothing are the ones that have been worth the most."

"Sometimes having a spec script is the only way to get started as a writer. You have to prove what you can do," says producer-director Jonathan Sanger. "In television, writers are always writing episodic shows, to demonstrate they can do that kind of writing in order to get a [staff writing] job. Those [episodic specs] are guaranteed not to get made . . . but they might capture the attention of somebody to try you on a new show." The television process reflects to a degree what has been developing in the feature market: Specs are a necessity for en-tering the game.

Selling the $1 million spec might be a quick way of making it onto assignment lists, but sometimes, as in Les Bohem's experience, the big money comes later. Son of Endre Bohem, a Hollywood screenwriter from the silent era, Les worked for years (on thirty-four assignments) prior to selling a spec script. Les took *Twenty Bucks,* a spec his father never finished, and turned it into a charming 1993 film about a $20 bill passing from hand to hand. He claims the curious distinction of having his first two specs (*Twenty Bucks* and *Kid*) *produced* on budgets less than what his subsequent two specs *sold* for: *Daylight* (for $1.2 million) and *Dante's Peak* ($1 million).

"I am now considered a much better writer because I've gotten a million dollars to write a screenplay," says Bohem. "But I'm not any better now than when I wrote *Twenty Bucks*. . . . The good news is that it's a little bit of recognition for [screenwriting] what I feel is the most important part of the equation. Like all writers, I belly-ache about how Hollywood studios are so stupid . . . but you know, if they're so stupid, why don't you have more of their money?"

With a spec, "your joy in the creation of the work is finished the day you hand the script over to your agent and producer to go sell it," says Bohem, also a musician, who likens specs to making demo tapes. "You're gonna get notes you hate, notes that are based on fear, notes based on stars, notes based on temperamental directors. You're gonna get rewritten. You're gonna get asked back to do something. . . . On some level you say, 'You want to pay me $1.2 million to go away? Great!'"

The ease of entry for new writers since the spec boom has also benefited established filmmakers. "It's great because the market has just totally broken open," says Dan Halsted, now Oliver Stone's producer at Illusion Entertainment. "I don't think there are any downsides to it, although I think for a lot of older writers who have been working on assignment for a long, long time—people in their forties and fifties—they're having a hard time finding jobs. [It's partly because of] ageism in Hollywood." Yet the ageism has a very practical side to it.

"Are you going to hire a mid-level $400,000 writer who's in his fifties, or do you hire a new guy for $100,000 and take a chance on them?" Halsted explains. A studio and producer "may want to invest in these younger guys, because their loyalty comes from executives working with a young person who they can call anytime and say, 'Hey, c'mon, do me a favor.' "

Tony Bill feels a writer must set sights on one of two things. "You can either say 'I'm not interested in writing an excellent script, I'm interested in writing one that will sell' or 'I'm not interested in writing a script that will sell, I'm interested in writing something that I like, that I think is good.' You have to make that seminal choice. And you can succeed on either level, but I don't think you can succeed on both levels.

"How many of these [big money] scripts get made? And of those that get made, how many could you honestly say were worth every penny you paid for them? Or should have been made at all?" Bill wonders. When William Morris's Jeff Field showed Bill a script called *The Baboon Heart*, it was presented in a stack of writing samples without any heat or hype attached. Tony Bill liked the title, and he and his producing partner Helen Bartlett gave it a read.

The script's writer, Tom Sierchio, had come out to Los Angeles after five years of part-time acting and stuntman roles in New York (on such B flicks as *Toxic Avenger*) and aluminum siding jobs to pay the bills. A reader for a low-grade Hollywood producer urged Sierchio to move west.

"You go to Detroit if you want to make cars, and Hollywood if you want to make movies," said the reader, who was fired for her unwavering support of Sierchio's early material over the dreck her bosses would make. Once in Los Angeles, Sierchio subsequently got his material in the hands of *Glengarry Glen Ross* producer Morris Ruskin, who introduced Sierchio's scripts to William Morris's Alan Gasmer. When Gasmer signed him, Sierchio delivered spirits for Vendome Liquors in Beverly Hills, and occasionally the agency would request deliveries from the store, putting Tom in a few awkward positions. But he didn't work at Vendome for long.

The Baboon Heart, Sierchio's tenth script, so enchanted Bill and Bartlett that they invited Tom over to their house. "I read the script, and I was crying for about ten minutes," Bartlett told Sierchio once he sat down. "I told Tony if he doesn't do this movie, then I will." Yet Bill warned Sierchio that his young love story, while precious in his and Bartlett's eyes, might be a hard sell.

Two days later, Tony Bill phoned up Sierchio.

"You know, I had a hunch," said Bill. "I have some friends over at MGM, and there's this guy there, Laddie, who's looking at your script. What are you doing right now?"

"Well, it's my birthday," Tom replied, who was turning thirty years old and was curious to know who "Laddie" was.

"C'mon over, we have to celebrate," Bill said. When Sierchio arrived at Bill and Bartlett's Venice house, a bottle of champagne awaited. "Alan Ladd [who ran MGM at the time] read the script and he wants to do it." By writing something from the heart after several previous scripts that anticipated the market, Sierchio finally made a sale. Retitled *Untamed Heart,* the 1993 release, starring Christian Slater and Marisa Tomei, became one of MGM's biggest hits that year.

"Now the funny thing is, the clientele list at the liquor store [where I worked] was the 'who's who' of Hollywood," Sierchio recalls. "And Alan Ladd was on that list. So I had a delivery to his house about a year before *Baboon Heart* and I snuck another script of mine in with his order. A couple days later, his assistant calls me."

Standing at the liquor store counter, Sierchio was elated to get the call, anticipating his first script sale. As it turned out, Laddie's assistant was none too pleased. "You don't do stuff like this," shouted the lady in Alan Ladd's office. "How'd you get Laddie's address? Don't you know things aren't done this way?"

THE RULES OF THE GAME

Like Wall Street, the spec market works in cycles, and the movie business isn't immune to the general rules of economics. "There's up periods and down periods, but it will always be around to some extent," says Paradigm agency's Stu Robinson. "The spec market seems to be kind of like a roller-coaster wave.

"It always happens when six or seven companies are spending a million or a million-five on spec scripts, and like *Radio Flyer* they lose money. Or worse, they make *Milk Money,* which tanks in eleven seconds," says Robinson of two separate million-dollar-plus scripts that damaged studio balance sheets, causing the spec waves to rise and fall. "And then they say, 'Let's go back to [internal] development.' What's here today will be gone tomorrow, and what ain't here today will reappear the day after tomorrow. I don't mean that to sound cynical. It's just a fact."

The feeding frenzies can be unsettling to those on the buyer side. "Something just sold in the past month for millions of dollars—it was a book—and there's just no way that anyone finished reading it," says Castle Rock's Liz Glotzer. "I think it would be nice if someone had twenty-four hours to read the script. It's advantageous to the writer, so that the person who buys it isn't getting a surprise. And it's advantageous to the studio because you then know if they really want to make the movie, or how much work it requires in the end. But sometimes the premises are so strong, people will respond to the premise.

"It used to go to a producer, a producer would read it that weekend, and said 'Yes' or 'No, I'm not interested,'" says Glotzer. "Now the minute producers get scripts they have to send them to the studio before they even *like* them, so they're really just—at *that* stage—not doing much except inflating the price. It wasn't usually an automatic thing to attach producers, and how are people deciding which producers to attach? I think that's why it's a more expensive process today. And the producers who are less expensive have a much harder time getting good material."

As Phoenix's Mike Medavoy notes, "we live in a market economy. We all want a piece of the few proclaimed box-office draws, and until there is a total collapse or we all agree to make a change, things will continue to escalate.

"Of course, it's not just the movie industry that's caught in this quandary," Medavoy said in a recent speech to industry leaders. "Clearly, when it comes to big names, executives in every branch of media and entertainment are acting like costs are no object. But the fact is, cost is not only an object, it's becoming an obstacle to our viability as an industry. We all make the decision whether or not to compete for talent. I paid for big names when I was at big studios. I also cut some wrong corners with talent. Telling Dustin Hoffman he was too expensive for *Gorky Park,* for instance, was what you could call a mistake.

"When I buy a spec script the idea is to make it. If we're going to pay that kind of price, I don't want it sitting in an inventory," Medavoy continues. "We're always making good and bad decisions, but if you believe that big stars or special effects will give you some kind of insurance policy, in my opinion, you stand to lose. You'll end up driving up costs and creating a product that looks like everybody else's."

Companies with a new regime and an influx of cash become suddenly active in the spec market where they might have been quiet before. "Certain companies have certain mandates," says Lynn Harris of New Line Cinema. "They may be looking for a certain type of movie: a broad comedy, or a vehicle for a particular star. They're looking at their development slate and seeing where the holes are."

But aside from the money, relationships are the key to getting prime material from agents. Janet Yang started her development career at Universal Studios, where she was hired to sell American movies to China, then worked with Steven Spielberg on 1987's *Empire of the Sun.* "I was one of the few people, I guess the only person in Hollywood, who had been traveling back and forth to China, and I had become very familiar with the film industry there. Spielberg's production company, Amblin, asked me to work on *Empire of the Sun,* which was a Warner Brothers picture, but I was essentially on loan for the movie for that period."

At the time, Amblin didn't have its own executive at Universal, "so they asked me to be the liaison between Universal and Amblin," Yang recalls. "I was primarily servicing the Amblin account. I'm sure my early days were very influenced by Amblin. I worked closely with Kathy Kennedy and her staff there. They too were just kind of coming into the spec market.

"Steven Spielberg started out really just making his own films, and they were obviously hugely successful," says Yang. "But the development game was also new to [Amblin] so I was learning with them, going out to lunches with agents, really trying to make contacts. I thought it was interesting that Kathy Kennedy, who was so successful, and even Steven still had to work *hard* at getting material because they had not previously been involved in the spec market. Although people respected their work, they were not an active buyer, so spec scripts were not frequently or regularly submitted to them.

"They felt frustrated that they couldn't get good material," says Yang, now a partner at the Manifest Film Company. "At the time, Steven was not represented by anybody. Everybody wanted to represent him. He hadn't decided, and later he went with CAA but that was a big step for him. So that's another issue that comes up—who is representing you— because obviously [an agency] favors [its] own clients, producer-wise. I got a taste of all that, and a sense of the high volume of spec scripts really out there."

The Studio's Almighty Franchise

Frustrated by a competing agent's sales of *Die Hard* on a bus (*Speed*), *Die Hard* on a ship (*Under Siege*), and *Die Hard* in a subway (*Money Train*), a novice agent suggests to his new client, "Why don't you go write *Die Hard* in a building" (forgetting that it was the original movie's premise). Such are the short attention spans in the frenzied world of specs.

Screenwriting today attracts those who feel it's one of the last places on Earth where you will find the "Horatio Alger rags-to-riches fable." Yet the pot of gold not only lures screenwriters, and producers hungry for fresh ideas, it's also especially desirable for studio executives who can locate a "franchise," a movie that spawns merchandising and any number of sequels.

"I knew *Alien* had the potential to be an enormous hit, but then there were hardly such things as franchises," says writer Ron Shusett. "*Star Wars* started the whole franchise thing, but *Star Wars* didn't open until 1977, two years before *Alien,* so it hadn't become a franchise yet. So I wasn't thinking a franchise as much as I was an enormous hit. . . . We made a huge amount of money, and in those days, you *did* see net points. [Today's movies] take in maybe double or triple the box-office grosses than before, but they cost five, or six, or ten times what they used to."

Sometimes projects initially designed with other intentions can be molded into a perfect fit for an existing franchise, otherwise known as a "tent pole," to maintain a string of long-running hits that the studios so desperately desire. *Die Hard with a Vengeance,* the third in the *Die Hard* series, was in fact adapted from a buddy picture that had not intended to be part of the *Die Hard* franchise.

"I was working with [screenwriter] Jonathan Hensleigh on something, and I just said, 'What else you got?' " recalls original *Die Hard* director John McTiernan. Hensleigh referred to the project *Simon Says* in development at 20th Century–Fox that kept being rewritten in circles. "People had been sending me *Die Hard* [scripts] for everything—including a building—for years. I talked with Larry Gordon over and over on a sequel, and I talked to Andy Vajna for several years. He had a project he wanted to turn into a *Die Hard* sequel, and I was never really thrilled with it. But I knew he wanted one."

Hensleigh's script had the elements for a *Die Hard* that wouldn't just be a remake of the first. "That was why I pursued it," McTiernan continues. "It could use the expectations of a sequel to *Die Hard* but spin along in other directions, sort of like an audience jiujitsu, to use what they *think* they know about what's coming and use that to surprise them.

"It all happened in four days," says McTiernan, who sent Hensleigh's script to Andy Vajna and Bruce Willis and promptly set it up at the Fox studio.

In fact, the original *Die Hard* also changed integrally from the initial 1979 novel *Nothing Lasts Forever* by Roderick Thorp, which was set around a genuine terrorist event. "We turned the story into a robbery, because I don't find terrorism entertaining, and I don't really think the movie audience does. Whereas if it's a good caper, you can root for both sides. You can enjoy both sides. You can even like the bad guys, or certainly find them interesting, even if you don't *like* them.

"When people start out to write sequels—the proposed sequels to *Die Hard* that people have . . . purposefully written—they have been pretty universally dreadful," says McTiernan. "They have no spark, no imagination. They don't really have any joy in them."

Likewise, many writers and script sellers make the mistake in thinking that filmmakers will be attracted to the same type of project that they have just completed. In fact, they more often go for something quite different, since filmmakers generally prefer to "stretch" or broaden their horizons. After Tim Burton made a surprise success with 1988's *Beetlejuice,* he was flooded with ghost-story screenplays that he had little interest in making. After Stuart Cornfeld produced the remake of *The Fly* in 1987, he got a script about a guy who turns into a donkey.

"It's astonishing how agents will send you a script . . . because it's like what you just did," says McTiernan, who after making *Medicine Man* found himself flooded with a number of "eco-movie" scripts. "Recently I got a script about a guy who's being sent from place to place by a telephone bad guy, and he's running up and down the hills of Hong Kong," says McTiernan, breaking into laughter.

"I said to the agent, 'This is a little similar [to *Die Hard with a Vengence*], isn't it? And he said, 'It's not, it's not at all. It's Hong Kong, it's Hong Kong!' "

Hollywood's Fear Factor

> ## SELLING IS A PASSION, BUT BUYING IS A FEAR.
> ## AND THE GREATER PRESSURE IS ALWAYS
> ## ON THE BUYER.

The race is not always to the swift, nor the battle to the strong, but that's the way to bet.

— DAMON RUNYAN,
LOOSELY PARAPHRASING
ECCLESIASTES 9:11

If we listened to our intellect, we'd never have a love affair. . . . We'd never go into business, because we'd be cynical. Well, that's nonsense. You've got to jump off cliffs all the time and build your wings on the way.

— RAY BRADBURY

AN OFTEN-TOLD joke about the studios goes like this:

After working on a spec script for months, a hopeful screenwriter manages to hand it to some seemingly stable studio executive.

Come Sunday night, the executive picks up the script. Could it be the next *Men in Black* or another *Heaven's Gate*? After about page forty, the studio guy grows worried that he didn't send it in to the studio's reader pool.

The writer calls on Monday morning. "Thanks for taking the time to read my script," he says anxiously. "I'm prepared to make changes, and I think it could be the Tom Cruise vehicle you're looking for."

"Yeah, I read it all the way through." The studio guy shifts and in a moment has a flash that the writer is actually right about this.

"Well, what did you think?"

"I, I don't know," the baby mogul responds. "Nobody else here read it."

You can bet the executive's still working in the business, while the writer is still waiting for somebody to read his script. Playing it safe can lengthen job security, but doesn't exactly result in courageous films. "It's always the fear factor," says Rima Greer of Above the Line Agency. "Will I get fired if I don't buy it?" "Will I get fired if I do buy it?" It can work either way.

"The industry thinks it knows what talent is bankable to that universe of people who actually pay money to see movies. So they're gonna be looking for material that will attract bankable talent," says Greer, who formerly ran Writers & Artists Agency literary department before establishing her own boutique agency. "If I read the script and have a reasonable expectation that Harrison Ford will want to make it, you bet I'll buy it. If I say, 'Is there any big movie star that I can put in this movie?' and the answer is no, you're gonna go, 'I'm not gonna buy it.' "

"You have to create competition," says Jeff Mueller, who with his partner Andy Licht produced such films as *The Cable Guy* and *Waterworld.* "You need to establish fear in people to sell a spec script," says Licht. "You need to have them afraid that you'll take the script elsewhere to make the movie.

"So it's the studio's job to be golden retrievers," Licht continues. "That's why there's all this wining and dining, and 'everybody wants to be your friend' kind of thing going on. But when it comes to actually buying a script, the people making the decisions are worried about what everyone else thinks. It's like *The Emperor's New Clothes.* People don't tend to listen to their own gut instincts."

"The problem with Hollywood," his partner Mueller cuts in, "is that the decisions aren't based on the material as much as they should be."

"You can lose your studio executive job and that's a really scary place to be, so they're justifiably cautious," says *Dante's Peak* screenwriter Les Bohem. "You like that six months where you can say, 'I've got a Schwarzenegger film. I'm doing a Demi Moore film.' What's that

mean? It's 'fame by association,' and it's a disgusting modern phenomenon. It's like, 'I'm riding in a limo with Mick Jagger, therefore, I'm
somehow important.' But all those sixty thousand people in the sta-
dium, they came to see Mick Jagger. They don't really care who's in
the limousine.

"You get these brownie points," Bohem says of thinking that goes
on behind studio doors. "Then there's the 'cover-your-ass' part. You
don't lose your job if you have Arnold Schwarzenegger."

"The stakes have gotten so high, if you're the person who occupies
that chair in a studio, your job security correlates with putting the biggest name you can in the movie and hiring the most successful director
you can attach, which cumulatively makes for these megabudgets,"
says producer Cary Brokaw, a maven in the independent world who
started his career as a 20th Century–Fox marketing executive. "Yet
when that film fails, you can't be criticized because you went with the
most reliable elements money could buy.

"That's what the heads of production do. They're trying to make
bulletproof movies, and it's always with hindsight: Who was last year's
star, who worked with what director, and so forth. Well, history has
proven that what worked last year usually doesn't work the following
year. But on paper, going into a particular movie, it looks good.

"It is the pattern of caution that keeps people in their jobs," Brokaw
concludes. "People write about the excesses of this business, but what
isn't spoken about very much is the *fear*—the fear of what it's like
when you're thrown out of one of those jobs. Or if you're an actor
who gets cold overnight, what that climate of fear is like when you're
living it and experiencing the volatility that characterizes this business
week in and week out."

According to Mark Johnson, who produced most of Barry Levinson's
movies before setting up his own company, the spec market has gone
from something really exceptional in the early 1990s, where the spec
sales were few and far between, to now where "it seems like everybody has to [write on spec]. It's almost more dictated by a writer's
pocketbook, and by his confidence in what he's about to write."

For a writer who could be making money on assignments, writing
on spec is a time commitment, although those such as Joe Esterhasz,
Shane Black, and Patrick Duncan often opt to write on spec because
it provides a comparable creative freedom. And the payday from a spec
is proportionally much greater.

"I don't think that most studio heads or most people working in the studios right now know the real basics of a screenplay, but [the decision to purchase a spec is] actually less that than the question of patience," Johnson continues. "To write a screenplay takes incredible time, skill, stamina, and a distinct methodology. . . . Nobody has the time to sit down with John Hancock once a day, two or three times a week, go over a script for two or three hours and say, 'All right this is what it should be.'

"Most people just sit down and say, 'All right, it's great. You're gonna do a thing about this guy, his daughter, and the wilderness. Where's it gonna end up?' 'Yeah, that's good' and 'Can you send us pages? Will you send us the first act?' If the writer is important enough, the writer could almost do anything.

"David Mamet is quite proud of the fact that when he takes [a job] he doesn't even have to listen to anybody's notes," says Johnson, referring to the playwright who wrote the screenplays for *Wag the Dog, The Edge,* and *The Untouchables.* "What you see is what you get. I think most buyers don't have confidence in their own ability of being able to develop a screenplay."

Total Recall writer Ron Shusett agrees. "Studios seem to have learned that an idea may be promising, but it takes *years* and years to get the script that big stars and directors say, 'Hey, I love that.' [Nowadays studios] are more receptive than I could ever have imagined, to anybody handing in a spec [that works]. They'll show it to a couple people they respect and say, 'Wow! Okay, we'll buy it no matter what it costs!' Because they realize that it's so precious to get a movie that *works,* they will pay disproportionately higher money, rather than develop their own ideas with their own staff."

Film historians recall that the original screenplay for 1942's *Woman of the Year,* by Michael Kanin and Ring Lardner, Jr., sold for a then whopping $125,000. "There was a spec boom earlier in the movie business, in the late thirties, early forties," says producer Thom Mount (*Bull Durham, Night Falls on Manhattan*) of the cyclical nature of Hollywood. But following the spec boom after the 1988 WGA strike, "the studios made a lot of mistakes, and the writers were very callow about it. It looked like a fertile market for a while, and it has calmed down a lot, which is good news.

"The bad news is that when writers sit around trying desperately to write something they think would be a big hit, they tend to write for the studio, and when they write for the studio, they tend to write in a formulaic way," Mount laments. "So we get a lot of scripts that you could plug Bruce Willis into, or Sylvester Stallone or Arnold Schwarzenegger, and crank out *Die Hard 17.* And studios, because they're under a lot of pressure every year to have a reliable flow of pictures, always reach for those solutions that look easy and safe.

"This means the kind of big action pictures we frequently see now are not very fresh," adds Mount, former Universal head of production in the late 1970s. "You think about the action pictures that were fresh in their day, *Star Wars, Raiders of the Lost Ark, French Connection,* even things like *The Omen, Terminator,* or more recently the original *Die Hard.* Many of those movies were really fresh at their moment. Unfortunately, they quickly spawn a sea of progeny, of imitators."

SHORT-ATTENTION-SPAN THEATER

A studio executive's search for a "commercial" property is by its nature ambiguous, because nobody can define what is commercial until after it makes a profit. Thus to studio execs, what makes a script commercial is its wide appeal. The only gauge Hollywood has to measure a script's appeal, once it's out on the market, are the judgments of the studio's competitors. But because studio buyers tend to live in an insular world, their only indication of audience taste is the success or failure of any movie.

As much as studios complain about the escalating prices of hot specs, the news stories that result from their mammoth purchases serve the studios well. "Studios don't simply get lost in the hype of [a spec] and then suddenly can't control their purse strings," says *The 13th Warrior* director John McTiernan. "Getting a script to the point where you can even send it to a star—let alone get a star attached to it—costs a lot of money. It can easily cost $2 to $3 million. There are certainly dozens—if not hundreds—of development projects lying in studios' bins, on the studios' books, where that much money is involved . . . and [the studios] have not yet turned them into movies." So in purchasing a workable spec, the studio's reaction in making a large bid isn't irrational, it's a justified business reaction.

Indeed, the process seems to be as mystifying to insiders as to those coming in cold. "To me, studios seem to be like that old-fashioned notion of God as a tapestry—where there's a grand plan, a beautiful design, and we're on the other side and we just can't see it," says Debra Hill Productions' Barri Evins. "But in the case of studios, I'm not convinced the executives are on the other side, either. I'm not sure who's looking at [the master] plan, because a lot of times I find the behavior of studios utterly mystifying.

"I know that their outlook is different from mine. I know that they're running a big, big business and that they need to look at things in terms of a slate, and in terms of many years down the line, and in terms of perpetuating this business, and anticipating the marketplace, and dealing with all kinds of things like foreign markets, and the marketing, and things that I don't deal with," Evins concludes. "But I still find a certain studio behavior inexplicable, because there are things, such as politics and behind-the-scenes pressures that I don't know about, that are influencing conditions."

Evins asks the following questions when looking at a spec: "What does this project need so that a studio will see what we see? Does this need a writer or a director for an auteur point of view? Does it need a star? How long will it take to get to whoever has to read it before it goes to the star? What does the project need to get it made, to sell it [to the public]? That is the central question. I think I have to have a really strong idea that it fills a need in the marketplace."

At the onset of the post-1988 spec boom, the "script chasers," also known as "golden retrievers," generally searched for what they personally would want to see, no matter how unique or offbeat. When *Good Will Hunting* producer Chris Moore was an agent, it was all he would hear from executives. "Do you have something you think is so genius that you've never seen a movie like it before?" Moore recalls the buyers asking him. "Do you have something that has a weird character you've never seen, a lead character in a movie—like a *Taxi Driver* kind of guy?

"It frees you up, because in a lot of ways, those weirder movies are from the better *writers*, the people who actually stick with it for a long time," Moore contends. "The view of movies now is, 'What's the package? Who's the director? Where's it gonna get made?'" says Moore. "The studio used to take that as *their* responsibility: 'We'll buy the script, we will put the movie together.' But now it's pretty much, 'Bring us the movie,' which in a way hurts the spec sale market because, therefore, just getting the idea isn't enough. Why spend a million dollars on an idea that might not get made?

"There are so many specs out there that were *huge* sales when I was coming up. Things like *The Cheese Stands Alone,* and all the stuff that never got made. . . . Then some guy comes in and looks at the books and says, 'Why'd you spend $1.2 million?' " says Moore, who left agency work to return to his first love, playground basketball, while producing his own movies. That so many of these big deals were never produced may sound nonsensical to many observers. Nonetheless, the screenwriters benefited, as such deals were still handsome for their bank accounts.

"To a certain extent [the studios and TV networks] have relaxed or even abdicated being aggressive and imaginative and doing the work that they used to do," says Paradigm agency's Stu Robinson. "It's the chicken and the egg . . . studios could be doing more work to develop stuff, but it's too easy to wait for somebody to come down the pike and say, 'Here's this script and Gene Hackman is in it, and Phil Joanou is going to direct, and blah-blah-blah.' You wait just for that package, like Jabba the Hut waiting to be fed. I think that has had an impact" on the buyer's market. "It's just something writers and their representatives never had to confront in that way before."

The studios also understand that the people making the movies, who are ultimately on the line, are the producers. If a studio believes in a producer and he believes in the material, it's a good situation for both. Generally speaking, the higher the executives rise up the studio ladder, the more they're motivated by relationships, and less by the material, because they understand they have benefited from the "you watch my back, and I'll watch yours" mentality. Junior executives at the studio tend to be more idealistic about their decisions; either they love the material or they don't.

The studios serve as sort of a balance between two approaches: buying specs versus developing material. It's an inexplicable process for which there are a million permutations. Many producers lament the spec market, preferring to develop projects wholly so they can create a more personal stamp on their movies. Others utilize the spec market primarily as a valuable resource for meeting new writers as they enter the game.

"Each picture is a different challenge," says Avenue Pictures' Cary Brokaw. "A great script is a great script, and that has a tremendous power to get a film made. Sometimes films get made with mediocre scripts because a particular actor sees something in a character that he likes. Or because of the filmmaker. Or for a variety of reasons. I approach each picture differently, saying, 'What are the optimal elements?' 'What is the optimal budget?' 'Who are the best and most appropriate financial partners?' and 'How can I do this efficiently?' It makes what I do fun. But it never ceases to amaze me how much easier the entire process is when you have a really good script."

A talented spec salesman knows when the script is ready to be exposed to the buyer's market. "There's a difference between getting feedback, and getting feedback from the people who might buy it," says writing coach John Truby. "As a writer, you need feedback from people who can give you really good information about what's working and what's not working, as well as to say, 'Hey, this is a great script, it's really terrific.' That's part of it too. But you have to keep those groups of people very separate.

"When you think it's done, then the agent's right for it. You have that agent use whatever strategy he's going to use," says Truby. "A lot of agents might send it to three or four people to get an initial response, because you may find out that all of the people you gave it to for feedback didn't give you the right feedback. All of the buyers are coming back with certain problems that they're having. It's useful to know that, because you can do yet another rewrite before you go out to a wider audience of potential buyers.

"At the same time, you're at the point where writers tend to write the thing to death. Every time they send it out and get a response from somebody, they try to make a change" to suit that person, Truby says. "In that way lies madness. You have to at some point say, 'This is what I wrote, this is the story I like, and there's either going to be a buyer who likes this or not.' Or a buyer who likes it enough to buy it as it is, and then if he wants to make certain changes then make those changes, but only once it's been bought. Otherwise, you just write yourself to death."

Any good salesman knows the best time to sell is when the buyers are buying. The same goes with screenplays. Hollywood follows trends; the week it finds a success in a particular genre, you can bet that it's looking for another. Action scripts are generally the biggest spec sales, and they are easy to time. Whenever a big action picture comes out and does remarkably well, agents will send out their action specs. Buyers will be more prone to respond on impulse in such a climate, and somebody will snap it up.

Oftentimes, studios stop buying scripts at the end of the year and during breaks at Labor Day and in August, when executives often take vacation. But in a 24/7 business, some of the more interesting sales occurred when nobody else was listening.

"I sold a million-dollar script two weeks before Christmas," says Justen Dardis, agent at Agency for the Performing Arts. "I sold one *just* before Labor Day for a million dollars. A good piece of material is going to find a home." In other words, timing is everything; you just can't chart it on a conventional calendar. Knowing the perfect moment to go out with a script is as uncertain as knowing which way the wind will blow. But if you can catch the right wind, as good agents do, a script can suddenly become a hot spec.

WHATEVER HAPPENED TO THE WEEKEND READ?

In years past, agents generally messengered material out around town. Studios were then known as "the Seven Sisters." Their executives would read a script and have a night to register their interest. Then that executive would decide whether or not to promote the project at the studio. When a script went out over the weekend, the bids would start coming in on Monday (the "weekend read" that agents such as Ziegler and Bloom began). If the Seven Sisters didn't bite on the submission, that would likely be the end of it.

Once the spec market began heating up, the studios in Burbank and Universal City felt slighted. "We want to get a jump on the material, your messenger always comes to us last," said buyers in the Valley, who weren't getting scripts as quickly from the Beverly Hills agencies. "We're two hours behind, so let us pick up the spec scripts from you."

"Sure, why not?" the agencies replied. After all, this process not only saved the agencies money, it gave the material even greater heat.

Now that the Valley-based studios could pick up spec scripts, they sometimes would make bids before the agency's messengers distributed scripts to all the potential buyers. Finally agencies said, "We'll have the scripts *here*, waiting for you. You guys send *your* messengers." Everyone wanted that first look. The buyers now had to read the spec script in two hours so they could make a bid before everyone else had read it.

The process got a little more complicated when "mini-majors" such as Cinergi, Savoy, Castle Rock, Turner, Propaganda, New Line, and Caravan began competing for the studio's material. With more and more buyers entering, such as Phoenix, Village Roadshow, Lakeshore, Bel Air, Mandalay, and others, the marketplace became even more competitive. Everyone was looking for that edge by controlling hot properties.

Occasionally, execs hurried through the scripts while sitting in the agency's lobby, then called their bosses with a verbal take and proposed bid. Of course, the agents were quite happy in the short run. In the long run, it can lead to not the healthiest of environments.

Certain agencies leaned more toward packaging feature film material with their clients rather than hyping particular specs. When Mike Ovitz and his brethren agents Ron Meyer, Rowland Perkins, Bill Haber, and Marty Baum defected from William Morris in 1975 to start Creative Artists Agency (CAA), they ultimately discovered an extraordinary method of doing business, which Ovitz had observed from Japanese management styles. Indeed, the teamlike packaging process allowed this upstart agency to surpass William Morris and International Creative Management as Hollywood's agency to watch. The package combined CAA's growing roster of directors and stars; therefore, studios could envision an actual movie at the point of making a spec purchase.

"Mike [Ovitz] is a very smart guy, as is Ronny [Meyer], and what they perceived . . . was a lack of strength at the studios. Darryl Zanuck did not exist, nor did Jack Warner, nor did Harry Cohn," says producer Leonard Goldberg. "A vacuum existed, so they put together, in the motion picture area, a list of talent: actors, directors, some writers . . . a very smooth working machine [so] that they could make the packages work and deliver them to the studios who were *thrilled* to have them.

"As their power grew, their roster grew. They said, 'Come with us, we have all these directors. You actors, if you come with us we'll get you working.' And 'You directors, if *you* come, we have all these actors.' They were very good at that, and their list grew like topsy," Goldberg continues. "They were courted by the studios, and they were feared by the studios. You didn't want to turn them down because, whoa, they might turn off that spigot."

Starting with 1982's *Tootsie,* CAA continued to package 150 movies throughout the eighties, a process that had a natural upside for the studios. But sometimes the packages didn't work, and movies such as *Rhinestone* and *Legal Eagles* were criticized for mixing the wrong elements. Nonetheless, the house that Ovitz built, on the corner of Wilshire and Santa Monica Boulevard, became the lodestone for most of the industry's top talent.

Then came the spec boom of the nineties, and the agents themselves who were very skilled at selling specs have become brand names. Every agency has one. A spec script submitted by them has a strong likelihood of attracting interest, because they have orchestrated the sale. They wouldn't spend their time on something they didn't think was a movie, or that they couldn't sell, so their scripts become presold in a way. Some agents and many producers have earned the title of "spec slingers": Some are sharpshooters who constantly hit bull's-eyes, and others toss wildly, throwing whatever shit they can against the wall to see what sticks.

Studios therefore created the process, and it's not necessarily a bad one for them. Why not spend a million or a million seven on a spec script, when in the past they would pump a fortune into a development project and never have the screenplay come to light? Spec scripts give the studios near completed material with which to work.

Selling a spec is "truly a science in and of itself, and there's a lot that can be said about the psychological aspects and psychological warfare," says writer Kurt Wimmer, who drove a taxi cab before nabbing several high-figure sales. "Probably the most salient aspect of selling scripts is the hype, but there are other routes to go. In fact, *not hyping* it is another route to go altogether—not letting anybody know about the script and just putting it out there."

So whatever happened to the weekend read? "Usually we'll go out with a script on a Monday. We'll know by Tuesday afternoon what's going to happen," says William Morris agent Alan Gasmer. "It used to be that it would take a couple of days. Now it's a couple of hours."

COURAGE AND THE ART OF ATTACHING ELEMENTS

Producers today may play a big role in the packaging process. "This has *such* a great role," Joe Singer thought to himself as he finished reading a movie script that he would eventually find some way to make. "*Courage Under Fire* is a script that went out, and I can't say everybody passed. But I can certainly say that all but one studio passed," Singer says of a script that ultimately sold for $2.5 million for a feature that made $54 million in the domestic box office.

"There I was, with a script that virtually everybody had passed on," Singer recalls. "Here was a script sitting there that was basically worth nothing, except it was a wonderful piece of writing and creatively something wonderful. But most important to me as a producer: 'This has such a great role; an actor's going to kill for this, and a director is going to kill for this.' " Singer's plan for Patrick Duncan's *Courage Under Fire* proved correct.

"You try to keep it as exclusive as possible, and that's why you show a script to very few producers," says Duncan. "You try to get them to do a battle plan where they don't just blanket the studios. You tell them you don't want it to go to a studio until an element's attached.

"You're looking for somebody with a good Rolodex who can call up Denzel Washington and say, 'I have this project,' " says Duncan. "He's right for the project, and the producer has the right track record. You are looking for good films, for a collaboration of a whole bunch of disparate people. They're looking for an initial foundation for that collaboration."

"The best star relationship I had at that time, early in my career, was Denzel Washington, who is incredible about reading," says Joe Singer. "I also had a few projects set up with Denzel at that time, and Denzel had a partner by the name of Debra Chase. So I called Debra Chase and sent her the script, and I called Denzel at home and talked to him about it and sent him the script."

It's rare for an actor of Denzel Washington's stature to read anything without a firm money offer, and a gesture for which Singer and Duncan were quite grateful. One word inspired Vietnam veteran Duncan to originally write this spec. "I wanted to do something about courage," he says about this story of an investigation into whether a military officer, played by Meg Ryan, should become the first woman in battle to receive the Congressional Medal of Honor. The movie reunited director Ed Zwick with his star actor from *Glory*, Denzel Washington, who played the complex lead role of Colonel Serling.

"He is as good an actor as anybody of our generation. Yet being a black man, quite often, people will offer scripts to Mel Gibson or Kevin

Costner *first,* which is happening less and less because [Denzel] is so talented," says Singer. "But Denzel, I really give him credit, because without an offer, from a producer calling him up, he and Debra Chase both read the script. Denzel called me about 11:30 after the day he had read the script and said, 'Okay, let's talk about directors.'

"It was this very funny moment, because I could hear the passion," Singer remembers. "I could hear the excitement. Before we talked about directors, we started talking about the role, and what was special about it, and we talked about a few different directors. One of them was Ed Zwick. Ed had *Legends of the Fall* out, which Denzel and I both felt was wonderful. I always loved Ed's work, and Denzel obviously had a good experience [from *Glory*]; so we decided to give it to Ed.

"I called Ed, and I think a lot of it was the fact that Denzel Washington was attached; obviously *that* interested Ed in reading it right away," Singer continues. "Although I do believe that if Ed had read this piece of material without any star attachments, he would have become attached. Ed is an incredibly bright man, and intelligent, and had a visceral and emotional response to the script because Ed's got this huge heart."

Now Singer had a hot property on his hands. "To digress for a second, what I really can't stand is these agents who will take a piece of material, give it out on a Friday to ten producers, take it to the studio, and Monday it's shot," says Singer. "You know, I didn't give a damn that *Courage Under Fire* had been passed on. I knew what it was, and I knew that I could put it together. So we sent it to Ed; and Ed called me back and we had a long talk about it. Then Denzel and I talked about it and Ed's response. Meanwhile, the two of them were not calling each other, even though they have this history together. I probably had four or five conversations with either one, and then we had dinner on a Monday night.

"At that dinner, it was great to see the two of them together," Singer remembers. "They hugged each other. You could see the chemistry and you could see how much these two people really liked each other; and they had gone through a movie before. When I started seeing Denzel talk about Serling's role—you know, Denzel is a method actor. When I talk to Denzel when he's in a movie versus when he's not in a movie, I feel like I'm talking to two different guys, because he stays somewhat in character all the time. I guess that's what makes him such a great actor. Ed was right about the script, and insightful, and we left dinner knowing we were going to sell it."

Assembling his army, and hot off his $1.2 million sale of *Daylight* to Universal Studios, Singer planned his new war strategy. "Fox 2000, to their credit, [President] Laura Ziskin and [Executive VP] Alex Gartner really stepped up and loved it. At that point, [Davis Entertainment Chairman] John Davis and [President] David Friendly came back in and they were going to be my partners on it. Pat had said he wanted to direct it, and for him not to direct it, he needed $3 million. And $3 million was not something that anybody was going to do. Because as good as the script was, it still needed work, which is not unusual in these specs that sell for so much money.

"It was a brilliant script with great characters, but it wasn't going to be a movie tomorrow," Singer continues. "We danced around with Pat for the better part of a week. Then Pat seemed to be getting cold feet, and Pat was at Sundance. I was sitting now with my new partners on the project, John Davis and David Friendly, and it was five o'clock at night. We said, 'You know, Pat's having dinner with Alex Gartner tonight, God knows how that is going to go. We're the real salesmen, we've got to get there.'" Singer and his shadow company saw this as *the* perfect opportunity to close the deal.

On January 18, 1995, knowing that Pat and Alex were convening at the Sundance Festival in Park City, the producers wanted to join in. "Why don't we charter a plane?" was Singer's first thought. "David Friendly and I will go in there and get the script. John Davis, to his credit, spent I think it was $4,400 chartering the plane, which is nothing in the whole scheme of things. I called Roger Strull, who's Pat's agent, and told him where to go at the Van Nuys Airport where the little private plane flies out.

"He didn't go home and bring anything, he came in a sweater," Singer recalls. "David Friendly and I at least raced home and grabbed stuff and had the cars pick us up, and we're dressed, but not appropriately for this huge snowstorm we were flying into, as it turned out. We flew into Sundance [and] there's snow all over. The plane was bouncing around, and David called John Davis. He's screaming at John about the weather report; the weather report said it was supposed to be clear.

"David's scared he's gonna die. He's calling John and telling him to get his wife, and I'm watching this whole thing go on," says Singer, as if recounting another D-Day invasion. "I'm thinking to myself, 'We're flying in because a writer won't take an offer of $1 million against $3. He wants $3 million.' We landed and took the car over the mountain, and in the snowstorm, the car basically didn't want to go over the mountain. We talked the driver into it. We found Pat walking down the street at Sundance, went back to his hotel room, and stayed up until 3:30 in the morning to close this deal.

"It was a great deal for Pat, and I am sorry that Pat didn't get to direct the movie because Pat created it, but I think Ed Zwick did a hell of a job," says Singer. "Pat wrote this with Denzel in mind. That's part of why he had given it to me, because I knew Denzel; and we closed the deal. Then things moved very, very quickly in getting this movie made."

"*Courage Under Fire* was turned down by one studio because they said they didn't know how to market it. I understand that," says Duncan, breaking into his warm Midwestern chuckle. "I'm not saying anything about the marketing department at *that* studio. But you know what I'm saying? That's one of their criteria: How do we sell this? Who will go see this film? I thought it was pretty much of a no-brainer."

THE MOURNING AFTER

Fear in Hollywood stems from filmmakers' own desire and need to make successful movies. Despite all the best intentions, their motion pictures might perform poorly, which always sets back the artists' next efforts. "As I look back on the careers of these fantastically brilliant guys like George Stevens, they had their flops too," says Ron Shusett, cowriter of *Alien* and *Freejack.*

"Overall, in that respect, I realized not every movie is going to turn out close to your expectations even," says Shusett. "*Freejack* didn't come out. It was a flop, both artistically and commercially. I had *great* hopes for it, and you know, I think we made a lot of mistakes in it along the way. Each person is part of the mistakes—maybe myself, the studio, the director, everybody—we made a lot of mistakes in it. It wasn't a bad movie, but it was mediocre; and I can't stand mediocre, it makes me cringe."

Whether or not a film will succeed is up to the gods of film. "[All] of us who make films try to figure out [the success formula] our whole career, and you never see it while you're making it," Shusett continues. "When you look back, you can say, 'Ahhh . . . that's what I didn't do right.' But when you're making the movie, you have no idea, you're just flying by the seat of your pants.

"*Flash Gordon,* if you look at the story, it didn't hold your interest, it was corny, it was this or that," says Shusett. "You look back at *Star Wars* and everything amazed you about it. You *can* see, especially given the history and perspective of time—not just after the movie comes out and everybody loves it—but years later, you look back and say, 'Wow, I made every decision right,' and it's a smash."

Just as likely, a script can have a premise that's good, but the movie's not wrought well enough. "Sometimes you just don't have a premise to start with; it's not a very stimulating potential. Other times you have got the premise and . . . it's not worked out properly so that the audience's interest is sustained throughout the movie; that's more often the case. Because usually if a movie gets made—it's so hard to get a movie made, there are so many premises—it's usually a decent premise in most movies even when they flop. They just haven't executed them properly, and so that's the biggest difference. . . . It's hard to get your powerful writers, directors, and actors to read scripts because there are fifty firm offers on the table, and they don't want to waste their energy reading things. Ninety percent aren't that good."

A big spec sale can either increase or decrease the chances of a movie getting made, depending on the circumstances. Obviously, a purchase like the $2.5 million spent on *Courage Under Fire* meant a serious investment, therefore gauging the studio's interest in the material. At some point, it's a commitment that the studio will make the movie. Second, it's a way the studio announces its interest to the town, and eating those costs by not making the project can create a lot of embarrassment.

On the other hand, if the spec requires a full-blown production commitment from the studio, even a million-dollar sale is a negligible expense in contrast to the risk of producing and marketing the finished film with a budget north of a hundred million dollars. So the studio might find it beneficial to cut their losses at an early stage if the script is ultimately deemed inadequate.

With the "spec scripts that sold for a lot of money, now you have a lot of money against them," says Interscope's Scott Kroopf. "In order to really take a spec up to the next level writing-wise, and also just in terms of cachet—to attract directors and talent—you have to get a big writer onboard. Big writers are not prone to want to write things where they are not going to get credit."

Each case varies, yet often even when the rewriter does an extensive rewrite, "the WGA protects the original writer, which is well and good. They should decide their own rules," says Kroopf. "But what I think happens is that now you have to build a spec script to a higher standard . . . to put together the actors, because actors' prices have gone up, and the directors, with what we pay high-level writers to rewrite now.

"Because those economics are so high, when you work with a spec and you think you're going to have to compete, you have to be saying to yourself, 'Okay, am I going to make this movie?' " says Kroopf of Interscope's criteria. "It has to be, because our agenda is to make five or six movies a year. So for us, if we are going to pay $1 million for a script, it's got to be a script that we're going to make. There's no question in my mind."

For a script to go to green light, it has to do with the person with the power to say yes, and the personal agenda lies with that person. "If their agenda is to satisfy relationships, then their friends—or the people who they want to be in business with—their movies will get made," says writer's manager Peter Scott. "If their personal goal is to make Academy Award–winning movies, and maybe at the expense of box office, those are the movies that will be made."

Going against the grain of a studio's prescribed formula produces the greatest fears, and oftentimes the greatest movies. This is another reason why specs by unknown writers are especially desired, because such writers' voices are untainted. And the spec world has provided an unprecedented power for both the new, and the experienced, screenwriter.

"The problem is fear on the part of the studios to just let a film be what it is," says screenwriter Shane Black. "I read so many letters from young writers, cover letters like, 'This new film is the most touching, visually interesting action-comedy thing you'll ever see. . . . It's a combination of *Terms of Endearment* with *Lethal Weapon,* all the action and adventure of it.' They have capital letters and exclamation points in them, and I'm thinking, 'Why?' This guy's selling me a circus. 'Is this what they really think Hollywood wants? A circus act?'

"Everyone's writing a script, but they're not really writing anything honest," Black says. "They're writing for the bull's-eye, thinking, 'If I can get the elements right, I'll hit it, and I'll get the money,' *not* do you have an interest in these elements? I mean, let's say the money were elsewhere. Would you still be writing this script because you're passionate?"

"I think for a writer, one really good spec script is the only great way to get a career going," says David Koepp, writer of *The Lost World* and *Bad Influence* as well as the first person in Hollywood to read the script to *Seven*. "That's all it takes. A lot of people think, 'Well, if I have two or three.' No, that's nonsense. Nobody wants to read two or three scripts. They want to read *one* really good one. That is still the thing that busts doors down."

Going for the Green, or Turning Around

Selling a script, and getting a movie made, are two skills that in many ways have nothing to do with each other, according to Universal Studios–based producer Joe Singer. "It's like the difference between running for president and serving the presidency. . . . I can tell you, getting a movie made is the most difficult part of the business that I've seen and almost pales in comparison to selling them."

The direction a script goes depends on the chemistry between the filmmaker and the studio. The process of getting to the green light is "horribly difficult, a lot of it's no fun," says Singer. "Getting the talent attached, getting the budget, moving it forward, those are the cards that really take you from a good poker player to a great poker player."

Failing that, a studio might put a dormant project in turnaround, at which point other studios can purchase it. Turnaround is when a studio gives up a project, expecting another studio to cover the costs it has so far expended. Although the deals are negotiable, the primary studio prefers to cover its previous costs, and the screenwriter's agent generally steps into the negotiation.

"If it's in turnaround from a friendly studio," says Above the Line agent Rima Greer, "you call them up and say, 'Pretty please, be good to us. Be kind. Don't hurt us with the money. We'll pay you later when the movie's made, and we're all rich. Just don't hurt us so we can get it back in development and activate it. You'll get some money back and we'll get our project back.' And some-times certain studios will be nice. Other studios will not. You call them up and say, 'Pretty please, can we have our project back? How much is against it?' And they tack on every lunch that anyone has ever had on their studio lot for the past two hundred years. They'll say, 'We want it all now, and you have twenty-four hours to respond.' So it depends on who you're asking.

"It varies by project too," Greer continues. "If Steven Spielberg comes and asks very nicely, you give him whatever he wants, thank you very much. Short of that, it really depends on the studio and what their policies are, because there are some studios that will be kind, and others won't. They want every penny they've ever spent on the script, on the producer's overall deal, whoever was attached to it, plus 33 percent overhead, plus prime, plus 2 percent interest. So if my writer got paid $100,000 to write some-thing three years ago, there's probably half a million dollars against the script now, which is really annoying. I have a project that's stuck at Warner Brothers forever. There's $2 million against it. It'll never get out."

In the meantime, the screenwriter receives whatever was obli-gated under the initial contract and most likely moves on to other assignments. Turnaround projects can be savvy acquisitions for the studios. When Brandon Tartikoff left the television ranks to become chairman of Paramount Pictures, he bought *Forrest Gump* in turnaround from Warner Bros. and was surprised to find that 35–40 percent of projects didn't originate at the studio.

For instance, *E.T. The Extra-Terrestrial, Young Guns, Major League,* and *Home Alone* were also turnaround projects, which like *Forrest Gump* ended up making huge profits for their ulti-mate buyers and often making the executives that let them go look like schmucks. Hence, studio reaction to seeing a block-buster like *Forrest Gump* is less likely to desire to make heart-warming stories, and more likely to refrain from putting anything into turnaround.

"Sometimes studios have invested a lot and don't know when they think they'll be able to make it, because they've got a plethora of that *type* of movie. By the time the script looks good to them, they're committed to three others that are in that category," says *Total Recall* cowriter Ron Shusett. "Sometimes that's the case: It's too late for that studio to hang around with that project anymore. Also, sometimes it's not the *taste* of the studio head after he's seen the script, even though he likes the concept. It might be excellent but just not strike his whim. I see that all the time; I wonder why they don't get made, they're so good."

Sin, Sacrifice, and Success

THE PATHOLOGICAL PATH OF *SEVEN*
FROM A SCREENPLAY BY ANDREW KEVIN WALKER
Purchased by Penta Pictures; acquired by Arnold Kopelson Prods.
MPAA Rating: R
Director: David Fincher

A serial killer stalks his victims in accordance with the seven deadly sins. The case joins a neophyte cop with a veteran detective, both of whom ultimately discover that one knows more than the other.

CAST OF CHARACTERS

David Koepp, Universal-based screenwriter
Gavin Polone, Koepp's agent at United Talent Agency
Missy Malkin, Polone's colleague at United Talent Agency
Phyllis Carlyle, manager-producer
Gianni Nunnari, president of Penta Pictures
Sanford Panitch, VP at Arnold Kopelson Productions
Arnold Kopelson, producer
Lynn Harris, VP at New Line Cinema
Michael DeLuca, New Line Cinema's president

NUMBER SEVEN IS a lucky one, magical in context. The Seven Seas make up the world's oceans, while Seventh Heaven is the celestial home to God and the angels in the Muslim and cabalistic systems. The number seven certainly proved to be lucky for Andrew Kevin Walker, who was working behind a counter at a Manhattan Tower Records when he chose it as the title for his spec script.

"Dark," however, became the word everybody in Hollywood used to describe *Seven*. At its nascent stage, Andy Walker's literate and chilling script was the type every development executive in town had to read; it had that lore of a great unproduced script that would have trouble ever getting launched. "Blockbuster" was certainly the one word that nobody, including the film's eventual backers, ever expected. And it all ended in a shocking surprise.

"*Seven* was always like a special son," says Gianni Nunnari, one of the project's fathers and producers. "Everybody would talk about it. Everybody would come back to me: 'I love the script, I want my client to do it.' [CAA president turned Universal Pictures chairman] Ron Meyer at a certain point was talking about it for Stallone. I mean, everybody was calling me back. So there was a hook. . . . Everybody would react, which is great."

Walker's tale of a veiled serial killer who commits murders in accordance with the seven deadly sins made it to the screen after initially being rejected all over Hollywood. *Seven* subsequently set box office records throughout Europe, earning over $340 million around the globe (and topping $100 million in the United States alone). Accordingly, this 1995 release caused the studios to rethink their agendas, prompting a flurry of inferior serial killer screenplays into the market. *Seven* was the picture Hollywood thought was uncommercial, and it turned out to be one of the most financially successful films of the decade.

Yet how would Hollywood ever know? After all, there wasn't a movie in history just like *Seven* to which it could be compared.

Seven follows the path of two detectives, the elder William Somerset (Morgan Freeman), whose metronome punctuates the sounds of horror that fill a city's night sky, and the neophyte David Mills (Brad Pitt), on the trail of serial killer John Doe. On a cursory glance, *Seven* could be written off as a one-note picture built around its provocative climax. On other levels, many consider it a cinematic masterpiece, with nuances in the photography, performances, and screenplay that make *Seven* one of the more brilliantly textured blockbusters to have ever come out of Hollywood. Released around the time of *The Usual Suspects* and on the heels of the phenomenal success *Pulp Fiction, Seven* was likewise a picture that had people talking. While its five-year path from script to screen was certainly not without roadblocks, *Seven* came about remarkably simply, considering the tremendous potential to impede it.

KNOCKING ON HELL'S GATE

After graduating from his college film program in Pennsylvania, Andrew Kevin Walker considered whether he would first set foot in Los Angeles or New York. Lacking the money for a car, he chose New York and began working as a production assistant, often for free, on such low-budget fare as *Robot Holocaust*. Walker's understanding parents viewed these ambitions as an extension of film school and thus supported him with loans while he picked up a little cash writing such B movies as *Brainscan* and *Blood Rush*.But the production work took time away from writing, so Walker accepted a run-of-the-mill job at Tower Records to provide him the structure of a forty-hour work week, which then gave him ample time to spec out his own screenplay instead of the straight-to-video fare that he was assigned. Walker chose to write *Seven*.

Its clear concept and subject matter was untested in a movie (although *Bedazzled* with Dudley Moore played with the seven sins, but comically). The script could draw upon great classic works of literature, notably *Paradise Lost,* Chaucer's *Canterbury Tales,* and Dante's *Purgatory,* as well as the polarity of good and evil within the human soul. This was all that Walker needed to begin writing. His script would employ "seven deadly sin" murders, and the sage cop would be the last survivor. For the last three years Andy Walker worked at Tower Records, he convinced himself that the preceding week was the last seven days he would spend at his mundane job. Walker felt confident that his spec screenplay was worthy of Hollywood notice.

But Walker failed to get any Hollywood agent to pay attention to his query letters. He decided that if agents wouldn't look at his script, he would find somebody else in Hollywood who would. One night in 1990, Andy went to the movies to see *Bad Influence,* a twisted psychological drama directed by Curtis Hanson and starring James Spader and Rob Lowe, which made an impression. So he wrote a letter to its young screenwriter, David Koepp. *Bad Influence* was Koepp's second movie after cowriting *Apartment Zero,* both spec scripts.

"I was working at Universal, and Andy had seen *Bad Influence* and liked the movie," Koepp recalls. "He didn't know anybody in Hollywood and sent what I thought was a very intelligent and direct letter. He seemed to have his head on reasonably straight and asked if I would read his script. If it's not someone I know, that's not a favor I will extend very often. But in Andy's case, there was something about him that seemed very worthwhile. So I did."

It was lucky timing. Walker, then living on Top Ramen from a countertop stove in his studio New York apartment, followed up with a phone call to David Koepp, then listed in the phone book and on his way to a roll of hits at Universal (including *Death Becomes Her, The Paper* with his brother Steve, *Carlito's Way, The Shadow, Jurassic Park,* and *The Lost World*). "There was just a seriousness of purpose about him," Koepp says. "Then once I read the script, it was just so good, and so original. He so *clearly* was a screenwriter, there was no question about it. So if it hadn't been me, it would have been the next guy he wrote a letter to."

Yet who knows how long it would have been before anybody in the filmmaking industry would have paid much attention. "My involvement was pretty limited," Koepp humbly adds. "All I did was read it, recognized that it was really good, and suggested to my agent that he read it. He did, and he too thought it was really good; and that was kind of where I left the process."

Koepp's agent Gavin Polone (then at Bauer-Benedek, which later became United Talent Agency) was a similarly on-the-rise player who thought Walker's script was brilliant and signed the writer. Andy Walker leapt for joy when he first heard from Hollywood that he had an agent. *Seven* began making rounds when *The Ticking Man* and *The Last Boy Scout* sold for $1 million and $1.75 million, respectively. With hopes for a big deal, Walker moved back to his parents' pleasant Pennsylvania suburb to prepare for his Los Angeles relocation.

"I just loved it immediately," says Polone, known for his sometimes pugnacious demeanor, his tae kwon do black belt, and his Rasputin-like hairstyle. "I knew there would be a problem, because I've gone out with stuff that was 'too dark' before. But I actually felt that because of *Silence of the Lambs* we would have a shot. Unfortunately we didn't."

Polone describes *Seven* as a spec script that didn't sell. Unlike the hot properties of the time that agents spun into huge feeding frenzies,

Walker's *Seven* slowly wandered through town, disturbing to conventional readers who only wanted happy endings, enticing to those speculative trendsetters who wanted to find some way to make Hollywood see this unique property as a commercial one.

"We went out with the script and we had some producers attached to it," says Polone. "All the studios passed. Everybody said they loved the writing, and immediately we got Andy a job so he was able to start working, actually for Joel Silver [*Lie to Me,* an adaptation of a David Martin serial killer novel]. So it launched his career and he was able to leave Tower Records and come out here. But nobody was willing to take a chance on *Seven.*" Koepp, in fact, submitted the script to Universal Studios with himself attached to produce. They passed.

"They found it a tad depressing, I believe," Koepp recalls.

"All the major studios passed on it," confirms Polone, who was then building a formidable client list that included Conan O'Brien and *Seinfeld* creator Larry David. "One of my partners [at UTA], Jim Berkus, gave the script to Phyllis Carlyle, who managed Jeremiah Chechik, director of *Benny & Joon.* He loved the script, and because they were very high on him at the time, they took it to Penta." Penta Pictures was an Italian company that took the first chance on *Seven,* continuing the domino effect that Koepp and Polone began.

"I think the truth is, [Berkus] gave it to me because he was trying to sign a client of ours," Carlyle says, regarding UTA's interest in Chechik. "We have a production side and a management side, and there was a client who he was angling toward, so he threw me a bone." Carlyle laughs a bit now at the thought of it, having such good fortune simply tossed her way. Upon reading the script of *Seven,* she too saw something distinguished in Andy Walker's writing.

"I was very impressed with how intelligent it was," Carlyle recalls. "It had a much deeper core to it, in terms of what it was talking about, than the normal sort of spec material you see. Most writers, I think, gear their material toward what they think is going to create that big sale, and Andrew Kevin Walker didn't.

"When we first saw *Seven,* it was in the first draft," says Carlyle. "It was the writer's first script, no one had ever heard of him. He wouldn't have sold anything for much money at all at that point, and *Seven* was a script that no one was interested in." With ties to international companies that perhaps would be more receptive to the dark tone of *Seven,* Phyllis Carlyle sent the script to Penta, giving its president Gianni

Nunnari an opportunity to take a low-risk involvement in something that turned into quite a big deal. But Penta had made a string of money-losing movies (*Man Trouble, Folks, House of Cards*) and therefore was reluctant to taking risks. Co-owner Silvio Berlusconi was on his way to becoming president of Italy, and projects at Penta stalled as a result.

"I had also taken it to all the studios, and they went, 'God, I don't think so. . . .' A couple of executives were intrigued, but just didn't think we'd nailed it," says Carlyle. "But nobody picked it up."

Nunnari had operated Penta's Los Angeles office since 1986, before European companies such as Polygram, Ciby 2000, and Canal-Plus arrived in Hollywood. When partners Vittorio Cecchi Gori and Berlusconi split up, it could have been a bad omen for *Seven*. But Arnold Kopelson, who had known both Nunnari and Cecchi Gori for over twenty years from his world travels as a foreign sales agent, had an employee who brought this dark script to light. Sanford Panitch, a young executive for Kopelson with a gift for getting material, got hold of *Seven* when it was slipped to him through a friend. Panitch knew about Walker from previously reading a *Sleepy Hollow* script the writer had written, and he loved *Seven,* although Panitch was aware *Seven* wasn't readily available.

Kopelson, a former lawyer and onetime pianist who became an industry figure when he and his wife, Anne, started their Inter-Ocean Film Sales company (sending titles such as *The Last Rebel* and *Porky's* into international distribution), was now one of Hollywood's most prolific producers, spearheading such pictures as *Platoon, The Fugitive,* and *Falling Down.* And it would take Kopelson's kind of clout for such an edgy piece as *Seven* to make it to the screen.

Kopelson hadn't heard of *Seven* when Panitch handed him the script, and was intrigued. So Sanford arranged a lunch for Kopelson with Nunnari and Cecchi Gori to see how they could do business. Penta controlled *Seven,* and if Kopelson wanted to make it at a studio, Penta would control the Italian rights.

"It was like asking me, really, to go on vacation with my daughter," Nunnari recalls. "When Arnold wanted it, I said, 'Listen, I want to be sure that we can put an enormous kind of strength in trying to make this movie.' They had already offered it to Warner Brothers. Fortunately enough, there was a good relation between me and Arnold, so that it helped in the switching of the property from Penta, which basically was abandoning it. We finally decided yes, and Arnold and Sanford also were very good at making sure that it still would be my son."

Fortuitous timing was around the bend. Ted Turner made a successful bid to purchase Robert Shaye's New Line Cinema in January 1994, infusing his new company with plenty of cash for spec purchases. Lynn Harris had recently landed a buyer job at New Line after working for Lynda Obst, the Fox-based producer of *The Fisher King*. Fortunately for *Seven*, Panitch had formerly interned for New Line years previously while he was on summer breaks from Tulane University.

Once Lynn Harris settled into her New Line Cinema office, she made a call over to Sanford Panitch in November 1993 to ask what scripts might be sitting on the shelf that he thought were really good. New Line could now be in a good position to make them happen. "Because the script had been around a long time, it had a certain buzz on it," Harris recalls. Brad Pitt's agent and managers had loved the script for a long time. At the time we were offering him this movie, he was being offered four or five other projects.

The movie begins with a ruse, that you're in a serial killer movie, "which you kind of are, except that you get to the crime scene after the crime's taken place," says Harris. "You don't ever see the murders. In a large way, the movie takes place in the mind of the audience, because you are left to imagine. You're told, partially, what might have happened, but you're left to imagine what actually happened. And in fact, you don't meet the antagonist until two thirds of the movie.

"So in that way, it's a ruse that you're about to enter into a typical cop thriller," says Harris. "In fact, it's a relationship story about these two cops. I don't know that I was smart enough to know that when I read the script. I just liked it, and I thought it was really cool and smart, and great writing."

By the time Harris saw it, *Seven* had already gone over to Warner Bros. under Kopelson's first-look deal there, and the Burbank studio passed on it. It was the third time it had gone to the Burbank studio, since Phyllis Carlyle had also tried that route twice before.

"It was *right* before *Legends of the Fall* was being released, and Brad Pitt had an incredible buzz on him coming off of *Interview with a Vampire*," Harris recalls. "He hadn't yet had a vehicle that was really *his* with the exception of *Legends of the Fall*, which hadn't come out yet. So there were really no obstacles. Brad's agents and managers loved it, got him to read it, and he loved it. He met with [director] David Fincher, and that's sort of how it all came about."

UNDERSTANDING THE DARK WORLD

Much of the inspiration for *Seven* came from Walker's experiences spending five years in New York City. Walker, who appears in the post-title sequence of the film as a blood-spattered victim of a gunshot blast, was never himself mugged in the Big Apple. But everybody he knew had been. Walker would get sick from the smell of urine everywhere he walked. In Walker's script for *Seven*, Detective Mills leaves the peaceful and productive life of "the country" for the hardships and disease of "the city." He expects to prove himself.

After the title credit sequence in which serial killer John Doe (Kevin Spacey) prepares for the busy seven days ahead of him, we see Mills's wife, Tracy (Gwyneth Paltrow), lying in bed with her head on Mills's arm. Mills lifts her pretty head, which would later wind up severed in a box, and sets it back down on the bed as Mills goes off for his similarly busy first seven days of work. A cocky newcomer who doesn't "get it," Mills gets off to a rocky start with partner Somerset, a police veteran of thirty-four years with seven days left before retiring from the police force; Somerset's initial suggestion that the two go to a bar to talk shop is rebuffed by Mills, who's eager to get down to the precinct. Toward the film's end, when Somerset finally gets his wish, he delivers another effective set-up at the bar: "You know, this isn't gonna have a happy ending." In fact, *Seven* would have one of moviemaking's unhappiest of endings.

"The thing about that ending—and I assume whoever's reading [this] will have seen it by now—is I remember during the development process how they tried to change it," says David Koepp. "But you couldn't, because the head in the box was just too perfect. It brought everything around full circle, it was brilliant. . . . It was just the *perfect* ending of the story.

"It was the resolution of everything, it was ironic, and there was just nothing wrong with it," Koepp continues. "I remember thinking that as I was reading the script. Every grisly turn the movie took, I would shudder and say, 'Oh my God.' But it was just, pitch-perfect, it was just right. So I think that what is a satisfying ending isn't necessarily what

is a happy ending, you know? What is satisfying to people is the tale
fully told, and in this case, man, it was fully told like a motherfucker."

While conventional studio thinking wouldn't stand for a head-in-the-
box finale, it piqued the interest of New Line's president Michael
DeLuca, himself a screenwriter of such movies as *Freddy's Dead: The
Final Nightmare* and *In the Mouth of Madness.* New Line Cinema naturally wanted to be in business with a producer of Kopelson's stature.
"We love this," DeLuca said in his phone call to Panitch. "We want to
do it."

New Line would make the movie with a particular cast and provided
Kopelson with a list. Johnny Depp was an early fan of the script, which
helped bring it initial attention. "Johnny Depp actually had always
wanted to do it," says Carlyle of the period before it had gone to New
Line. "We made offers to Pacino, De Niro, Denzel Washington. I think
there might have been maybe one other actor in that mix. There was
some discussion about Michael Douglas . . . pretty much the obvious
men who fit the right age and have that kind of factor.

"They threw very heavy offers out there. Michael Mann (*Manhunter,
Miami Vice*) received a *major* offer to direct it, Pacino and everybody.
But at that point, it was not a project people were paying much attention to," says Carlyle. "One person who actually sticks out in my mind
was Kevin Huvane at CAA, who represents Brad Pitt. I had shown the
script to Kevin about a year before New Line picked it up. We had
talked at length about the script, on and off, for a year. He had said to
me, 'You know, I really think this would be good for Brad.' That's
actually how Brad came about. Once we got the movie set up, Kevin
gave it to Brad and called me and said, 'Brad wants to do it.' " And on
the set of *Outbreak,* Arnold Kopelson personally handed the script to
Morgan Freeman.

Since Jeremiah Chechik had gone on to make another movie, two
meetings had occurred with Michael Caton-Jones, the British director
of *Scandal* and *Doc Hollywood,* who very seriously wanted to direct.
"Then a movie that he had been trying to put together for a long, long
time came together and that was *Rob Roy,*" says Phyllis Carlyle. "And
there we were. At that moment, Fincher wasn't anybody's idea, except
CAA's, and they were quite committed to resurrecting Fincher's career
as a feature director."

Indeed, David Fincher was looking for a career revival. Mention the
name Fincher around a hip Hollywood happening and most guests

will drop to their knees and murmur, "We're not worthy." (At least those who had worked in the music video business, where Fincher was an early innovator.) At age twenty-four, this former Marin County neighbor of George Lucas was part of the original directing stable at Propaganda Films, the visionaries of what defined the MTV language at its birth. Some of his credits as a director include the Rolling Stones' *Love Is Strong;* Madonna's *Express Yourself, Vogue,* and *Oh, Father;* Aerosmith's *Jamie's Got a Gun;* and Don Henley's *The End of the Innocence,* all high-budgeted, in some cases, multimillion-dollar videos.

One time early in his career, Fincher met with George Lucas's former president (then a Sony exec) Sidney Ganis, who assured the wunderkind music video artist that no studio would give him $35 million to make his first feature.

"Of course not," Fincher quipped. "What would a studio do with a thirty-five-minute movie?" With *Seven,* Fincher gained prominent stature as a feature filmmaker.

"I think the rap on Dave was that he didn't have any story sense, and I think that's a very unfair assessment of his talent," says New Line's Lynn Harris. "He's a phenomenal filmmaker with an incredibly good storytelling sense, and an incredible knowledge of movies." Fincher's marred reputation at the time was the result of the critical and commercial backlash to his first feature, the $60 million *Alien³,* which Fincher himself says he hates as much as any of the picture's detractors. But Fincher's agents at CAA stood behind his talents and encouraged New Line to go with him to helm *Seven.*

At the start, Kopelson felt determined not to make a movie that ended with a head in a box. Previous drafts had watered down the violent ending. Walker had to search for new ways to script the finale, and all kinds of ideas were kicked around. Perhaps the box could contain a video-feed showing Mills's wife being held captive. Perhaps Mills would die alone. None of it sat well. There was also concern at New Line about the "lust" sequence, where John Doe forces a john to penetrate a hooker with a strap-on blade. When the script went to Fincher (of several drafts floating around town) he happened to get the one with the head in a box. Immediately, he loved it.

"Fincher came in, was just smart as hell about the material, and was a guy that we all believed in despite the buzz of him being incredibly difficult," says Harris. "If you look at *Alien³,* it's clearly phenomenal visually. The failure in that movie, I believe, is that he didn't have a script to work with when he started shooting. Was he difficult on that movie? Probably. But you know, I didn't find him difficult."

Fincher's talent developed from making commercials for Nike, AT&T, Chanel, Levi's, Coca-Cola; his aesthetic tastes developed from years of music videos. Walker loved Fincher right away, and they worked furiously to put together the picture. The development process was a joy for both Walker and Fincher, who later collaborated on 1997's *The Game,* starring Michael Douglas and Sean Penn, after *Seven* was released (Walker did not get a rewrite credit for *The Game,* which had been bandied about Hollywood for years but was always considered too highly budgeted).

Seven was green-lighted with a version in which it was actually Somerset's character shooting John Doe; the movie sets this up with Somerset saying that in his thirty-four years he had never fired his gun. But with Pitt agreeing to the picture, Mills's character became central, and it made more sense for him to play off the final moment.

"Most producers, and I think most studios, are a bit too quick to replace a writer," Carlyle says. "It was discussed a couple of times, and I won't say it never came up. . . . But this was a damn good script from day one. So when Fincher came onboard, and it was about the script and what in the script does one want to address, there was nothing we thought Andrew couldn't deliver."

While the message of *Seven* could be considered "dark," it was similarly thoughtful and resonating. Pitt was determined to end the movie the way Andy Walker designed it, and his onscreen chemistry with Morgan Freeman made this motion picture a hard-edged buddy cop classic. Having killed an "obese, disgusting fat man," a lawyer who "dedicated his life to making money by lying to keep murderers and rapists on the street," a woman "so ugly on the inside she couldn't bear to go on living," "a drug-dealing pederast," and "a disease-spreading whore," John Doe was ready to finally complete his heinous design.

"The ending *would* have changed if it weren't for Brad Pitt," Gavin Polone contends. "He's the reason why it didn't change because once the movie's going, he's got a tremendous amount of control and he exercises it. It's a terrific thing."

The final screenplay was the culmination of Andy Walker's trips back to the drawing board, from which the writer could assemble the best elements. "We went through about four or five drafts. There was one draft that was so brutal there was no way [that] it was going to get made," says producer Phyllis Carlyle. "There was always a debate between whether Mills would die, or [the killer] would die. There were several drafts where Mills was the one who died.

"In the original screenplay, Somerset was white," Carlyle continues. "Mills's wife . . . was more clearly defined in all of our drafts than I think she ended up being in the movie. Her story was that she'd been a schoolteacher, and she loved Mills from childhood—childhood sweethearts—and they got married. She was quite happy, loving him, being a schoolteacher, and living in a smaller town. It's really Mills who has to go for the bigger city, the more dangerous, cutting-edge life, which she does not want, but she gives it all up to go with him. Which I always thought was very key to the story. . . . Obviously he leaves her alone, she's quite frightened, she cannot get a job in the city. She's basically a wasted human being.

"She and Somerset actually come very close to having an affair in the original script," Carlyle continues, "and they *don't*. Then to cut to the end, in this [version of the] script with Mills dying, it's not like Somerset ends up with her. But there is this moment when they part, and I think the audience is left thinking that after the tragedy settles and people heal, they find each other again. So *that's* the difference between what you saw, and what the original script had."

"There are those movies with maybe one, two, three great lines," says Gianni Nunnari, "and they'll make the movie. There are other movies that you can somehow relate [to], or dig into, and learn. Like a great book. There is always a part that is like a mirror that you keep moving so the light can go this direction, that direction, so that you learn. When you watch *The Godfather,* you can watch it forever, because there are lines of dialogue that you can keep and relate, 'That's wise advice.' There are lines in *Scarface* that come just through the script and the setting; they're great lines, great attitudes, great characters. And *Seven* also I think is one of those, because basically you can understand the dark world, and it's like bringing the darkness of this world into the reality of the everyday."

MARKETING MAMMON TO THE MASSES

Since filming *Seven* began when rain showers are seasonal in Los Angeles, Fincher chose to make all the scenes rain-drenched to avoid any mismatched scenes, as well as provide the look of a veil of tears pouring over a dark city. On December 28, 1994, eleven weeks of shooting commenced on the $31 million film, at the time a very high budget for New Line.

Chris Pula, then head of marketing at New Line, had a sizable advertising budget of $19 million to play with (the industry average was $15 million at the time and continues to grow), and this project took careful strategizing. If Pula had approached the film as *Legends of the Fall II* or *Driving Miss Daisy II,* he feared the Pitt and Freeman fans would go screaming out of the theaters, thus handicapping the potential word of mouth for *Seven.*

Pula instead chose the advertising to look slimy, dark, and menacing, consistent with the film itself. "Here we are, this company that was doing a lot of low-budget stuff, and now we have these two huge stars," said Pula in a *Daily Variety* interview. "And I take their big mugs and smother them in grease." The print and TV advertising also had a somber, gritty look.

New Line also took what was then the clever step of promoting this motion picture online: For the seven days leading up to the movie's release, they sent press members a screensaver a day—one for each sin—which downloaded video clips from the film. Pula drowned a demonic-looking typestyle font called Manson (designed, incidentally, by the psychotic Charles Manson) in a blood-red color for the television spot ads, which made up two thirds of his budget expenditures.

"We're a very, very market-driven company, *Seven* was not a particularly easy movie to sell, and they did a *hell* of a job selling it," Harris says. "I mean, 50 percent of this movie, in terms of its box office success, [was marketing]. The campaign was *phenomenal. . . .* And we had a movie star at the *moment* at which we needed to get him. An extraordinary actor in the body of Morgan Freeman, who was a *prince* in the way he worked with the movie after it was made. . . . We had three incredible actors, Kevin Spacey, included, and an amazing director who all believed in the material and worked for it well after it was in the can."

Upon its release on Friday, September 22, 1995, *Seven* seemed to strike a nerve in the public psyche, opening pain that rocked the hallways of studios that had passed on it. Reporting on the New York premiere at Alice Tully Hall, *The Village Voice* called *Seven* a "pretentious, portentous, pointless thriller" and also a "weirdly low-brow *pièce de garbage.*" Other critical reviews were equally as scathing. Gene Siskel and Roger Ebert, however, both offered an enthusiastic thumbs up (Ebert called it "filmmaking of a higher order . . . well made and uncompromising"), and suddenly there was an "interest factor" in seeing the film that attracted younger audiences that wanted to be "in the know."

Seven enjoyed the highest-grossing September opening weekend in history ($14.5 million in 2,441 screens), knocking out the previous record holder, *A Nightmare on Elm Street 6*. It held the box office lead for several weeks. Upon the closing credits at the film's premiere, *Boyz N the Hood* director John Singleton stood up to shout, "That had balls, yeah!"

"Audiences reject what they don't like, and they won't go. It doesn't matter what the movie costs, or who's in it, or how well it's marketed. They just won't go," says Lynn Harris. "They'll go the first weekend out of curiosity, but they'll reject it [if it's not a good picture]. So I don't think we're lowering our standards as an industry because the audiences are lowering theirs, or vice versa. I think if you make a good movie, people will go see it."

"Even if you know that they were going to kill the wife of Brad Pitt in *Seven,* it is like you're living that moment," says producer Gianni Nunnari. "It's almost like a virtual reality game. You are there. But in a way you suffer because somebody's going to get killed. I'm not saying that you really need to surprise. I'm not saying that's the technique."

"*Seven* was a good movie, and people wanted to go see it. We had *no* idea," says Harris. "There's not a single person in this company, and they'd be *lying* to you if there was anybody in the world, who said they knew this movie would make over $300 million worldwide. Nobody knew. We made the best movie we knew how to make, and then we had a team of marketers and distributors, thank God, we're happy enough to work with; and then we held our breath." The movie's success from small town to big city showed that the typical pat Hollywood ending is not to the audience's liking anymore.

FROM *SEVEN* TO *8-MILLIMETER*

"I've had a lot of clients who had scripts that I thought would sell and didn't sell, but then years later, they come back around," agent-turned-producer Gavin Polone says. "But with Andy, I don't even think he was working full-time at Tower Records in New York; he was borrowing money from his parents, doing anything he could. We had to get him some money so he could come out [to Los Angeles] and live and write scripts. So the immediate thing was to try to get him solvent, and we did by selling it to Penta."

As producer Phyllis Carlyle explains, "Two and a half to three years after I had gotten the script, I had seen all the studios. ICM, which at that time was [Jeremiah Chechik's] agency, had talked about Richard Gere and Denzel Washington. The one important factor, if we're talking about the script, is that each actor who saw it—or almost everyone who saw it—responded on some level of being somewhat intrigued by it.

"But they all wanted to sit down and throw a lot of notes at everybody," Carlyle recalls. "Between Johnny [Depp] and Denzel [Washington], both who I have great regard for, we thought by the time we got done with each one's notes and the contradictions of how each one sees this movie—and what we would have to do to turn it into a vehicle that they would both say yes to—it got quite complicated. I fear that type of stuff in a way, because you either believe in what you've got, or you don't. Once you start ripping something really apart, I think you lose it."

Seven reflected the different stages of innocence that a culture and a society pass through to get to the other side. The more astute film critics recognized this as the zeitgeist of an anguished society. "I think *Seven* indicates the passage of a certain level of innocence and safety and security that people no longer feel, and I believe that that is the chord we struck," says producer Phyllis Carlyle. "I was somewhat saddened that Gwyneth's role didn't fulfill itself on paper the way I had wanted it to," Carlyle adds of the character Andy Walker identified with most, expressing the fears and anxieties he himself experienced while living in New York. "I mean, there's obviously more than one victim in this film. . . . She gave up her job, she gave up her marriage, and she gave up her life. As a woman, I felt *that* message [resonated] as well . . . that's a chord I think we struck.

"I think we were very fortunate," Carlyle continues. "The gods sometimes just make [the process] all go the way it's supposed to. I think that Fincher added a hip edge to *Seven* that made it different, on top of its message and its strength and its intelligence."

There were many layers in this script that the viewer could participate in, perhaps a reason why viewers at all levels of society responded favorably. Those who wanted bloody gore and tragedy would be fulfilled with the same sick thrill sensed from driving past a bloody traffic accident. The highbrows in the theater embraced the film's mystery and enjoyed unraveling the scheme at the movie's center. Many critics, however, lambasted the film for being pretentious, possibly a reaction to Fincher's maverick visual style that the studios ultimately embraced. Some critics noted that both *Seven* and *Theater of Blood*, a 1973 English film starring Vincent Price and Diana Rigg, toyed with systematic death; the latter utilized the concept of a London acting company seeking revenge on its critics with gory Shakespearean finales.

"Darker material has always been perceived as selling bigger overseas than it does here," says Gavin Polone, who subsequently left United Talent Agency, and in June 1997 as a partner in a production company with Judy Hofflund, sold Andy Walker's spec script *8-Millimeter* to Columbia Pictures for $1.25 million. "Coming on the heels of *Silence of the Lambs*, you would think that people would not have a problem with something like *Seven* in America. But [the buyers] can't get out of that certain frame of mind." While the studios couldn't get out of it, both American and worldwide audiences embraced it.

"Movies that are different often have more trouble getting made, and it's very fortunate that [Penta] was not a traditional American company and understood the material; because I don't think it would have gone any further had Penta *not* gotten involved. I think that script was just dead in the water," Carlyle believes.

"*Seven* did well because I think any Brad Pitt movie was going to do well at this particular point in time. He is one of the very few actors who people are going to go see [regardless of] the movie, especially women, I believe," says Gavin Polone of a movie that in a strange way became a popular, albeit twisted, date movie.

"After the initial flood of people going to see the movie because Brad Pitt was in it, I think ultimately it came down to word of mouth," says Polone. "People go back to work the next day and say, 'You've got to see this movie, it was amazing.' I think it was really shafted at the Academy Awards, because it was not a Christmas movie, therefore they forget. But I think it was certainly a better written film than a lot of things that are out now." *Seven* did in fact win MTV's Best Movie award, Best On-Screen Duo, and Best Villain, and Richard Francis-Bruce was nominated for an Oscar for his editing.

"People will want to go see the movie stars," says Polone. "A lot of these studio executives were so myopic they couldn't see that a role like this was going to attract Brad Pitt and Morgan Freeman and a real visual director. Ultimately *that's* what gets your movie put together. You have to have something really interesting about a script. You can't just keep making movies like *Assassins* or something like that. . . . So I think that if you want Brad Pitt, you have got to offer him something that's really different."

While waiting for *Seven* to find a home, Andy Walker wrote TriStar's *Hideaway,* a TriStar release that novelist Dean Koontz wanted his name removed from; Walker's name remains on the poster, although the final product literally had just five lines and half a scene that he wrote. Other assignments that came Andy's way included *X Men* (from the Marvel comic books about a group of mutant freaks fighting among one another) for Richard Donner and Lauren Shuler-Donner (who also took an initial interest in *Seven*); the W. Somerset Maugham classic *Of Human Bondage;* and the *Sleepy Hollow* project for Scott Rudin, which Tim Burton directed.

Polone's greatest joy in the process was helping to get Andy Walker his start. "To me, it's really about representing the client," says Polone. "It's about the point where we could call Andy and say, 'Andy, your life's going to change.' It wasn't even selling *Seven,* because that came later. It was about using that script to get Andy his first job so he didn't have to work in a record store.

"Over the years, when I think back on the situations in my career that I've been most proud of or felt most satisfied in, it's when I've been able to say, 'You're getting a big check and now you can leave wherever it is you live or get out of that crappy apartment, and your wife can have a baby,' things that really change people's lives," says Polone. "As of now, over a long period of time, I represent a lot of writers who make a lot of money, a lot of people who make well over a million dollars a year. You go out and say, 'Okay, look, we'll get another deal for you, for $800,000 to do a rewrite,' or something like that. And by that time, it doesn't really have any kind of impact on their lives.

"But that first couple of deals *does* change their lives," Polone continues. "It allows them to quit whatever crappy job they were doing to support themselves and just focus on [their writing]. That's what I find most memorable.

"Andy Walker, one way or another, is brilliant, and whether or not he had met me and Missy Malkin, and the agency, he would have been very successful," says Polone. "Maybe if I helped to speed that up, then that's really satisfying. On top of which, he's really a terrific person and that makes it even better; because when you meet Andy and spend any time with him, you can't help but really adore him and want to help him out and want to be part of that."

In the final version of the movie, the audience is not left knowing what happened to David Mills. But regardless of whether the good cop is given jail time for murdering the serial killer, Mills's act reinforced everything that John Doe said in his speech in the squad car: "Only in a world this shitty could you even try to say these [victims] were innocent people and keep a straight face." The statement seizes the thematic quotient of *Seven*. Mills's awakening, as a result of his final action, was his coming of age in the big city. For Walker, the whole movie would have made no sense had it not ended with a head in the box.

Despite the fact of the success of *Seven,* it's doubtful to many of the people involved that the studios would purchase the script if it crossed their desks, even today. "I've never worked anywhere else as a buyer," says New Line's Lynn Harris. "People tell me that movies like *Seven* wouldn't have been made anywhere else in town." Warner Bros. came out around the same time with *Copycat,* about a murderer who copies the crimes of previous serial killers. By comparison *Copycat* was considered contrived and failed badly at the box office. The next year Warner Bros. released another serial killer thriller, *Glimmer Man,* which also came out to lackluster critical and box office results. Paramount's 1997 release of *Kiss the Girls,* also starring Morgan Freeman, got off to a great opening, but didn't sustain its audience as *Seven* did.

When the script to *Seven* made the Hollywood rounds and Andy Walker relocated to Los Angeles, he and David Koepp became good friends. In the span of the few years since *Bad Influence* came out, the two scribes have become among the most highly regarded screenwriters in Hollywood. Koepp subsequently wrote Spielberg's *Jurassic*

Park, its 1997 sequel *The Lost World,* *Mission: Impossible,* and *Snake Eyes,* as well as directing his first feature, 1996's *The Trigger Effect,* which starred Kyle MacLachlan, Elisabeth Shue, and Dermot Mulroney.

"I followed [Andy's development process with] *Seven* in the way that writer friends bitch and moan about what's going on with their projects," says Koepp. "I don't think *Seven* had any better or worse development experiences than anybody else's. . . . I think the best part is that I read several interim drafts in which Andy was asked, or arm-twisted, into making changes that he didn't really love. When I saw the finished film, I remember thinking how it was so remarkably similar to the very first one I read that I couldn't believe it. He really managed to wrangle it back to his story, and that's great, that's a real gift. To be able to do that as a screenwriter, to win those battles, that will serve you well."

Global Gambling: Rolling with the International Marketplace

Along with love, filmmakers might refer to their work as the international language. Hollywood is indeed very cosmopolitan, both in its talent base and in its intended market, yet the love produced can often be unrequited. To create an industry analogy, imagine if Hollywood scoured the earth looking for the world's top furniture designers. The studios would inevitably bring them all to Los Angeles to design six-dollar plastic chairs to sell at the local Wal-Mart.

Yet because Hollywood has become so lucrative, many of these designers wouldn't hesitate making the leap. "The big sea change in the business is in the international market. Basically it's the impact on who is a brand-name star, who guarantees a certain amount of business worldwide, and what you pay for them," says Columbia Pictures' Doug Belgrad. "It's both supply and demand: The demand on the part of the audience is that it's harder and harder to get people out of their houses, and because of home video, it's harder and harder to get people not to wait [to see the video]. So you have to make movies an event to make them successful—what's going to lure someone out of his house, not wait to see it on HBO or on video."

There are only a handful of names that guarantee worldwide business, Belgrad explains. "Studios increasingly understand that their businesses are for the most part really sustained on huge, blockbuster hits, rather than by 'successes,' because the ratio of success to failure hasn't really changed. You're still lucky if you're making six hits for every four failures. But what people realized is that the failures are getting bigger and the fixed costs are getting bigger, therefore it's more important to have bigger hits to cover all those costs. Studios are willing to pay more, the audience demands more of an event-type environment, and the overseas marketplace has grown. That's why you're seeing increasing prices for stars, which in turn makes it again more expensive to make movies and again feeds on itself to increase the risk."

On the other end, studios are more receptive to new talent and apt to take actors for starring roles from a hit television series, rather than grooming them through supporting roles as they did in the past. Such motion pictures therefore intend to create stars or be fashioned in a way that the risks are lower. "You'll make the $70 million movie with the $20 million movie star. But you won't make a $40 million movie with a $5 million actor [in the cost range of 1988's original *Die Hard*].

"Instead, you'll make a $25 million movie with a $2 million actor and a younger director. Movies are adjusting on that basis, and I think it's polarizing the way the business operates," Belgrad continues. "You either have to make them below a certain price and limit your downside, or you've got to make them big—with big stars and big concepts—so that they become potential blockbusters." If a feature creates such an "event" environment in the United States, it stands a good chance of spiraling out the same way into other territories around the globe.

"The international market has become *so* important to the industry," stresses New Line's Lynn Harris. "In general, you can no longer find something that works for a small slice of an American audience, because the budget range is a certain size. It's got to appeal to a worldwide audience, and action movies work overseas and make companies a lot of money.

"We live in a world in which we can't be so egotistical or naive to think the American audience is the only one that's going to go see the movie," Harris continues. "American film is a worldwide business: Half of these companies are financed by foreign dollars, and the rest of us have money coming in from all over the place. We're not just making movies for an American audience anymore. We're making them for a world audience, and we have to know what the world audience likes if you're going to spend that kind of money.

"We know certain things play overseas, certain actors play overseas, and certain directors play overseas," Harris concludes. "Physical broad comedy translates no matter what language it's in. Exciting action translates no matter what language you're in. Terrific visual effects translate no matter what country, what culture, what language you're talking about. Subtle, quirky, interesting adult drama and black comedy sometimes translate and sometimes not. You're taking a pretty big risk if you're putting a lot of dollars behind something that may only play to a specific section of an American audience, or a specific section of an international audience."

"It's more about what *doesn't* work," says Miramax's Jack Lechner, regarding international tastes. "There are certain things that just don't translate. Stories about race relations in the United States tend not to play. Stories about American politics don't tend to play. There are all kinds of things that are taken for granted—all kinds of cultural context in an American movie about American politics—which just don't translate. Stories about baseball don't tend to translate, as you would figure.

"We faced that in reverse on a [British] Channel 4 movie that Miramax bought called *True Blue*, which is the true story of the Oxford-Cambridge boat race of a couple years ago, in which Oxford recruited a number of world-champion American rowers who turned out to be complete prima donnas. They ultimately had to be kicked off the team and were replaced at the last minute by a bunch of the B team who hadn't gotten to row all year. And they won the boat race." Lechner begins to laugh. "But this is a story in which the Americans are the bad guys, and as we found out at a test screening, that's not very easy to sell to an American audience."

American comedies, if verbal rather than physical, tend not to translate, yet sometimes they do better, Lechner says. Independent filmmaker "Hal Hartley is infinitely more successful in France than he is in the United States. Another movie that people were really shocked at: *Father of the Bride* did as well in Europe as it did here. It was Steve Martin's real breakthrough movie, whereas almost none of Steve Martin's previous movies really managed to sell as well in Europe. Go figure.

"Very dumb, *Dumb and Dumber* kind of movies do well all over the world," adds Lechner, who worked three years at Channel 4 in London before returning to New York. "In terms of cable movies, especially because the kind that HBO makes are very political and hard-edged and keyed into American social concerns, a lot of those movies don't actually translate. We did a movie called *The Infiltrator* about an Israeli journalist who went undercover with neo-Nazis in Germany, and needless to say, trying to find a German partner for that movie was not very easy. We had to fully finance it."

A foreign filmmaker's orientation brings a fresh perspective, but for Icelander Sigurjon "Joni" Sighvatsson, it also meant a particular improbability about his survival in Hollywood. "I'm one of the few executives working in this industry who's non-American, and non-English. There's certainly no Scandinavian, and so very few executives from other countries.

"Maybe my fortune was that I was one of the first students to come and study film in America. There were a lot of very good film schools in Europe, particularly in the sixties and the seventies—we had the German schools and all the great Czechs and Poles, and eastern Europe, and the Swedish Film Institute, maybe one school in each country—and there wasn't really such a demand to become a filmmaker.

"One of the reasons that those countries had such great film periods in those years was that they had very, very good schools that turned out good people," says Sighvatsson, who came to L.A. on a Fulbright scholarship and later attended the American Film Institute. "There weren't many foreigners studying film in America in the seventies. I came here in the late seventies, and I remember at USC, among the student body of three hundred or four hundred people, there were *five* of us who were foreign. That was it, everybody else was American. So I think I was lucky, in a sense, that I got in at the right ground level, and even though I wasn't planning to live here and stay here, I started to get work.

"I have been here for a long time, but it's been an interesting dichotomy for me," says Sighvatsson, who cofounded the phenomenally successful Propaganda Films with Steve Golin and a handful of music video directors. "I always said one of the reasons that I succeeded in the business was that I was working with an American partner, and not only did we work well together for many years, but he also had a very distinctive American perspective that I think was helpful. It didn't mean that I tried to become an American myself, but I always found that [partnership] very helpful to me; because very often then people would come and say, 'If you can do it, I can do it, and how do you succeed in Hollywood?' What people very often don't understand is that it's *as* much about the culture. When I think of all the films that I made, some were intrinsically American in an un-Hollywood way. They're not mainstream movies, but they're very American movies; I think particularly *Wild at Heart* and *Red Rock West* were very, very American movies.

"What you get in film school is five years of indoctrination, not only in American film, but also you're learning the culture at the same time," Sighvatsson explains. "You're understanding the real politics, so I think those things were really helpful in navigating me in a totally different cultural environment. Because *now,* in the nineties it has changed, and there's such an 'appetite' here that they're willing to take a director who's done one successful Spanish-language film and hire him to make Hollywood movies.

"That didn't happen ten years ago; no, no way, they didn't even *see* those films," Sighvatsson concludes. "They wouldn't even bother to look at them, so the marketplace has changed. It's still as competitive, but it's been easier, particularly I think for directors, to come here now to Hollywood. But then they get accustomed to a specific brand of a movie. Hollywood's been more open to hiring foreigners, probably because the marketplace has become so international."

Winding one's way through Hollywood Oz has interested explorers since Warsaw-born Samuel Goldwyn and Hungarian William Fox first set their feet on this foreign soil. Money men such as John F.'s father, Joseph Kennedy, Howard Hughes, and William Randolph Hearst followed. Hollywood always has and always will translate into money for those seeking fortunes in its whimsical fantasyland.

"People just show up with millions of dollars, rich people from around the world, who somehow want to get into the film industry," says entertainment attorney Dennis Cline. "Independent filmmakers are a natural fit, because the people from around the world aren't necessarily glazy-eyed with Hollywood. They are willing to take a chance on other kinds of things.

"For a writer, it depends on what you like to write and what you really like; that's idiosyncratic in and of itself," Cline continues. "It depends on who you know and who you get to know, and that's idiosyncratic in and of itself. But opportunity? There will always be opportunity."

Lightning Bolts and Train Wrecks

IN A WORLD WHERE MATERIAL DRIVES EVERYTHING,
THE GODS OF FILM ULTIMATELY DETERMINE
DISASTER OR SUCCESS FOR AN ENTERTAINMENT
FORM THAT CAN CHANGE THE CONTEMPORARY ZEITGEIST.

In every work of genius, we recognize our own rejected thoughts.

—RALPH WALDO EMERSON

Better to write for yourself and have no public, than to write for the public and have no self.

—CYRIL CONNOLLY

WHEN A MOVIE unexpectedly bursts through at the box office, as with *Seven* or *The Full Monty,* it's as if a lightning bolt has pierced the sky to ignite popular culture. Likewise, a studio can have the highest hopes for a project and watch it crash and burn when it opens. Numerous factors play into any motion picture's success or failure, but at the root of each is a screenplay bound by the rules of storytelling. That's what an audience responds to. Yet the most extraordinary screenwriters have a special talent for breaking those rules to create the most unique conventions.

Quentin Tarantino's *Pulp Fiction* relied on its narrative, but scrambled and interwove its structure, resulting in one of the most significant pop-culture phenomena of its decade. Like *Easy Rider* did in a previous era, such motion pictures reflected and propelled the cultural spirit of the times (as well as prompting a number of imitators who failed). In neither case did Hollywood convention back these films. But today Hollywood is a place that responds to success, rather than creates it.

The script alone is central to the process. "Material drives everything," says Interscope's production chief Scott Kroopf. "It's what gets actors; it's what makes movies. The [stronger the] voice and artistic integrity to the script, the better chance you have of getting a really good director and really good actors. Now that the market has opened up, you see more offbeat material succeeding, like *Pulp Fiction* and *Seven*.

"I've had to go back and think of some movies in the seventies because I was really hard-pressed," says Kroopf, in trying to think of a movie with such a tragic ending as *Seven*. "In the eighties the happy ending was totally de rigueur. Now *Seven* really opened up the field. You can play on both ends of the spectrum now, better."

Says screenwriting instructor John Truby, "The writer cannot control many of the factors that go into selling a script. Typically we cannot control who gets attached to it. We may certainly want somebody, but getting them attached usually—for most writers—is pretty much impossible. We can't affect whether or not somebody thinks that our idea is commercial. The only thing that we can control is the level of craft that goes into the script itself."

You can't tell a writer to write a commercial script or premise, says New Line's Lynn Harris, because it simply doesn't exist. "Sometimes he delivers a great piece of writing that catches our attention, and we know who the writer is. We can keep that person in mind and his next movie will be something that we buy. . . . The scripts that are great scripts come out of things the writers are really passionate about. Sometimes those are very commercial premises, and sometimes they're actually not. It's our job when we buy a script to figure out whether or not it's something people will go see, and whether or not we can cast it and find a director to bring it to light.

"The marketplace is constantly changing, and you can't judge what's going to be popular," Harris contends, in reference to the time screenwriters waste trying to second-guess the market. "Frankly, if you write what you think is going to be popular today" you are already behind the learning curve. If you happen to be lucky, "your movie's not going to get made for a year or two anyway, or more. So you write the best possible screenplay you can write about the best story you have to tell, and hope."

John Truby agrees. "If you think you can play some kind of a game from a selling point of view, you're going to lose. Number one, you do not know the market the way an agent will know the market; number two, you can't possibly know what the market will be when the script is finally ready. If you start playing that game, you're always going to be behind, and you're always going to be writing something that's really derivative. What you need to do is work on the areas that you *can* control, and you hope you come up with an idea that a lot of other people think is commercial.

"If there's any change I've seen [lately], it's that agents have become sharper at creating an environment where competition is going to drive the sale," says Truby. "But again, writers do not have control of that. So to me, you can't even get to the spec sale type of situation unless you come in with a script that is perceived to be professional.

"That doesn't mean there aren't spec sales where you'll say, 'My God, how did that script even get read?' Really, it's just because it was only driven by an idea," Truby explains. "Maybe you come up with an idea and somehow people think they're going to buy that, but this is the kind of mythology that drives lottery analogy. Therefore, it's a trap for 99.9 percent of writers. So I tell them, 'Don't play that game.' If you want to play the lottery, go play the lottery. But if you're going to write scripts with that lottery mentality, you're going to really be disappointed."

Spec scripts designed for the quick sale tend to be of a certain ilk, according to Manifest Film's Janet Yang. "They're often very concept-oriented and they're often really good in the beginning and fall apart at the end. Some writers are in such a hurry to finish they often haven't worked through the ending carefully. So a lot of people read the first thirty pages of a spec, which are fantastic, and are eager to jump into a bidding war, only to later find there's no ending. It's hilarious."

IF IT AIN'T ON THE PAGE, THEY WON'T BE ON THE STAGE

Savvy actors constantly search for material that will elevate their careers. They want dialogue they can chew on, or as Matt Damon and

Ben Affleck did with *Good Will Hunting,* they will write it themselves (actually the same path as actors-turned-writers such as Horton Foote, Billy Bob Thornton, Tim Robbins, Dean Devlin, and Carrie Fisher). "With low-budget movies, you see writing that is more distinctive, much stronger, purely good writing, and you *will* figure out how to make those kind of movies at a good cost," says Interscope's Scott Kroopf. "You find that's probably the only way you can get really good actors to work for less. It's because in their minds they're working on something that has absolute artistic integrity."

In a real sense, "the stars," who by their celestial position reside closer to those gods of film, are the ultimate buyers, not the studios. You can't make a buyer purchase a script, nor can you make an actor perform in a picture they do not like. To the studio, the script itself is never really commercial or noncommercial, that is, until a star enters the picture. But when a Mel Gibson or a Tom Cruise or a Julia Roberts says, "I want to do this," then the word "noncommercial" would never, ever leave a studio executive's lips.

"I have read *great* screenplays that can't get made because they can't attract a talent base around them," says producer Jonathan Sanger, a former documentary filmmaker in South America before arriving in Hollywood to participate in the Directors Guild assistant director's training program. "As soon as acting talent starts to buzz around a project, then all of a sudden the project takes on a whole different [convention]. If an actor is involved in a script that the actor wants to make, it automatically makes the material visible. It doesn't mean it will get made." Occasionally, says Sanger, a Bill Murray will get to do a *Razor's Edge* because he did *Ghostbusters,* but stars can't keep coming in with noncommercial projects, because that's not what the studios want them for.

Actors with vanity deals at studios are able to get projects made that a producer couldn't bring in off the street and get made. "The reason they get made, never stated, but always unstated, is that having a relationship with Robert Redford or Tom Cruise is going to mean that down the line maybe that studio will have a project that they will be in, so we'll do the small project," Sanger continues. "That's never alone enough of a reason, but it's always a reason to get in the door. And that is a big issue: getting in the door."

If a spec is in fact castable, attaching the actors whose cachet translates into wealth for the studios will naturally improve a deal. Oftentimes it benefits a producer to attach the right "element" before making a sale. Producer Joe Singer offers the example of J. J. Abrams's screenplay *Rest of Daniel* (released in 1992 under the title *Forever Young*). "Would that script have been a $2 million script without Mel Gibson attached? I certainly doubt it.

"I think the script was a very good script," says Singer. "But probably it would have sold at that time, in that market, for half a million dollars or for $700,000. Mel Gibson's attached and it's a $2 million script! The agent did a great job on that and really fulfilled his responsibility and *duty* to that client who wrote it. But that is the exception, not the rule."

The bowling comedy, *Kingpin,* by veteran television writers Mort Nathan and Barry Fanaro, failed to attract an offer when United Talent Agency placed it on the spec market in 1993. But when Michael Keaton became interested two years later, his CAA agents were able to put together the movie (Woody Harrelson replaced Keaton in the 1996 release). The once-dormant property, which had simply been making the rounds as a writing sample, brought the writers an unexpected million-dollar paycheck.

There are plenty of good scripts, as well as plenty of bad scripts, sitting around at every studio. "But the real process is out of the producer's hands and is really in the studio's. They control the green light at a certain point," says literary manager Peter Scott. "Some producers argue that if they get Michelle Pfeiffer in a film, and they attach Harold Becker to direct and just keep moving forward that they force the studio to say, 'Yes, we'll make this film. How can we not make this film with all this talent attached?'

"They just keep on attaching and attaching and moving forward, and they don't wait for the studio to say, 'Okay, you have a green light.' They get to the point where the studio just can't say, 'No.' That's an interesting kind of green light, that's like wishing a green light onto a studio," Scott says. "Now, that strategy can work very well. But if a producer cares more about a final product (i.e., getting the movie made) than the product itself, and if he has strong relationships, he might see a really bad movie getting made because he's attaching really talented people to a script that doesn't work yet. There are some checks and balances, because you don't expect Michelle Pfeiffer or Harold Becker to attach themselves to a movie if it's not good. So it depends on the integrity of each of the people involved."

CUTTING THE DEAL BEFORE CUTTING YOUR WRISTS

Dorothy Parker once said that Hollywood is the only place where you can die of encouragement. Chasing after that gold nugget can also lead to despair for screenwriters who seize the big deal and never get to see their intended pictures produced. Yet sometimes having a film made to less than the scribe's expectations can be a screenwriting career's worst ordeal.

"I can't even tell you how *right* that is," says Ross Hammer, formerly a development executive for *Friday the 13th* creator Sean Cunningham. "A friend started with . . . *Friday the 13th: Part 9.* He wrote *My Boyfriend's Back* before he moved out here. Disney purchased it, and he got four writing deals based on that script.

"His price was suddenly going up after his first sale, and suddenly he was making hundreds of thousands of dollars," Hammer recalls. "His first two movies . . . were both released a week apart, and they both *bombed* miserably. Since then, his price has gone down significantly . . . and he's brilliant! It's not that he can't get a job; he's working now. But he's not writing scripts for half a million dollars, which is where I think he should be."

What winds up on film may not be any indication whatsoever of the credited screenwriter's initial work, or their true talent. Most movie critics, and practically all of the public, who are not otherwise informed of the inner workings of the script's development, readily perceive that the final cut is all the credited screenwriter's contribution.

"The connective tissue of the stories in films tends to get cut out first, rather than the action sequences, when a film is running too long," says David Twohy, one of the rewriters of Peter Rader's original script for *Waterworld.* "They'll take out a scene that shows why a hero knows how to get from point A to B and find the bad guy there. But since it's only a talk scene, somebody at the studio says, 'Let's just lose all that talk and get straight to action.' So you have these glaring holes in the continuity of the story, which oftentimes are attributed to the writers, but are more often than not the responsibility of the editor and the studio people."

While writing his master's thesis at the University of Southern California (USC), Michael Beckner spent his days transcribing director Barry Levinson's notes and lines of dialogue for Levinson's Baltimore Pictures. Beckner took stabs at his own writing, and after selling *Sniper* (directed in 1993 by Luis Llosa and starring Tom Berenger), Beckner jumped into the high-stakes spec world with his million-dollar-plus sale to producer Larry Gordon of the as yet unproduced *Texas Lead and Gold,* cowritten with Jim Gorman.

At Baltimore Pictures, "I wrote four or five scripts, and Levinson's producer Mark Johnson passed on all of them," Beckner recalls. "Then I wrote the movie *Sniper.* I figured there's no way that Mark Johnson and Barry Levinson are going to make a movie that has to do with snipers murdering people. I didn't want to go to the well one more time; it's getting embarrassing. So I didn't give him the script."

Dan Halsted was Beckner's agent at the time, and he began to circulate the script to potential buyers. "I got married when Larry Gordon's Largo was interested, and Joel Silver was in there, and I'm off on my honeymoon." Gorman, who was attached as a producer, called Beckner.

"Mark Johnson is buying the script," said Gorman.

Since it was a long-distance call, the newlywed Beckner tapped on the telephone and replied, "Do we have a good connection here?"

"Mark Johnson had gone into my office to find a story report or something and saw the script on my desk," says Beckner. Johnson had never seen *Sniper* before and sat down to read it. He called Halsted, to Beckner's surprise, to say he was making the movie.

Beckner still wasn't ready to quit his day job until *Sniper* got made. "I worked for [Baltimore Pictures] for about another two years—through *Avalon*—but at that point my writing career was kind of taking off on its own."

The million-dollar sale of *Texas Lead and Gold* boosted Beckner's bank account and Hollywood profile. Then Beckner and Gorman wrote *Cutthroat Island,* a pirate adventure that sold for a hefty $2 million. *Cutthroat Island* sold almost a year to the day after *Texas Lead and Gold.* "It was one of those deals that was weighted more on the back end, whereas most of my spec deals have all been guaranteed, because spec scripts often don't get made."

Under a deal at Hollywood Pictures at the time, Beckner and Gorman shared an office on the Disney lot. "With *Cutthroat Island,* they had a first look at it. They could've gotten it for $200,000. They passed, but Danny Halsted and everyone at Hollywood Pictures and Ricardo Mestres were saying, 'We gotta make this movie,'" Beckner recalls. "Jeffrey Katzenberg says, 'No pirates. There's no way we'll do it.' But again, with that one, it was all about passion. No one would want to make a pirate movie. I didn't even want to make a 'pirate' movie.

"When I wrote *Cutthroat Island,* it was the same [reaction] as *Texas Lead and Gold:* No one wants to see swinging on a rope, no one wants to see swordfight duels with two ships next to each other broadside, because it's been done," says Beckner. You can take Errol Flynn as inspiration, "but in watching an Errol Flynn movie, you want to see Errol Flynn. But I discovered there's so much about pirates that we never saw, and that is so much fun if you can make it different.

"In my first meeting with [*Cutthroat* director] Renny Harlin, he said, 'I am doing this movie as a tribute to Errol Flynn.' And I thought to myself, 'Oh, noooo. . . .' Actually, I got paid for a rewrite I never did; they never wanted it. They just went off with other writers, and then it became a love letter to his wife, I think."

Industry wags retitled the movie *Cut Wrist Island* after the swashbuckling adventure, starring Harlin's then wife Geena Davis, bombed. Beckner now carries the stigma of a major misfire on his writer's resume, while Gorman has since retired from the business altogether after marrying an extra he met in Australia during the filming of *Sniper.*

"When my scripts go out now, there's an automatic million-dollar price tag, which can kill me," says Beckner. "I'd be perfectly happy to take $100,000 for something. Maybe I'm being facetious there, and I don't know what the other guys say, but it seems there's a double-edged sword. [The studios] know that they can't even come in with a bid if they like it, but say, 'Oh, it needs to be developed.' They're afraid if they come in with a bid of $300,000" that it's insulting.

"I harbor fantasies that twenty years from now they'll make [my] *Cutthroat Island,*" Beckner sighs, before talking about his recent foray into novel writing, the subject of his USC education. "With books, you don't get a *Cutthroat Island* out of them. If I write a shitty book, it's shitty because I wrote it. But *Cutthroat Island* has *my name* on it— my name's on it more than anyone else except Gorman. Beckner, Beckner, Beckner, it says it all over the place. I'm embarrassed! I'm embarrassed because it's not what I did."

CHASING DREAMS AND CHASING DOLLARS

Genre movies, such as horror or film noir, often depend on studio whims rather than needs. Yet such flicks can be a great means for a writer to get started, so newcomers will often spec out a slasher picture to, at least, interest a B-grade financier. Because of the phenomenal success of the *Scream* series, written by Kevin Williamson and which revived the moribund horror genre, today's studios rediscovered an interest in material designed to shock and surprise.

Just like action pictures, some of these pictures win, and many of them lose. It's primarily an impact of the international audience that studios are willing to risk multimillions on motion pictures about gigantic bugs; after all, we relate universally to things that frighten us. Today's studios have found a potential goldmine in their making. It wasn't always the case.

"When I did *Nightmare on Elm Street,* the conventional wisdom was that the horror film was burned out," says director Wes Craven. "There was a desire to be politically correct—although at that time the term wasn't around—a feeling that horror movies were nasty and ugly. There had been so many reactionary articles against [Sean Cunningham's] *Friday the 13th,* about violence and its effects on kids, that *no one* would go near *Nightmare.*"

Prior to such critical and commercial successes as *Platoon* and *Apocalypse Now,* Cunningham and Craven cowrote a Vietnam script based on a soldier who had been an inspector general and had been courtmartialed for reporting American atrocities. "Everybody talked about Vietnam, but nobody wanted to do a movie about it. The feeling was that nobody wants to pay to go see it in a movie, because Vietnam was a failure. . . . So the studios just closed down to it.

"Doesn't *that* create the vacuum where an audience gets hungry for something? If you make all your decisions politically correct, the first guy who comes out with something horrendous, awful, and *blows* your *ears* out, then a lot of kids are going to want to go see it," Craven contends. "But studio executives at their cocktail parties aren't going to want to have to admit that it's *their* film. . . . It makes it very hard to sell [a more complex fright-fest] to a studio, unless it's a very clever, escapist, roller-coaster ride."

Says *Alien* cowriter Ron Shusett, "I write for the fantastical, so I am always for something that's totally unusual, a movie that's never been made. The studios hate that, because it's always *risky*. It's weird, it could go through the roof, or it couldn't draw well at all. Unless I *force* myself to write something that isn't particularly imaginative, I won't write something that they are likely to buy.

"It presents a problem that's unique to my own personality," says Shusett, who produced local theater in Beverly Hills before getting together with a young director named Andrew Davis (who later directed *The Fugitive*) to begin producing movies. "They don't want to buy the things that I write until I get a package, and that's very hard to do—the chicken and the egg—without a studio interest, at first.

"Yet I *loathe* writing something that's formulaic, another *Die Hard*–type movie," Shusett says. "These kind of nonstop action movies always work for the studios: 'We'll do one! We'll do hardware.' I like a story that's mind-boggling, and the studios *hate* that. The more imaginative it is, the more frightened they are unless it comes attached with a name director. So I usually ignore what I'm supposed to do and write through my heart, and that's perhaps why I get so few movies made; it's painful. I get them made, and they're usually smashes . . . probably half my movies have been major hits. But each one is so weird."

It was Dan O'Bannon's collaboration with director John Carpenter on 1974's *Dark Star* at USC's film school that prompted Shusett to contact him. After working on *Alien,* the two started writing *Total Recall* in 1974, when there wasn't yet much concept of "virtual reality" and the studios scoffed at characters purchasing artificial memory to plant in their minds. " 'Baloney, the audience won't accept that it seems real to him.' In the 1980s when *Total Recall* went into production, virtual reality started coming about, and the critics said, 'What a great premise.' Then critics and audiences embraced it when it came out, but of course they were probably ready to embrace it all along."

Few people knew of Phillip K. Dick when Shusett optioned his short story, *We Can Remember It for You Wholesale,* which became *Total Recall.* "Studios don't like to option short stories because it's so hard for them to see a whole structure in it. So they're not looking very hard, unless the guy's *really* a huge name, and Phil Dick wasn't at that time. . . . That was *way* before *Blade Runner* [based on another of his short stories]. Basically no one even knew who Phil Dick was, but O'Bannon, a science fiction buff, knew the story and loved it.

Phillip K. Dick had "written *We Can Remember It for You Wholesale* probably in the sixties, and I optioned it in 1974, and it was peanuts.

I optioned it for a thousand dollars. I had the rights to buy it for $10,000 total, another $9,000 if we made the movie. So it *isn't* too hard to option short stories if you look through pulp magazines, and the writer isn't [yet] famous. Now William Gibson, he's become the new Phil Dick in an *established* way. There are other young science fiction writers who you can option if you admire their work and they're not yet made. The studios don't even bother looking at them."

Two thirds of the structure of *Total Recall,* in which Arnold Schwarzenegger's character goes to Mars, was invented by the screenwriters. Paul Verhoeven eventually directed the 1990 release, which earned $261 million in worldwide gross receipts. The project went from Disney to Dino DeLaurentiis to TriStar as Shusett and O'Bannon developed the picture. Director Bruce Beresford (*Driving Miss Daisy*) was set to direct it in 1988, and Patrick Swayze, coming off *Dirty Dancing,* would star. Then Dino DeLaurentiis's company went broke.

The movie was called off, until Carolco, which subsequently would also go broke, bought the rights from DeLaurentiis. "Schwarzenegger always loved the script and wanted to do it," Shusett recalls. "He wasn't a big enough star when he first read it four years earlier. But by this time, Arnold's become a superstar, and he told Carolco, 'I want to make this movie.' They said, 'Fine.' They bought it in Dino's bankruptcy, and Arnold got Paul Verhoeven interested in directing it." The movie was made a year later, in 1989.

"It's so subjective that you can't tell how things get made," Shusett contends. "*Alien* didn't get made at first. They optioned it, but they couldn't get a star for it, nobody wanted to do a monster movie, and no name director was interested in it. Ridley Scott was a budding young director who had only one movie." Scott's *The Duellists,* produced by David Puttnam, was a box office dud but a visually stunning film that earned Ridley Scott, then a dazzling London commercial director, some Hollywood attention.

"It's all luck, and intuition, and timing, and a certain powerful person," Shusett explains. "How did *Alien* get made? Fox optioned it, but they weren't going to make it. At the last minute, the costs were too risky. As we were designing it and drawing it, it got to be three times the average budget, and no star. They talked to Jane Fonda, Candy Bergen, all these women who were hot female stars at the time. Sigourney Weaver had never made a movie.

"They'd already sent us a letter [that] they decided not to make it.

They couldn't get a star and they couldn't get a hot director. So they *passed* on it and put it in turnaround." George Lucas had directed *American Graffiti,* so it made sense for Fox to take a chance on him with *Star Wars,* says Shusett, "but we had no film. We didn't have Ridley Scott then, or Sigourney, or any of these people. Steven Spielberg happened to read the script. And I have never even met Spielberg, after all these years, to this time."

Alan Ladd, Jr., ran Fox at the time and asked the boy wonder Spielberg his opinion of *Alien* in 1975. Nobody wanted to risk missing out on another *Star Wars.* According to Shusett, Spielberg (who had just directed *Jaws,* then the highest-grossing film in history) told Ladd, the Fox chieftain, "This is amazing, what do you mean, hesitate? Get the best talent you can and make it. I don't care if anybody ever heard of them. . . . It's phenomenal, it's hugely commercial, and it's an amazing movie. I am just too busy to do my own projects that I've had my heart in for a long time, or I would do it myself."

"Dan O'Bannon and I were total novices, and these guys Fox made the deal with were not at the top level," Shusett continues. "Gordon Carroll hadn't made a hit in many years. Walter Hill was doing low-budget movies that looked promising. David Giler was a pretty successful writer, but none of them had had big hits; and this movie *Alien* was *escalating.* Within an hour, all of a sudden we get a telephone call, and a letter the next morning" that Fox reoptioned *Alien.*

"Within six months, they were shooting. They just went out and hired Ridley Scott, who was eleventh choice as director. They screen-tested a lot of people, Sigourney gave a dynamite screen test, and they made the movie. What made them do it? They liked it on the strength of the script, but it wasn't enough backstop. So nothing seems to change, you know. It's a guess, it's intuition in getting the right people involved with you. Or if Spielberg had said nothing, I don't know, I don't think any other studio would have made *Alien* either.

"It's the same way they seem to operate now," Shusett concludes. "You wouldn't think a goddam giant *Alien* lizard coming out of your chest would be commercial. You'd say, 'Oh, that's gonna be a grade-Z horror movie.' But who knew that Ridley Scott, a genius visual stylist in the tradition of Spielberg, would be hired somewhere down the line and help make *Alien* into a classic?"

A PERFECT HOLLYWORLD

Steven Spielberg was also a prime mover for 1993's *A Perfect World.* Its writer, John Lee Hancock, was a lawyer from Houston, Texas, who bagged his safety-net career to roll Hollywood's dice. "I just wanted to be around actors, and I wanted to have the experience of putting a production up. Then I started directing some theater and worked with a couple of different theater companies.

"One of them was with an Okie named George Davis, a Texan named Bill Allen, myself, and Brandon Lee [son of Bruce Lee], who's now deceased. We had a theater company called 'Legal Aliens,' none of us being from here, and Brandon being from Mars basically. But we had a ball," Hancock recalls. "We were like brothers—the four of us— and we did real guerrilla-type theater. We would go up for four weeks: 'If you want to come, come.' We gave all the money to charity."

Hancock began using his middle name, because another Screen Actors Guild member was known as John Hancock, a popular large black character actor who played a judge on *L.A. Law.* "People would get in touch with me: 'We'd love for you to come in and talk with us about a project.' I think they were pretty disappointed to see a skinny, white Texan come in if you're thinking about a four-hundred-pound New York black man. So it's my middle name, and I decided to stick with it," says Hancock, who bears much more resemblance to singer-actor Chris Isaak than to Shaquille O'Neal.

Hancock survived on a variety of low-paying jobs, did a little acting and production work, and was a freelance reader at the now defunct Triad Artists where because of his excellent coverage the department heads recognized he was a natural storyteller. After writing several specs, he came up with *A Perfect World,* about a Texas Ranger (Clint Eastwood) on the trail of an escaped convict (Kevin Costner) who has taken a little boy hostage. Hancock was soon to become a "pocket client" of Ronda Gomez, then an agent at Triad.

"I wrote *A Perfect World* and [Ronda Gomez] liked it a lot and felt there was a market for it," Hancock recalls. "The funny thing is, at the time they had a system where she wanted to sign me, she wanted to make me official, but none of the other agents there could agree.

"Some of the agents said, 'I have no idea how to sell this. Why are we going to bring in another client who writes this character stuff? There's not a single car crash. There's not much gunplay. It's got this thing with the kid. What are we gonna do?' I'm sure that was up-setting to Ronda," Hancock recalls of the reaction to his rather dark drama. "But she came to me and said, 'You know, if you don't mind, you won't be signed, but I will work as hard for you as any of my clients.' I trusted her, and I believed she did have a plan for selling a script. Because my idea was, 'Okay, I'm gonna go independent with this.' "

Gomez submitted *A Perfect World* to such producers as Scott Rudin, Paula Weinstein, Jim Brooks, and Mark Johnson. "It was a slow-play process. It wasn't Ronda calling producers and saying, 'We have a bidding deadline at 5 P.M.' She knew it wasn't that. . . . They were go-ing to read it, they were gonna like it, and it was going to haunt them. If someone forces you to say, 'Buy it or don't buy it,' he's going to go, 'Eyeee, okay, no. I'm a little afraid.'

"I had met with all these different people and everybody loved the script and seemed to be interested, and the wheels were kind of turn-ing," Hancock says. "Mark Johnson optioned it, and then things started happening very quickly. It was very strange. People were passing it around as a writing sample by then. Next thing you know, you're get-ting calls." Mark Johnson had been friends with Spielberg since work-ing as an assistant director on Spielberg's early movies.

Spielberg called Johnson when he heard about the option, at first hassling him playfully about not sending it to him in the first round, then prompting Mark to send over *A Perfect World.* Johnson laughed, telling Spielberg that *Jurassic Park* was already on his schedule.

Johnson then called up Hancock. "What are you doing Saturday?"

"I don't have any plans," Hancock said.

"We're going to lunch at Steven's," Johnson informed him.

"Oh really?" John beamed.

"So we drove up to Steven's house," recalls Hancock, greeted by Spielberg's wife and fellow Texan, Kate Capshaw. "It's a really com-fortable place. There's dogs and kids and you feel like it isn't anything ostentatious. I remember leaning back against the wall, feeling com-fortable enough that I could lean back I suppose, and something rattled on the wall behind me—a painting—and I just had this image of a Matisse coming down and crashing over my head. I turned around and grabbed it and looked and it was Rosebud [from *Citizen Kane*], which he had purchased. I was holding this, it was in Plexiglas, and I was just staring at it, one of those weird, odd moments."

Johnson, sitting next to Hancock, said, "Don't worry. They threw the good one in the fire. It's the second one."

"Right when this happened, Steven walked in, and I turned and said '*Rooseebuuddd,*' " Hancock remembers.

"Pretty cool, huh?" Spielberg asked.

"Yeah, it is," said John. "I'm glad I didn't just turn it into kindling."

Hancock spent the next couple of weeks at Spielberg's house developing *A Perfect World* while the director waited for Industrial Light and Magic (ILM), George Lucas's Marin County–based special effects company, to finish designing dinosaurs for *Jurassic Park.* He told Hancock that he was pretty sure ILM wouldn't have the computer graphics ready in time.

"He thought it was going to be later, at least two or three months pushed," Hancock recalls. "So he was going to do this little character movie first, then do *Jurassic,* which he had completely worked out, boards and everything else."

Then Spielberg told Hancock to stand by until the following Wednesday. When that day came around, Spielberg called Johnson to tell him ILM swears they're going to be ready, effectively scrapping *A Perfect World.* Johnson's partner at the time, Barry Levinson, wasn't as keen on the project, so Johnson decided to split off on his own and somehow make *A Perfect World* happen.

"Steven was really good to me, because you know how spin control is in this town," Hancock remembers. "Somebody says one thing, and all of a sudden something's dead. It would have been very easy for Steven to say, 'Yeah, I was thinking about doing it, but I don't think I'm going to do it now.' Then it becomes 'what's wrong with it?' Instead of that, Steven basically let it be known that 'this is the script that I desperately wanted to do, but because of time and scheduling, I couldn't,' which is 180 degrees different, which makes *everybody* want to be involved."

In the meantime, Clint Eastwood had read *A Perfect World* as a writing sample for the novel *Midnight in the Garden of Good and Evil,* which Warner Bros. had purchased for him. "I think he surprised everyone when he said he wanted to direct it. We went and met with Clint, and this was before *Unforgiven* had come out. Mark Johnson and I walked out of the meeting and looked at each other."

"He was so honest about the script," said Hancock. "I could tell that he got it, which was the main thing. He told me that it reminded him of *Lonely Are the Brave,* to which I went, 'Okay, he gets it. He gets it.' That's one of my favorite movies, the Kirk Douglas–Walter Matthau thing. In some places it's a little silly; but it's a good movie and it had that resonance. Mark and I got in the car and said, 'It seems like the right fit.' "

"I've heard *Unforgiven* is wonderful," Johnson continued.

"So that was how Clint got involved. He was going to do it, and we were very happy with that," Hancock says. "I knew that other people were reading it. And then one day Clint called me."

"What are you doing tomorrow?" Eastwood asked him. "You want to come by the office around ten o'clock or so? We really haven't sat down and talked about anything since our one conversation. . . . Do you mind if another actor might join us?"

Hancock thought to ask who, then refrained. "I thought that if he wanted to tell me, he would. Every time the phone rings, it's only good news or better news," Hancock remembers.

"This is pretty wild," Johnson and Gomez told Hancock. "This doesn't happen on every movie, John. You do understand now?"

"I understood that, but basically I was pretty loose about the whole thing," says Hancock. "I mean, after you go to Spielberg's for lunch, you know you can handle it. Everybody's normal and nice and all, *plus* they like the script, which is your entree. You're on some level of confidence right there."

The day for Clint's meeting arrived and Hancock entered the Warner Bros. lot to obtain his drive-on pass. But the security guard misdirected the hopeful scribe to the far end of the studio lot. When a distressed and sweat-drenched Hancock arrived at Clint Eastwood's Malpaso Productions office a quarter hour late, he burst into the room and looked over to the couch. There sat Kevin Costner. "The first thing that came to mind was something my father used to always say, and I quoted him: 'If this isn't a dollar waiting on a dime, I don't know what is.' "

"They laughed, and we were fine," Hancock recalls. After Hancock caught his breath and took a seat, Kevin Costner turned to the screenwriter.

"I just have to go on record and say that there's *absolutely no way* that I can do this movie," Costner began. "My schedule's just too full, my plate is crammed, and there's just absolutely no way I can do this. I've got too much to do. There's no way, just no way . . ."

Hancock recalls the moment his heart skipped a beat.

"But I want to," Costner concluded.

"That was one of my Hollywood lessons: 'No one has time to do anything.' These movie stars are always booked," says Hancock. "It's a matter of getting them to *want* to do something, and he wanted to do it."

Spielberg then called Warner Bros. to tell them he wanted a blind-picture deal with Hancock, coaching the screenwriter in further lessons of the game.

"What's a blind-picture deal?" the former lawyer asked Spielberg.

"We get together and pitch ideas to each other," Steven explained. "And when we decide on one, Warner Brothers pays for it."

"So we had a ball. During this time I was meeting with Steven and Clint and obviously they're good friends, but they're very different: With Clint you sit and you have conversations, and he's relaxed," says Hancock. "Then you go to Steven's office, and you're talking about ideas, and you're crawling around the floor describing shots." Hancock went on to also write 1997's *Midnight in the Garden of Good and Evil* for Eastwood.

"I had these strange fathers at the same time: one very passive and strong and quiet, and one more manic and excitable in talking about ideas," Hancock says. *A Perfect World* went on to make $31 million domestically, causing many in the industry to feel it underperformed. Yet the picture grossed over $135 million in the world's box office, with long runs in such countries as Japan and France. Regardless of the box office, the process was a particular joy for Hancock. "I had a great time on the set of the movie. I spent a lot of time down there. Let's face it, at that point, I had two Academy Award–winning directors to talk to about directing."

BACKLASH OF THE SPEC BOOM

The spec market has its pros and cons, or its professionals and its con men as the case may be. It's generally agreed the marketplace fury from spec frenzies can be detrimental to the studios, the writers, and ultimately the agents. In such an environment, the studios don't feel they have time to make intelligent decisions, and the writers' hopes are dangled by the quick sale, or an otherwise tainted project. If what's expected to be a hot spec doesn't sell, it can be hard to ignite interest around the project later. On top of that, the agents are prompted to one-up deals to keep clients happy.

In real estate, if a house doesn't sell right away, its price continues to drop, and it leads to a skepticism regarding its value. Such is not really the case with specs, since they can more easily "build on" an element.

"The agents who are doing the best in the spec market are not necessarily doing a service to the business or their clients in the long run, because a lot of material's getting bought for the wrong reasons at inflated prices," says one studio executive. "And these movies either don't get made or they're not successful, and then there's a reluctance to do it again and make movies with that particular piece of creative talent because they've failed.

"People in this business are smart enough to understand that people who get movies made—who write movies—are a scarce commodity. So you don't quickly dismiss talent. But you might if their representatives are inflating the value of their work. Also, it's a precedent-based business. . . . If an agent is unable to sell someone's material for what he got for his last script, the writer [might tell the agent], 'Well, am I at the right place?' "

Says producer Mark Johnson, "I've never been involved in one of those deals where somebody calls you and says, 'Twenty-four hours and we've got a sale. If you're interested, you've gotta meet us all in a room and work things out.' Yet all of us have someone on our staff whose job it is primarily to track spec scripts. And I'm not sure why, because I doubt that I will ever make a spec buy. I temperamentally resist having a gun to my head, saying, 'All right, you gotta read it overnight.' I sort of resent the game rules."

Producer Ross Hammer suspects that 75 percent of what's sold for half a million dollars or more in the last few years is a large-scale action picture. "That's because the Jim Camerons and the Philip Noyces and the Mace Neufelds in town who can produce these big action pictures, attract big stars, and actually make significant amounts of money at the box office provide more of a sure bet than by making a smaller character piece, or an interesting little thriller with a great story. It becomes an issue of profile, and a lot of stars are very concerned about that.

"If you try to interest a star in a picture, the first things his agent or manager is going to ask you are: 'How are we gonna promote this movie?' 'How widespread is this campaign gonna be?' 'Is this gonna give my client the most and best exposure possible so that my client has a hit, so that my client's price will then go up?'

"More often than not, it's much more attractive for executives to be associated with a humongous picture that makes decent numbers at the box office than to be associated with a small picture that makes *great* numbers at the box office," Hammer concludes. "Executives want to be associated with that bigger, higher-profile picture."

Thus what the spec process leads to, says producer Thom Mount, is too much standard studio fare. "When you wander around America—and I've spent a lot of time out there in what are nominally called at the studios 'the fly-over cities,' the places where people actually buy tickets to movies—the human cry is always the same: 'Not enough interesting films, not enough diversity of product.' One of the reasons the independent market has prospered was by its obvious financial pitfalls. You can have a *Four Weddings and a Funeral.* You can have a *Sense and Sensibility.* You can make pictures of quality that actually do business, everywhere. There is a market in Kansas City for *Sense and Sensibility* . . . who would've thunk it?"

After numerous bidding wars that go out of control, the bottom falls out, and "then agents complain, 'Oh, nothing's selling for a lot of money now,'" says Liz Glotzer of Castle Rock. "I tend to think writers are, dare I say it, underpaid. I mean, without a script you don't have a movie, and that's the most important selling point. Actors, they can't *act* without the script, so a good script is really hard to find. It's really a precious commodity." To reach the screen, those scripts require a champion with the intuition to not only sell them, but then guide them through Hollywood's labyrinth that is so prone to damaging their original vision.

According to former Sandollar President Scott Immergut, "A lot of scripts sell because they're easy to pitch in a staff meeting. It's easier to say 'I've got a great script about *The Cable Guy* from hell' than it is to pitch *Diner,* which is unpitchable. If you try to pitch that to Joe Roth or Jeffrey Katzenberg or any of these guys, they'd look at you like you were crazy. That's one of the reasons the spec market has evolved the way it has. It's also the reason why so many remakes of television shows hit the big screen. You can go into a staff meeting and say, '*Hawaii Five-O.*' Everyone knows exactly what you're talking about.

"The blockbuster has driven what people like," Immergut continues. "If *Sense and Sensibility* grossed $150 million dollars in three weeks, believe me, we'd all be doing that. The other thing about the spec market is that it's relatively rare in studio jobs when you actually feel like you've accomplished something. When you buy a spec script, there's all sorts of back and forth, everyone's calling everybody else, everyone's writing big checks, you get your name in the trades: You've *done* something. That is very rare. . . . You can read a script, write a check for $800,000, your name's in the trades, and everybody else hates you cause they didn't get it. It's a whole big '*to do*,' whereas most of making movies is pushing a big piece of granite up a really long hill, and you go inch by inch.

"It's partly to do with big blockbusters, and also partly to do with the agency side and the studio side of business becoming more prominent [in the last decade]," says Immergut, formerly a *Premiere* magazine editor before entering the studio ranks. "The agents controlled us. It used to drive me crazy that an agent would call up and say, 'I've got a great script.' Well, that means I have to shut my door, cancel my day, and read this thing, which is almost always a piece of crap."

Studio executives aren't driven by the same goals as their writers. As those who must struggle with the art versus commerce issue rather than deal with it day to day, writers often don't fit in or find the same satisfaction in what *is* popular to the masses. Producers have a goal somewhere in between, harkening to Joel Silver's famous words by searching for material that is *uniquely generic*. "While Hollywood wants you to be fresh and new," says director George Huang, "they also want something very familiar. That's why you always pitch an idea as 'so and so' meets 'so and so.' "

Mark Johnson feels that we as a culture are to blame for the current cinema's lack of diversity. "When I think of my favorite movies over the years, I don't think they would fare very well today in Hollywood. I don't think *Lawrence of Arabia* coming out today would be a particularly successful movie. Most people would find it too long, too talky, and too exotic, or whatever. We don't have the patience, as moviegoers.

"When *Die Hard* works, I'm the happiest moviegoer in the world. But I also want to go see *The Conformist*, or I also want to go see *Raging Bull*," says Johnson, who experienced one of his greatest joys producing 1995's *A Little Princess* (which critics adored but didn't garner much box office upon its release). "I think what's happening is that we've become a society that's only going to see the *Die Hard*s.

We don't have the patience or quite frankly the discipline to really appreciate some of the more demanding movies.

"Some of my favorite movies, the movies of the seventies, the movies with a certain amount of paranoia, be it *Three Days of the Condor* or Coppola's best movies, I just don't know if an audience today—forget about sophistication—really has the *patience* or the interest to sit through something like that, and to work with it," says Johnson, who earned an Academy Award in 1989 for producing *Rain Man.* "I love the idea of a movie business that has room, that has broad parameters for what we can and cannot see. I'm not asking that *My Dinner with André* make the same money as *Twister.* But I am asking that *My Dinner with André* has the possibility for making a profit.

"What's happened is that we're becoming a film industry in which we're only making the big event 'movie star' movies, or the tiny little go-for-broke movie," Johnson concludes. "When those [smaller movies] work, it's great; and when you see a *Walking and Talking* or any John Sayles movie, you want to cheer. That really invigorates the area I think is most in danger, in terms of the business. The mid-level—where you need a budget to do something a little bit bigger than *Lone Star* or *My Dinner with André*, with subjects that aren't big 'event movies,' but nevertheless have movie stars and certain production values and aren't done on the cheap—I think we're in danger of losing those."

It's perhaps unavoidable that screenwriters allow commercial notions to affect their work, but it's a result of the great emphasis their industry has placed on the "bottom line." A picture's box office receipts are reported in the media in the same manner, and to an even greater degree, as a baseball player's batting statistics or a new automobile's zero-to-fifty time and braking distance. The latter's statistics validly measure a ball player's or a new car's value. But because a picture does phenomenal box office doesn't necessarily mean it has redeeming value as art for our society.

"I don't know what commercial is, I really don't. I only know what I care about," says Michael Kalesniko, who broke onto the scene by winning a script competition with *Botch* and has done well on spec and assignment writing since, including 1997's *Private Parts.* "The truth is, if it's really passionate, *that* will sell. But you have to know when you're working with the studios, they make the rules and you decide if you're going to play by them."

Unlike the studio executives, screenwriters don't generally watch a film with the thought of running to the Internet on Sunday night to see how much money it made on its opening weekend. They tend to just look at the film for the story's sake. If it told a story that interested them, that's all that mattered. Good writers will always appreciate good writing. Many don't really care how a picture does at the box office, so long as it plays in the theaters long enough for all their friends to see it.

The Three As to Defining a Literary Agent

As it should be very clear to this book's readers by now, agents play a pivotal role in any spec script's sale. To consider this "power" is a misnomer, as every agent will agree that the capability to make a sale ultimately belongs to the studio (or the entity supplying a project's financing).

As a conduit and commercial access point in the process, an agent's particular power depends almost entirely on the abilities and loyalty of his or her clients, as well as the agent's relationships with the buyers. And a wise choice of an agent can make all the difference in a writer's career.

Smaller agencies can sometimes be more adept at selling spec scripts, because oftentimes they're more likely to offer them, while the larger agencies have their clients booked on assignments. Thus, there's no reason to feel a small agency is less able to sell spec material. In fact, smart buyers often give greater attention to "boutique" agencies for that very reason.

Sometimes studios will accept material from a lawyer's submission, although it's generally agreed—even by lawyers—that agents are more keen at evaluating the spec-buying game. Therefore agents will often develop relationships with lawyers who can forward them spec material.

"Fortunately, lawyers have sort of replaced agents as the bad guys," says Paradigm agent Stu Robinson. "There used to be agent jokes, now there are lawyer jokes. I think, quite frankly, over the last thirty years, the quality of agents has improved enormously, because there is no cliché of an agent anymore. It used to be the gravel-voiced guy climbing up the fire escape with Jesse White's picture in his hand, and that just doesn't exist anymore."

The Three *A*s (Access, Attention, Aggression) can lead a writer to the right choice of an agent, depending on one's personal sensibilities and needs. An agent may be strong in two *A*s and weak in the other, although that may provide a perfect complement to a client. But any successful agent needs at least a portion of all of the the three *A*s:

• *Access*

"Access" is the agent's relationship to the town. Can the agent get people on the phone? Does the agent know the people in the moviemaking community who a writer needs to reach? Is the agent well liked? Is the agent's taste well regarded? Ultimately, does the agent have access to information? Keep in mind that information works both ways, since sometimes the client can have as good (if not better) access to information. Some clients simply do not need as much access as others do.

Access also means how high up the Hollywood ladder a given script will be submitted. If the agent's submissions can get the genuine attention of the president of production at a studio, then that agent has good access. An agent with limited access will have submissions go to the lowest rungs, where it may be passed off to an intern to read over the weekend. Access to information relates to the agent's knowledge of what will spark the market at a particular time, when to go out with a project to enhance the chances of selling it.

• *Attention*

"Attention" is the client's personal day-to-day interaction with the agent. Does the agent listen to the client? Does the agent figure out a client's strengths and needs and direct the client in that particular path? Does the agent understand what path the client wishes to go on? Does the agent have a good enough level of communication with the client?

What a good agent does, in essence, is not just service the client to maintain a status quo, but rather elevate the writer from whatever level he or she is presently at by bumping the client up to the next level. To plateau a client is easy, but having the vision, energy, and passion to accelerate a client's career is a sign of an agent who pays good "attention." Getting personal attention from an agent is always comforting, but a client must discern whether that agent is really working for them, or just stroking their ego. Large agencies are less likely to give attention to lower-rung writers, for obvious reasons.

• *Aggression*

"Aggression," the third component in the equation, is how aggressively an agent sells his or her client. If a writer has a high-ranking agent, that agent not only has great access, but also the potential to be aggressive for the client. A writer can have an agent who talks to his client four times a day because the writer makes him laugh, or for whatever reason, but that doesn't mean anything if the agent's not selling the writer. Time is money, and agents guard their time tightly. An agent can be a busy guy who calls clients all the time, but if he never lifts the phone to sell for the writer, then that time's not well spent. A writer can get all three of these *A*s from an agent, but every writer has different requirements.

There's nothing wrong with a client feeling that his agent's a shark; the client would just rather have that agent swimming in "somebody else's pool." Nor does a particular agent have to be a friend. "I've spoken to clients who have had the same agent for a long time, and they're not friends; but you don't have to be 'friends' with all your clients," says Stu Robinson. "That happens, or it doesn't happen. You can't really work at it. I knew one guy who had been with somebody a long time and said, 'Look, he's a good agent, he's not Mr. Stylish, and I wouldn't go to the opera with him; but he does the job.' Fine, that works. I think the most important thing is the communication. And obviously, honesty, and returning phone calls."

Emerging screenwriters don't necessarily need great access, because such writers are at a stage where they'll be meeting story editors and directors of development. If their agent can't get a studio head on the phone, it doesn't really affect them, because they're not going to be meeting a studio head, or being read by one, anyway. They're at a different level of their career.

But they need somebody who's aggressive, and everybody needs a different level of aggression. Somebody who sells themselves doesn't need somebody else selling. Instead, they need an agent to negotiate deals and to legitimize them and send out material to somebody they might have met at a party. The best agents are those who provide their clients with paths to make the films the clients *want* to make.

The agent's role, on a creative basis, ends once the deal is done. "If you really have creative instincts, the job of an agent can get very boring because it's just one deal after another," says Justen Dardis, of Agency for the Performing Arts, who prefers developing material with clients before submitting it to the town. "Sometimes you may want to see a movie get made, you know?"

When the spec script meets a screenwriter's best intentions, it's time to evaluate and target an agent who can best play the role of Virgil in guiding your Dante through Hollywood's own *Divine Comedy*.

Shooting for the Stars

THE SCATTERSHOT ORIGINS OF
IN THE LINE OF FIRE
FROM A SCREENPLAY BY JEFF MAGUIRE

Purchased by Castle Rock Entertainment and Columbia Pictures
MPAA Rating: R
Director: Wolfgang Petersen

A cat-and-mouse suspense thriller in which Secret Service agent Frank Horrigan, haunted over the loss of John F. Kennedy, follows the trail of a skilled assassin determined to kill the current U.S. leader during his presidential campaign. A younger woman supports Horrigan's intuitions, rejuvenates his search, and invigorates his life.

CAST OF CHARACTERS

Jeff Apple, producer
Scott Immergut, creative executive at Hollywood Pictures
Mindy Marin, casting director and budding producer
Jeremy Zimmer, partner at United Talent Agency
Liz Glotzer, president of Castle Rock Pictures
Mark Canton, chairman, Columbia Pictures
Barry Josephson, executive VP, Columbia Pictures

THE DEPARTMENT OF Water and Power came to disconnect Jeff Maguire's lifeline on the day his screenplay sold for $1.4 million. At the time, Maguire had tapped out every credit card, had borrowed the last dollar from all of his relatives, and was also about to have his phone shut off. Maguire's wife began asking whether they'd be better off if he pursued another career rather than plugging away at screenwriting while earning a little cash waiting tables at a restaurant. Maguire had crossed these doubts before in his hopeful writing career. Fortunately, he decided to keep taking a shot at it.

When most people in their right minds would have abandoned hope, Maguire clung to it, given the long A-list of stars supposedly interested in his spec screenplay that had been bandied about by Hollywood's leading talent broker Creative Artists Agency (CAA) for over six months. Then Maguire met Jeremy Zimmer, an agent at CAA's competitor United Talent Agency, who within a couple days began fielding offers for Maguire's story about a seasoned Secret Service agent hunting a warped, CIA-trained assassin intent on killing the U.S. president.

It was in April 1992 that Zimmer landed the big deal to boost Maguire's bank account to an unprecedented sum. That paycheck allowed Maguire to send the electric company on its way, so he wasn't forced to feed his family by candlelight that night. As a story of a struggling screenwriter breaking through a gossamer complex of "oh-so-close" deals, Maguire's success depended on the vision he shared with a producer whose obsession sprouted over ten years before the stellar sale of *In the Line of Fire*.

Fascinated with the Secret Service since he was a kid, native Floridian Jeff Apple remembered seeing the Treasury Department's sunglass-wearing agents protect Lyndon Johnson in a dazzling motorcade through Apple's sunshine state. "Why would somebody do that?" Apple thought. "It takes a special kind of person to say, 'When the bullet rings out, I'm gonna step in front of that bullet.' " The image buried itself deeply in Jeff Apple's mind, prompting a desire to some day make a film.

1973's *The Day of the Jackal*, based on Frederick Forsyth's best-selling novel about a skilled assassin plotting to kill French president Charles de Gaulle, garnered acclaim as a taut, brilliantly adapted film. But no picture had adequately explored the Secret Service, and Jeff Apple foresaw an ample opportunity. After attending NYU, where he learned filmmaking skills from such teachers as Martin Scorsese, Apple came to Los Angeles to make pictures with Bob Rosenthal for B moviemakers Crown International Pictures and formed Apple-Rose Productions. 1982's *Zapped!* might have made a chunk of money and delighted a number of hormone-enraged kids, but Apple-Rose's production (in which Scott Baio's character telekinetically removes women's clothing) wasn't exactly heralded by the critics. Apple sought a more serious moviemaking mark.

"I raised independent financing in 1983 to do a movie about the Secret Service," explains Apple, who then hired another NYU alumnus Ken Friedman (writer of *Heart Like a Wheel* and *White Line Fever*) to draft a script. Apple called Secret Service agent Bob Snow to get some information.

"It's very simple," Snow replied. "Just come on out to Washington, D.C." So Apple jumped on a plane to bury himself in research. About a year later, Ken Friedman finished his *In the Line of Fire* screenplay.

"For a number of years, I had been through a lot of ups and downs on the Ken Friedman draft," Apple recalls. "I knew it wasn't working, [but] I even had Dustin Hoffman attached and director Michael Apted attached to the project for two years." At one point, Columbia Pictures wanted to make the picture (an ironic footnote, given that the studio ultimately had to pay a large sum for Jeff Maguire's spec script years later). When British producer David Puttnam took over Columbia, squabbling with Hoffman—then starring with Warren Beatty in the studio's ill-fated *Ishtar,* and a project Puttnam publicly fought—caused Hoffman to pull out of Apple's project and opt for 1988's *Rain Man,* for which the actor won an Oscar.

Over lunch one day, Hoffman asked Apple about having his character live down Kennedy's assassination, suggesting what ended up giving *In the Line of Fire* much of its depth. Apple saw something strong in having this backstory haunt the hero, so he then pitched Ken Friedman on the concept of Frank Horrigan feeling responsible for the loss of Kennedy, always feeling he could have prevented it. "The pivotal thing that really made a lot of it work was the concept of Horrigan having to live down the past and now having to deal with this new threat. Can he convince these people?" says Apple. "He's coming to the end of his career. He's not the same guy, and it's an uphill battle."

To social historians, John F. Kennedy's death marked the end of American innocence. In the screenplay, villain Mitch Leary, eerily played by John Malkovich, became the personified by-product of the nation's degeneration. "Having a great villain paired with a very empathetic character, whose backstory relates to American history, was something members of the audience can all relate to," Apple contends. The villain's character, a CIA-trained assassin, relied equally on his own strength of conviction. "A lot of the things [Mitch Leary] says are true. You understand what happens to him.

"We've all made mistakes in our lives, but I wouldn't want to be Frank Horrigan," Apple says, "a character who knew if he had only gotten there earlier to catch Kennedy's bullet, the world would have been a different place. There aren't many things *we* do in our daily lives that we can say would have much of a difference." Apple then summoned screenwriter Jeff Maguire.

"I had written another project that was developed with Jeff Apple, which was in the arena of racing cars," Maguire recalls. "It sort of got sidetracked after *Days of Thunder* came out and bombed." But the Secret Service idea so intrigued Maguire that Apple sent over Friedman's screenplay. "Ken Friedman's written a couple of pretty good scripts and everything, but this one I didn't think was all that strong."

Maguire suggested starting from scratch. Agreeing, Jeff Apple provided Maguire with a five-page treatment that was the genesis for what eventually became the film. "[From Apple's treatment] I came up with an action-packed, high-tech kind of thriller idea for us to pitch to a guy named Scott Immergut," says Maguire, referring to a rising executive at the Disney studio's Hollywood Pictures. "They were interested in the project for Tom Selleck."

ROUNDING UP THE USUAL SUSPECTS

In late 1990, Apple and Maguire went in to Hollywood Pictures to pitch their new story. "You know, what I'm really interested in is more the idea of what would happen if you get this incredible assassin and this incredible Secret Service agent, and they lock horns," Immergut notioned. Maguire didn't want to make the killer a foreigner, such as an Arab on a holy mission or a Russian saboteur, since that would require a whole separate agenda, which Maguire felt had been done too many times before.

"How do you do that?" Maguire thought. "As soon as the Secret Service agent has identified an assassin, they're going to pick him up. What American would be deadly enough? Or capable enough? Just by process of elimination, it came out that he's a CIA-trained guy. That's when the whole disenfranchised aspect came to mind." Maguire collected his notes, thinking about Immergut's concept, then wrote that story into a little treatment, which he and Apple went in with again to pitch to the executive in January 1991.

The new pitch positioned the Mitch Leary character as a CIA-trained operative turned evil, allowing a rich subtext about the government collapsing from within. At that time, however, there wasn't much research regarding the Central Intelligence Agency. "The CIA doesn't acknowledge that it has ever hired a killer," Maguire says, "so I called a friend of mine who is connected with people in Washington.

"I need to know, what do the CIA call their killers?" Maguire asked. "I know they used to call them *mechanics* or something like that. What's the name for them that they use now? I just want to make it accurate."

Ten minutes passed. Maguire's Capitol contact called him back.

"Are you ready for this?" prepped Maguire's deep throat. "They call them *wet-boys*." Maguire had never heard that before and worked it into his script.

"It was certainly easy enough for him to find out what they call their killers, even though they would deny ever having killers," Maguire chuckles. By now, Apple and Maguire felt they had the story locked.

With the January 1991 pitch, Immergut told Apple and Maguire their story was exactly what he wanted. "Jeff Apple and I left there all excited, thinking, 'Oh, we're gonna have a development deal, this is great,' " Maguire recalls.

"I loved the idea, and I loved him," Immergut says of his first meeting with Jeff Maguire. "I'll tell you, and I'm not keeping any secret about this, when I was a kid I had seen *The Day of the Jackal* many times. One of my suggestions was inspired by that movie. I mean, it wasn't that I'm such a genius. I love that movie. [But] I was low level, the lowest-level creative executive at Disney. I pitched it to my then boss and, you know, I probably didn't pitch it very well either. Because I wasn't very good at it at that point."

After a couple of weeks went by, they still hadn't heard from Immergut. "What's going on?" Apple finally asked.

"I just can't get my boss to go for it," Immergut replied.

"I've since spoken to Scott and he laughs about it," says Maguire. "But he says, 'You know, in the end, you were blessed that it turned out the way it did. Face it, Hollywood Pictures with Tom Selleck would have been a completely different movie.' But I was broke, and I think I would have gone for it with Bob Denver in the lead.

"About four or five months went by and Jeff Apple tried to talk to a couple different people about the idea, and nobody was really interested," Maguire recalls. "It just seemed to be dead in the water."

Maguire finally called Apple in July 1991. "Look, these characters are so vivid in my mind, and I've got the story worked out beat by beat. How about if I just write it on spec? You'd be attached as producer. I'll be attached as writer, and we'll take it from there." With nothing to lose, and having vested as much time as he had in the project so far, Apple agreed.

About a month later, Maguire completed the screenplay, turned it in to Apple, who then submitted it to the powerhouse Creative Artists Agency. Within a couple of weeks word came back that they really liked it. "They were trying to package Robert Redford and the usual suspects over there," Apple recalls of casting the Horrigan role. "We realized that we had not really taken this to any of the studios, just sort of shopped it around on a very small level."

Hearing that CAA liked the script was music to Maguire's ears. As the predominate packaging agency in town, CAA and Redford had the omnipotence to make Apple and Maguire's dream come true in a heartbeat.

"This is great. We'll be skiing in Sundance this winter, and he'll make us do some rewrites and get the script going," Maguire remembers. But six weeks dragged by, and still no word from Robert Redford. "At one point I was even told that CAA chairman Michael Ovitz was having dinner with Redford and had urged him to do it, and then finally after six weeks we got word that he had passed."

Meanwhile, Maguire still didn't have an agent. "I was asking Jeff to ask CAA if they would represent me, because he had the contacts there," Maguire remembers. "He apparently mentioned it to them a couple of times."

"If we take him on, he's just another out-of-work writer we got to find work for," was the agency's response to Apple. "Let's try to sell the script first and see what we can do."

"I've since found out that CAA didn't realize they would have to deal with me," says Maguire. "I think they thought that Jeff owned the script outright, that he'd developed it with me and paid me, which wasn't the case." Times were getting tougher for Maguire, whose personal debts were mounting. And at that time, things weren't a whole lot better for Apple.

FROM A SUBLIME START TO A FORECAST FINISH

Jeff Maguire originally came out to Hollywood from the East Coast in late 1976. After growing up in Connecticut and New Hampshire and studying biology at college in Massachusetts, Maguire met the writer Djordje Milicevic in New York and drove cross-country with Djordje's family of four.

Maguire's introduction to Hollywood was rather sublime. He sold four screenplays within a year, two of which ended up getting made. "One of them was *Victory,* for Sylvester Stallone, and I don't take the credit, or more often the case, the blame for that one, because it was pretty much substantially rewritten from the work that I did," says Maguire of the 1981 John Huston film. "Djordje Milicevic and I had written a bunch of scripts and sold a bunch of scripts, and then I couldn't figure out why I was not feeling fulfilled.

"I ended up taking a couple of years off when I just didn't write. I went on kind of a spiritual search and traveled around and came to grips with at least my understanding now of God and my purpose here," Maguire reflects. "Then I came back into writing again. I didn't really get into it in full force until I got together with my wife, in 1983. Then I got a couple of development deals going during the eighties. But nothing ever came of the scripts that I wrote.

"I was working as a waiter, and just barely kind of scraping by, and then when our son was born in 1985, I began to kind of panic a little," Maguire continues. "I would get a development deal and make just enough money to squeak by, but never enough to relax. Then the Writers Guild strike in 1988 was just a real hard time. I had a couple of deals pending when that strike began, and they all fell through in the six months of waiting. I finally ended digging into our savings and going through our credit cards."

In another bit of irony, one of Maguire's development deals was at Columbia, Maguire recalls. "A guy named Robert Lazarus was Bill Block's assistant at ICM, and Bill Block represented Djordje Milicevic. Robert was going to try to sort of carve a niche for himself as an agent.

" 'Why don't you take Jeff and see what you can do with him?' " Block told Lazarus.

"I had this development deal at Columbia that Bill had kind of negotiated for me . . . it was a foot in the door," says Maguire. "At this point, Djordje Milicevic and I were working separately from each other. He went on to write the movie *Runaway Train* (a 1985 Mena-chem Golan Production starring Jon Voight, Eric Roberts, and Rebecca De Mornay).

"Lazarus then took the script I did for Columbia around to some people and one of them was Jeff Apple, who was looking for some-body to write this race-car movie," says Maguire. "He and his partner at the time, a guy named Jake Hooker, then hired me to write this race-car movie, and that's how I got to know Jeff [Apple]. That led eventually to *In the Line of Fire*."

Apple and Maguire's concerted efforts turned the spec into a hot property. Creative Artists continued to package the project, this time with Michael Douglas, who read it and passed. "Then they said that Sean Connery was interested, but he didn't know how he could be a foreigner playing a Secret Service agent," Maguire recalls. "We did a little research and found that you can be foreign born. I ended up writing up a little biographical sketch of Frank Horrigan, showing that he was an Irishman who came here, went to Boston College, and saw Eisenhower's Secret Service detail go through town with the president and thought, 'That's what I want to do.'

"He had fallen in love with America. And then of course when Ken-nedy came along, when he heard there was a young Irishman in the Secret Service, he had to have that guy in his detail and they became fast friends," Maguire explains. "I wrote up this whole thing, and I wrote up a couple of scenes to show how this could be integrated into what I'd already written. We sent it to Sean Connery, who had then gone off for the holidays. That was now Christmas, 1991. And in Jan-uary 1992 we got word that Sean Connery had gone on to do *Rising Sun*. He was now out of the picture, so once again I'm broke, I've got credit card guys calling me. There's no money for the rent, and I've tapped out just about all my uncles and everybody else.

"But now the hope springs eternal because Harold Becker is inter-ested in maybe directing *In the Line of Fire* because he's looking for a project to do with Warren Beatty," Maguire says of the director of *Sea of Love*. "He came up with some really good structural ideas. The third act had been a lot weaker than it currently is, and he'd come up with some really great suggestions." If Maguire made those changes, Becker might be interested in taking it to Warren Beatty.

"Still not seeing a dime from any of it, I went back and did a couple weeks' work on it. At the end of those two weeks, as I went to turn in the script, I found out that Harold Becker had gone on to do *Malice* with Castle Rock, so he wasn't even going to read it now," Maguire continues. "Once again, I was kind of devastated, and now, everything still sort of stopped dead. We did hear rumors that Robert Redford was interested again, but who knew?"

Toward the end of May 1992, Jeff Apple called Maguire with some great news: Imagine Entertainment, a company founded by Ron Howard and Brian Grazer, was interested in the script for *In the Line of Fire* and a meeting was set with their executives to discuss purchasing it.

"Do you have an attorney or somebody who can represent you?" Apple asked Maguire. "Because if Imagine *does* decide they want to do it, a deal will be forthcoming pretty quickly, and I don't get the feeling that CAA really wants to represent you."

"Well, I don't really have anybody offhand who I can get to do it," Maguire replied. "I'm sure I can come up with some attorney or something, but I'd really like to get an agent out of this whole thing." Maguire continued calling CAA but didn't get his phone calls returned.

"I had never been very comfortable with the whole agent thing," says Maguire. "The whole business end of Hollywood had always kind of sickened and intimidated me."

By then, a casting director named Mindy Marin entered the picture, one of the essential keys to the script's sale. With aspirations to produce, Marin was looking at several writing samples. After reading Maguire's screenplay, she called him to say, "You're too good a writer not to have representation." So Mindy gave the script to one of her friends, United Talent's Jeremy Zimmer, who for some reason still unbeknownst to him, read *In the Line of Fire* that night.

"So I called Jeremy," says Maguire, "and I said, 'It looks like there may be a deal with Imagine Entertainment and are you interested in representing me?' He said, 'Why don't you come in tomorrow and let's talk.' So I went in and we met." Maguire now prepared for his meeting at United Talent Agency, whose Beverly Hills offices fill the space on Wilshire Boulevard once belonging to junk-bond king Michael Milken and his Drexel, Burnham, Lambert clan.

"If Jeremy Zimmer calls you up, says 'I've got a great spec,' you're gonna sit down and read it, no question about it. If Joe Blow, junior agent, calls me, I'll probably get it covered," says Scott Immergut. "Clearly, Jeremy read something that he connected to, and that clearly he was right about. No question about it, he was right about it. My only regret is that I couldn't do a better job over here. . . . That was *my* shortcoming, not theirs."

"I had heard a little of Jeremy's reputation for being a bit of a shark and all, but we got along fine," says Maguire. "When I got home that night, I called Jeff Apple and said, 'I got somebody to represent me,' and he said 'Who?' And I said 'Jeremy Zimmer.' He goes, '*What?* Are you crazy, that guy, he's *hated* by people at CAA! You can't have him represent you.' "

"Well, I just shook hands with him," Maguire responded, "and that's that." At night Jeff Maguire got his first call from an agent at CAA.

"How could you do this to us?" the agent pleaded.

"But wait a minute, you guys didn't return my calls," Maguire responded. "I would have loved to have gone with you, but I didn't think you were interested!"

So the next day, Maguire and Apple met with Imagine Entertainment.

"We love the script, but we'd like to consider changing it, because we have a really good relationship with Tom Cruise and we're looking for a project for him," said Imagine's executives. "If you can make it for a twenty-eight-year-old agent, that would be great."

"But then you'd lose the whole Kennedy backstory," Maguire replied.

"Well, you'll have to come up with a new backstory," was the answer. Jeff Apple and Maguire looked at each other, disappointed.

"We'd really rather try going down those avenues and go with the older stars and see if we can get any of them first," they responded.

"We understand that," the Imagine execs said. "But we would have loved to do it if you could have accommodated us."

In the search for stars, it's remarkable how moving the telescope by an inch can put the focus in an entirely different universe, because making *In the Line of Fire* with a younger lead would mean an entirely different story than Apple and Maguire had originally planned. As Maguire got up to leave, all he could think was, "God, I've got to go back and tell my wife, who doesn't have money for groceries, that I turned down probably a hundred grand, or whatever it would have been, to rewrite it for Tom Cruise." Maguire was equally uncomfortable about reporting this event to his new agent.

"I called him to tell Jeremy Zimmer how the meeting went, and I thought maybe he's going to say, 'You asshole! You should have taken the money. Are you crazy?!' But instead he says, 'A twenty-eight-year-old agent? What's the matter with that?' I started to explain. He said, 'Better yet, let's make it an eight-year-old agent. We'll get Macaulay Culkin to play the part! Look, forget about those guys. I've slipped the script around to a couple of people and I have a feeling we're gonna get some action on it.' This is on a Friday afternoon. 'So have a good weekend and just take it easy. I think something's gonna be going on once the new week starts.' "

"WHAT ABOUT THIS SCRIPT FOR CLINT?"

"I sent it to some friends of mine at Warner Brothers who were looking to bring something in to Clint Eastwood," Zimmer recalls. "Their initial response was they passed: 'Nahh, I don't know, I don't think it works.' I said to this friend of mine, 'You know, you're crazy. This is really good. You and I have known each other a long time. You are making a big mistake by passing.' 'Really, you think so? Okay, let me read it again.' "

The Warner executive rang Zimmer back. "You're right, it's fantastic. I didn't really read it [the first time], I had someone in my office read it, and now, to tell you the truth, I fucked up."

"In the meantime we'd given it to Billy Friedkin, who was a client, who read it and loved it and had submitted it to Paramount," says Zimmer. Paramount wanted it for Friedkin to direct. "At the same time, we had shown it to other people . . . Interscope, and Hollywood Pictures wanted to buy it.

"We're willing to make an offer on the script but we're offering $250,000, that's it," said the Hollywood Pictures exec.

"Okay, that's very nice of you," Zimmer responded. "We'll get back to you." It also went to Castle Rock, who "read it and said, 'We'll buy it.' We got into negotiation with them pretty quickly. At the same time, we're in negotiation with Paramount, who wanted to buy it for Friedkin."

"On Monday, the new week starts," Maguire recalls, "and Zimmer says there's some interest—of all places—at Disney, at Hollywood Pictures. But this time [the bid] was in league with Interscope and producer Bob Cort. Then I think the first solid offer came in on Wednesday. For the next two days, it was just like every time the phone rang, it was Jeremy telling me that the bid had gone up, and that there was somebody else involved. Everybody at Paramount stopped taking meetings for an hour and a half so that all the executives could read the script, because Billy Friedkin wanted to direct it. It was pretty heady stuff for me."

Paramount wanted the script, but wouldn't agree to the terms Jeff Apple wanted as producer, which would compensate him for the many years of perseverance he had put into the project. "We're negotiating with him and we're negotiating with Castle Rock, and in the meantime we're trying desperately to get the Warner Brothers guys to read it for Clint," Zimmer recalls. "Now the producer's taking it to Warner Brothers and Warner Brothers read it. But the guy on the Clint account is in New York, they were faxing him pages, and I guess he couldn't read the fax or something."

Meanwhile, back at Castle Rock's Beverly Hills offices, partner Rob Reiner was wandering the hallways in search of a script. "What's going on? What's new?" Reiner asked Liz Glotzer, Castle Rock's president of production.

"Well, there's this script everyone's talking about it." The executives all closed their doors and read it, and Reiner liked it.

"Very early into the script, I was on page thirty or forty, we kind of regrouped," Glotzer recalls. "Unless something goes terribly wrong, this is a great script. So then, we just scurried back and finished reading it and made an offer that day."

"Warner Brothers ended up not reading or buying the script," says Zimmer. "We ended up making the deal at Castle Rock, who basically gave us everything we wanted, and they were complete mensches about the entire negotiation. . . . Then the guys from Hollywood Pictures called and they were irate."

"How could you do this?" the Disney executive hollered.

"You said $250,000 and you wouldn't spend a nickel more. I took you at your word," Zimmer responded. "I'm sorry. We had $250,000 and we got offered a lot more."

Over at Columbia Pictures, a rumor was buzzing that Clint Eastwood was interested in the script for *In the Line of Fire*. This accelerated their curiosity in the script, so Columbia's Barry Josephson began circling the project. "The power of talent—the fact that Clint Eastwood even expressed interest—all of a sudden made this a very hot property," says George Huang, who worked on Josephson's desk at the time.

"We all canceled our lunches, stayed in, read the script right then and there."

Columbia wanted to get involved. "Nobody would have stopped business to read the script otherwise. It would have just stayed there, somewhere downstairs, waiting to be covered for months, if someone hadn't mentioned 'Oh, Clint Eastwood's interested in doing this.'

"Barry canceled his lunch, every executive canceled his plans and read it," Huang recalls. "By the end of lunch we decided 'this is a great script. Let's do it.' Of course by that time, Castle Rock had already been on it, so the deal was structured so that Castle Rock and Columbia would cofinance it and we'd work on it together. It goes to show the power of talent . . . just a rumor that Clint Eastwood was even remotely interested."

Yet at the time, Eastwood had not even seen Maguire's screenplay.

"You know when you read a script that you want, usually there are other people who want it," says Liz Glotzer. "Early on, we knew a big bidding war was going to erupt. Always, the concern is that if you make the first offer, they'll use the offer to make you the stalking horse. Are you going to lose out just because you were first?

"I don't know what order our offer came in, but I do know we had an advantage," says Glotzer. "We don't have a lot of precedents, such as, 'We won't pay this amount for some producer.' Jeff Apple was not a first-time producer; he had produced *Zapped,* but he wanted a lot of money. Paramount wouldn't pay him a lot of money. They would have paid Jeff Maguire probably *more* money than we offered, but they were not willing to make a deal [that Apple wanted]. He had a control in it.

"It's not often that you read a script that you really want to make," Glotzer continues. "We knew this was a movie. It didn't need much work. We thought, 'That's the price of getting into business,' so we had no problem [satisfying Apple]." As a leaner company, Castle Rock didn't have a rigid rule book.

So within the few days that Zimmer represented the property, rooted in ten years of perseverance, Castle Rock chieftain Martin Shafer and Columbia Pictures president Mark Canton partnered up to take *In the Line of Fire* off the market (as they had done the previous year with *A Few Good Men*) for $1.4 million, the majority of that going to Maguire. At last, Apple and Maguire were about to see their project get made. "As I remember, I read it, I met the guy, I loved it," says Zimmer, snapping his fingers. "We went to market. It happened. It was fantastic and it turned into a great movie. . . . Usually, it goes wrong somewhere.

"Usually the guy turns out to be a complete fucking asshole, or the movie turns out to be a piece of shit, or something. This was just all harmony," Zimmer recalls, breaking into one of his trademark chuckles. "One bad thing that did happen, I guess, was that we got fired by Billy Friedkin. But that was a little while later.

"It was a time in your life where, as an agent, you can make a difference [by prompting] someone to buy [a script], make a lot of money, and be involved with a product that you're proud of," says Zimmer. "So it was a rare triple."

News hit the trades with an announcement in April 1992 that Castle Rock bought *In the Line of Fire*. "This script was *very* far along, we made very few changes," says Liz Glotzer. "There were maybe three big things that came out of our meetings. The first time I read the script, it was Rene Russo's character at the end who yells 'gun' and saved the day. Which made me, like, *throw* the script across the room, I was so frustrated." Maguire changed the script so that Frank Horrigan unequivocally redeemed himself at the end. Additional plot twists Castle Rock provided, such as having Mitch Leary's bank teller wear a Minnesota T-shirt (thus requiring him to murder her) and more back-and-forth interplay between villain and hero, enhanced Maguire's script.

"We did our notes, and then Columbia became involved, which was unusual for our company," says Glotzer. "We usually finance our own movies, so we're not used to going to other people for notes. That's why we can guarantee artists that they are not going to be tampered with, which is something that we couldn't really do on this movie."

While Columbia wanted more of a "popcorn" ending—more action to charge up the audience—Glotzer feels the picture remained very true to Maguire's original vision. But the question remained, who would finally play Frank Horrigan?

When Clint Eastwood's longtime agent, Lenny Hirshan at William Morris, read the trade article about the spec's mammoth sale, he phoned up Castle Rock.

"What about this script for Clint?" he asked Glotzer, and Castle Rock loved the idea. Thus Eastwood, whose Malpaso Productions is an institution on the Warner Bros. lot, was going to make a motion picture released by rival Columbia Pictures, the Sony-owned studio that distributed Castle Rock's productions.

"We wanted to make the movie with Clint Eastwood," says Glotzer, who knew if Castle Rock had waited for another financial partnership they could have lost what turned out to be ideal casting. "Then Columbia came in. We had already had our initial story meetings, because we had already gotten Clint Eastwood involved." The production came together very quickly with German-born director Wolfgang Petersen (*Das Boot* and *Shattered*, a picture that bombed, but Clint liked) taking on the directing reins. Lenny Hirshan also represented John Malkovich, the gifted actor from Chicago's Steppenwolf Theater who performed in the films *The Killing Fields* and *Of Mice and Men*, who signed on as Horrigan's nemesis.

Mark Canton, then president of Columbia, pushed to get Rene Russo on board as Lilly Raines, Clint's romantic interest. Hot off *Lethal Weapon 3*, a franchise Canton had developed while at Warner Bros., Russo played the Secret Service agent who had the compassion to stand by Frank Horrigan when the rest of the U.S. government flew their flags against him. "It was *easy*," says Glotzer about the casting. "We got our first choices for every part."

Jeff Apple felt that because Wolfgang Petersen (whose TriStar office sat next to Columbia's on Sony's Culver Studio lot) was relatively new to this country, he brought a special kind of reverence to Horrigan's role. "If you look back at some of the great films of Americana, they've been done by foreigners. Look at [Australian] Peter Weir's film with Harrison Ford, *Witness*, and [Italian] Sergio Leone's *Once Upon a Time in America*. They capture Americana with an interesting perspective."

In the Line of Fire provided a technological challenge, containing scenes of Frank Horrigan protecting various former presidents, somewhat of a chore to accomplish. "Clint was only out of a cowboy uniform starting in 1970," Apple explains. "I had to go home one night and look at all of his movies after 1970 to get close to 1963 for the age difference. And I looked for movie shots that might work with footage we picked up from Dallas. I isolated those myself and sat down with the special effects people to see what might work. It seemed pretty off the wall at the time."

The clip of Clint Eastwood with John F. Kennedy was inserted from 1971's *Dirty Harry*, and Apple gave Eastwood the first digital haircut in motion picture history. Effects for *In the Line of Fire*, totaling $4 million of the film's $40 million production budget, were the precursor to 1994's *Forrest Gump,* which incidentally Mark Canton's wife, Wendy Finerman, produced.

From the time Apple started the project in 1983, it was his intention to mix reality with fiction and to shoot against real events. Bob Snow had since retired from the Secret Service, so he became the film's technical consultant, which enabled Apple to send crews around the country during the 1992 presidential campaign. "With the use of digital compositing—getting to the point where it was then seamless—it was the perfect opportunity to do what I always wanted to do," says Apple.

In the Line of Fire unloaded its final shot and finished postproduction so far ahead of schedule that Columbia considered swapping its release date with their much touted *Last Action Hero.* "It was basically when the studio was riding its high: 'Look, we've got Arnold, now we've got Clint . . .' and everyone was just ecstatic," George Huang recalls.

Columbia slotted *In the Line of Fire* for a late August 1993 release, says Huang. "By the time they were done with it, they were finished way before *Last Action Hero,* and there was actually talk of swapping the dates because *In the Line of Fire* was done well before August. We could have met the June release date if we wanted, whereas *Last Action Hero* was still shooting and we had no idea if it was going to get to the theaters for the June release date. But the exhibitors wouldn't go for it. They wanted AH-nold!"

"Castle Rock shepherded more of the creative process," says Huang. "There was a big brouhaha between the studio and Castle Rock . . . because we were intent on Clint doing a Dirty Harry–type thing, a line like 'make my day' or 'did he fire six shots or only five?' In fact, we had gone through the script and even chosen the line: 'That's not gonna happen.'

"We marketed the whole film around that [line], with John Malkovich saying, 'I'll see you standing over the grave of another dead president.' Clint turns to the camera and says, 'That's not gonna happen.' That was Columbia's one note, and we all basically went to war with that one note. Clint said, 'I'm not gonna say that.' John Malkovich said, 'He shouldn't say that.' Wolfgang, 'It's inappropriate for the ending.' Which caused a lot of friction between the filmmakers and Columbia, especially at the end, when the film was a success. That's really why Castle Rock went to war over the credit-grabbing thing, because in everyone's mind, the only thing Columbia was trying to do was screw it up." Thus the line "that's not gonna happen" didn't, although Columbia otherwise handled the picture's marketing and distribution plan.

Castle Rock's Reiner and Shafer later felt terribly squeezed by their financial deal with Columbia, which didn't result in a sizable profit (less than $10 million) despite Castle Rock's creative role in the project. "Columbia, they had some pretty good input. But it was really a battle," says Maguire, recalling the studio's desire to remove the phone calls between Leary and Horrigan, fearing that an action-oriented audience wouldn't sit still during such scenes.

Columbia also felt there needed to be more at the picture's end than the fistfight on an elevator, Maguire recalls. "They discussed having a bomb placed in the hotel that would blow up the hotel. And finally, they even had discussed bringing in another writer.

"Clint Eastwood and I had gotten along very well on the shoot," Maguire continues, "so at that point, Clint called Mark Canton and said, 'Let's leave Jeff alone. I signed on for this script and I don't want to make any more changes.' So I felt like [In the Line of Fire] had the potential to go the direction of Last Action Hero if some of the cooler heads hadn't prevailed."

LEARNING LESSONS THROUGHOUT THE LAST SHOT

The final film ran 123 minutes and opened on July 9, 1993, eventually earning over $187 million worldwide. Not only was In the Line of Fire the first picture made with cooperation from the Secret Service, but it was also the first non-science-fiction film to use digital compositing. Renting or physically re-creating the U.S. president's $500 million airplane, Air Force One, was out of the question, so the plane's exterior was digitized at a cost of $300 a frame (Wolfgang Petersen subsequently directed Columbia's 1997 blockbuster, Air Force One, set aboard the plane).

"For me, there were some real spiritual lessons along the way," says Maguire. "I had to learn to relax amid all the chaos of my life while I was waiting for [the film] to happen. It was about a six-month period where one actor or one director after another looked like they were interested. We kept thinking, 'Oh this is it, now it's gonna go,' and we got all excited; and then it all fell apart.

"But in the end, I think it worked out for the best for everyone,"

Maguire says. "Because had it not been Clint and had it not been Wolfgang, I don't think it would have been nearly as good an experience or a movie as it ended up being. My feeling would be that there was kind of a divine hand at work that held everything up until I learned a few lessons and until the timing was perfect, because *so* many things went right once it all started. Castle Rock bought it on April 3, I believe, and by the end of the month we were in preproduction. We were shooting in October, and it was out [in theaters] the following summer."

That summer was one of the toughest of recent history, with *Jurassic Park, Schindler's List,* and *The Fugitive* competing for the market share, Apple recalls. "It was clearly a summer movie, it was a very tough summer, and Columbia did a very good job of marketing it. I think we came out two weeks after *The Fugitive* and *The Fugitive* had twenty to twenty-five more theaters throughout their whole run. It was a tough summer, but it shows the strength of our movie within the context of tough competition."

"Wolfgang wanted me on the set every day," says Maguire. "I mean, Wolfgang wouldn't change a line without looking to me and saying, 'Well, what do you think?' People came up to me all the time saying, 'Do you realize how blessed you are to be on the set and to be given so much respect and creative input on it?' I said, 'Yeah, I really do.' I felt like I'd earned it with all the aggravation that I had gone through for the years beforehand."

The benefit of writing a spec script rather than running through pitches was another lesson Maguire learned. "If I were a young writer, I wouldn't even waste my time to perfect pitches at this point. I would be writing spec scripts. They always say, 'Yeah, but you can't get agents to read them.' I've always felt maybe the best way to go is what happened to me, when Mindy Marin—somebody who was in the business but was not involved as an agent or as a writer—read the script and recommended it to an agent."

"When you realize you're in the hands of a great writer, you don't look at the concept. You're not analytical from a concept point of view," says UTA's Jeremy Zimmer. "You're too involved in the story to sort of take a step out and say, 'Oh, what a great idea. Secret Service agent, dah-dah-dah.' Now subsequently everybody says, 'Secret Service, that's a great place to hang a movie, and that's terrific.' But I didn't look at it as a concept movie, I didn't pitch it that way. I pitched it as just a great script. Great writing.

"Often, I will read a piece of material and go out with the material based on the concept," Zimmer continues. "I'll read it and say, 'It's not a *great* idea, it's not a great script. But, boy, it's a good idea for a movie.' Usually I fail with those. Usually I don't even sell them or decide not to go out with them. But I entered this movie through the writing. Within the first ten pages, the opening sequence where he's playing the piano, I was just so totally taken in."

The period during which *In the Line of Fire* bounced around in search of a package, Zimmer feels, weakened the perception of how salable the script was on its own. "They probably had read a multitude of drafts and had lost perspective. I think CAA didn't know what they had. They weren't going to it with fresh eyes. I read that script for the first time and thought, 'This is just fantastic.' Maybe if that were the tenth time I was reading it, I wouldn't have the objectivity to recognize how great it was."

Creative Artists Agency's participation certainly helped shape the final product through its clients' input along the way. "From day one when Maguire finished it, you just knew this was turning into a movie, because [people were so] unequivocally receptive to the story," says producer Jeff Apple. "It shows you: In real estate, it's location, location, location; in movies, it's script, script, script. You can't stop a great script."

Eventually Ted Turner's purchase of Castle Rock allowed them to play more freely in the spec market. "We haven't made a lot of action movies at our company. . . . I always fell asleep at action scripts, which are just boring chases or lots of violence. *In the Line of Fire* had people you really cared about, who were psychologically interesting, so I thought that made it special."

Because Turner eventually merged with Time-Warner, Castle Rock projects fell into a complex transition of how their pictures would be distributed. Working out such business wrangling is the stuff Jeff Maguire would prefer to avoid. Today he's quite happy just being able to pay off his electrical and phone bills. "When I write, I rarely know where all this stuff comes from. It just sort of pours out," Maguire explains. "In retrospect, I think, 'Well, where did that come from?'

"I've gone through long periods of time where it wasn't coming and I'm thinking maybe I shouldn't be in this business," Maguire continues, "both before and after my so-called success." But with an agent who does enjoy the business wrangling, and who returns his phone calls,

Maguire regards the process of screenwriting much more comfortably than before.

"He's been great," says Maguire of his agent. "He's been really very supportive, and when I told him that I had to cut back and bail out of one really high-profile project, he wasn't at all upset or annoyed. He said, 'You know, I understand. You've got to process all of what's happened to you.'

"I talk to Jeremy Zimmer maybe once every six weeks or so, and usually it's because he's telling me about someone who's interested in me," says Maguire, who adds that he is very selective of his current assignments. "I don't say that arrogantly at all, it's just that for a while after *In the Line of Fire* came out, I was afraid to turn down work. I got myself buried under a bunch of projects and began to have anxiety attacks, and then bailed out of a couple of them and finished up the others. Now I just do one project at a time and don't really want to talk about any other projects.

"In terms of real solid advice it's hard to know what to say, just because I think everybody you talk to has a different wrinkle in their success story. I don't think there's any one way to go about it," says Maguire. "At any rate, I don't read people's scripts anymore. But I tell them: Don't necessarily go to a writer and ask them to read your script, but see if you can get maybe a set designer or a casting director."

After all, it's a strategy that worked splendidly for Jeff Maguire.

Who's Got the New Football?

It is indeed a seller's market, otherwise studios would simply hire some secretary to take all of those thirty thousand projects registered at the WGA each year, buy them up, and pass them out to directors and talent based on the studio's needs. The fact is, workable material is hard to find, so the studios combined spend over half a billion dollars yearly on script purchases and development costs. The lack of quality scripts floating around means that if you have one, *you've got a lot of power.*

"It's about making it impossible for them to say no. That's what this town is ruled by," says writer John Lee Hancock, regarding the writer's next passage from writing to directing his own material. "It's not about fairness, it's not about them seeing a short film, it's just not. There are millions of dollars on the line, and they don't make those kind of business decisions, nor should they, based on 'This is fair' or 'He's a good guy' or 'He's done well for us' or 'I think you can do it.'

"All of those may play a part, but when it comes down to it, you can never forget that when they're allowing you to direct for that first time, they're putting themselves on the line," Hancock continues. "It's not necessarily that their job's in jeopardy, but it might well be, by making those kinds of decisions. It's very easy to sit on this sideline and say, 'They're so obstinate, they won't let anybody direct.' Every writer I know has a writer-directing deal. Have any of them ever directed a movie? No. I can name fifteen people. It's a joke."

Hancock recalls *Waterworld* director Kevin Reynolds talking about writing in terms of getting into the industry, which applies equally to directing:

"Okay, you're a kid and you moved. You've changed towns, you're in elementary school. It's really tough to move at that age because you don't fit in. It's hard to make friends, et cetera. Let's say you moved during the summer, and you noticed every day the kids playing football at the corner vacant lot. You're building up your courage because you want to get in that football game, desperately. So you go down there, and you kind of stand around, and when they're picking teams, they don't pick you. So you go home.

"The next day you go back, and you're a little more vocal: 'Heyya I wanna play' or 'If you guys need somebody else, here I am and I live in the blue house.' *That* doesn't work. Nothing works, until it's your birthday, and you open your present and your father's given you a brand-new football. You walk down and somebody sees you standing there with this brand-new football, and they all perk up and look and say, 'Hey, kid, throw me the ball.' And you start to throw it, and then you pull it back. 'I get to play.' They go, 'Okay.' Now you may start out hiking the ball, or rushing, or something that's not glamorous. You're not going to start at quarterback.

"But you're in the game now, and then it's up to you," Hancock says. "You have a product: It's all about that. I think it's the same with it being impossible for them to say no. This little kid with the football made it impossible for them to say no."

Once somebody says yes, that buyer sets off a chain reaction throughout the town. "Nothing is ever as good as it seems when you know that other people want it," says *In the Line of Fire* writer Jeff Maguire. "Whether it's a car, a house, or anything else. There's something in the human animal that if three or more people are all hungering after something, it's got to be great."

"We're always looking for good material," says Castle Rock's Liz Glotzer. "It can come from any source, anywhere. *Extreme Measures* was a book that was given to me at a traffic light, literally" as she was leaving on Christmas vacation and glanced out her car window at an agent she knew. He handed her the novel by Michael Palmer (made into a 1996 release starring Hugh Grant) that she read on the airplane. Once her flight touched down, she called her office to make a bid.

"Things come in in the strangest ways, and I think you have to be open to wherever it comes from," says Glotzer. "You always hope there's that diamond in the rough, that your neighbor will give you a script, or the bartender, and it's really good. You can't be too cynical about that."

Jonathan Sanger affirmed that theory ever since his baby-sitter's boyfriend handed him the spec screenplay of *The Elephant Man.* "There was no agent involved. And it kind of set the tone for the material I received that has come from odd and different places. With *Elephant Man,* my baby-sitter's boyfriend was Chris DeVore. He and Eric Bergren had written a draft of this script, and they had no agent. They'd never written anything—certainly had never sold anything before—and I met with them. I read their script, optioned it, and from there the rest was history. It didn't take very long to get moving."

The 1980 release of *The Elephant Man,* produced together with Mel Brooks and Stuart Cornfeld, earned Oscar nominations for director David Lynch (who would later make *Blue Velvet* and *Wild At Heart*), Best Picture for Jonathan Sanger, and Best Screenplay for DeVore and Bergren (along with Lynch).

With *The Shawshank Redemption,* "someone handed it to us, we loved it, we bought it. And it wasn't like a big bidding war, a frenzy," says Castle Rock's Liz Glotzer, regarding Frank Darabont's adaptation from a Stephen King short story. "Frank wanted more than just money. He wanted to make *his* movie *his* way, and so you have different requirements."

Darabont's "main concern was that he was going to be able to make the movie he wanted to make, at a price he wanted to make it at, without someone saying, 'Okay, you have to cast this person, that person.' He knew that we were the place that would support that vision. I think *that* was very important to him. Sometimes people look for a personality fit. I mean, there's other things, some people don't just put $2 million on the table."

In describing what grabs a studio's attention, director George Huang says, "You've got to have such colorful prose that the words leap up. A lot of writers write to be entertaining. Other writers say, 'Screw that, I'll concentrate on what makes a movie.' You kind of have to do both. Think about the people who make the decisions. They're taking the script home for the weekend; they won't get to it till Sunday night at midnight. They're going to be sitting in their bed, and if this thing doesn't absolutely *rock* and just *jump* at them from the page, they're asleep by page thirty. . . . The spec script, especially, isn't so much a blueprint as it is a sales brochure. Like 'Glengarry Glen Ross Islands. Gorgeous.' It's that color glossy brochure that's going to get someone sucked in and want to buy and plunk down for that investment.

"I'll be honest, a lot of the best scripts I have read don't make good movies," Huang says. "The writer's done such a fantastic job of writing it, but there's no way to convey that visually. It just dies. . . . You read the script and go, 'Wow. This is fantastic.' Then you see it and go, 'What the hell happened?' Sometimes writers do such a great job, it doesn't get any better than that."

Slick Tricks Studios Play

9

OR, HOW EXECUTIVES LEARN TO STOP WORRYING
AND LOVE THE OTHER STUDIO'S BOMB. *THE PLAYER* IS
ALIVE AND WELL IN LOS ANGELES.

Without limitations, there is no creativity.

—ORSON WELLES
(VIRTUALLY BANISHED BY THE STUDIOS
AFTER MAKING HIS CONTROVERSIAL
MASTERPIECE *CITIZEN KANE*,
WHICH INFURIATED MEDIA
MOGUL WILLIAM RANDOLPH HEARST)

"I'm a writer. . . . I write. What can you *do?*
—SCREENWRITER DAVID KAHANE'S LAST WORDS TO
STUDIO EXECUTIVE GRIFFIN MILL IN
THE PLAYER (GRIFFIN ANSWERED
BY KILLING HIM)

DIRECTOR ROBERT ALTMAN and writer Michael Tolkin's tribute to Tin-
seltown terror, *The Player,* showed a studio world afflicted by avarice,
trickery, and mischievous lies, not to mention a covered-up murder.
In the 1992 release, Griffin Mill, played by Tim Robbins, is a pandering
miscreant who tramples on the creative endeavors of the genuine
writer and winds up with the promotion, the mansion, and the gor-

geous girl. Could the real-life studio game really be so wicked? "Are you kidding?" Producer of *The Player* Cary Brokaw responds to those civilians outside the industry who ask. "This movie is a valentine. It's *so* much worse.

"And I think it is," Brokaw continues. "What [characters] Larry Levy and Griffin do to 'the movie-within-the-movie' in *The Player* isn't an anomaly. That's commonplace. Previewing, what goes on, the catering to superstars, those things aren't aberrations. That's business as usual."

Hollywood's "business as usual" has now become so ingrained in the American psyche that the process is not about to change. If studios appear to be dens of iniquity, perhaps they are simply reflecting the demoralized nature of celebrityhood that their best-laid plans promulgate. Dirty deeds, and the scandals that follow them, have—and always will be—a natural byproduct of Hollywood's business as usual.

The industry's forefathers were opportunistic newcomers to the United States who parlayed their keen business sense, ambition, foresight, and chutzpah into building movie palaces and grand studios while establishing themselves securely as oligopolistic leaders of the market. The Zukors, Foxes, Laemmles, and Warners stand alongside the Rockefellers, Mellons, and Morgans as institutional forerunners of the postindustrial American economy. By the 1930s, they were the movie moguls whose foundations were there to stay.

These moguls capitalized on a number of innovations in cinema's beginning years while the megastructure of Thomas Edison's Patent Company continued to stagnate (Edison secured the first patent on the movie camera, although his apprentice W.K.L. Dickson is now recognized as the actual innovator). As brilliant an inventor as Edison was, he clung to the shortsighted idea that the general public would be satisfied with a Kinetoscope, allowing only one viewer at a time. Edison figured he would collect a royalty off each patron to thus add to his growing fortune.

Savvy fur traders and glove cleaners realized that they could gather small audiences and show their crude movies in converted backrooms. The moguls' lower-class roots may have benefited them in giving a humanistic touch in guiding film's evolution from a lower- to middle-class entertainment form. And despite Edison's attempts to limit the field of entry and maximize his profits from the invention, filmmaking was a new phenomenon and thus an expansive and open one. Had the moguls' challenges to the system remained sheltered desires, who knows what course the movie industry might have taken at its earliest stage?

Thus began the theatrical motion picture industry. Problem was, most of these immigrant entrepreneurs were too close to Edison's New Jersey headquarters for comfort. To fend off the gate crashers to their budding creative empire, they took Horace Greeley's advice and headed out west.

Los Angeles proved to be a suitable spot for their growing empire. It was sunny most of the time and housed an emerging population of potential talent; those who worked in the business were known as "movies" and were often refused room and board by locals who feared that moviemaking would tarnish or ruin Hollywood's then pleasant and puritanical image. Mexico served as an easy getaway should Edison's Trust come calling.

In time, the maverick immigrants succeeded in breaking the trust and a legitimate industry was born. Operating from New Jersey, Edison was too busy making new inventions to bother with renegades. Lawsuits took an inordinate amount of time, and the hassle of countering public opinion wasn't worth the effort; so trendsetters Carl Laemmle and William Fox fortified their empty desert. Looking back to its roots, it's no wonder filmmaking has always been considered an outlaw business.

"Hollywood has become the last frontier. It's the last Wild West we have—not only in America, but in the world—where you can come in with no qualifications needed, write a hot spec and sell it, and you can go from obscurity to celebrity even in a few weeks. And there's a great attraction to that," says producer Joni Sighvatsson. "But what that promotes—because it's the only place left—is *so* much desperation. There *was* 'honor among thieves' before. [Now] I think that's changed tremendously.

"There's a whole new breed of people who I don't believe are here necessarily because of their passion for film," says Sighvatsson. "They think it's the easiest way to make a dollar, and they think it's a fun business to be in. . . . That's what I call the 'ruthless young executives' willing to do anything. They'll sell anybody down the river, and maybe it's because I'm nostalgic and getting older, but I don't think it used to be that way. . . . There used to be a certain honor among even those ruthless studio executives we all knew. Their word was their bond, and I don't think anybody's word is his or her bond anymore."

The Hollywood players continue to stand above the law. From Fatty Arbuckle to Heidi Fleiss, the outrageous actions of celebrities have garnered headlines in both the tabloid and general press. From Charlie Chaplin's paternity scandals to Robert Downey, Jr.'s drug busts, the carefree antics of those who dared step into the limelight have attracted international media notoriety. When Hugh Grant was caught with a Sunset Strip hooker, or Woody Allen had an affair with his stepdaughter, or Eddie Murphy played Good Samaritan on Santa Monica Boulevard, it may have made the covers of *The National Enquirer* and provided fun fodder for the Howard Stern show. But it hardly hurt their careers; it may have helped them.

An "if them, why not me?" attitude pervades the industry, extending to its slick tricks as well. Everyone accepts a little bit of underhandedness, because they can always point to somebody who's done something much more malignant. Honesty is always highly regarded, but if morality ever becomes a question, the standard Hollywood reply would be "What's the big deal?"

WENT TO HOLLYWOOD AND A HOCKEY GAME BROKE OUT

Although those who have yet to play in Hollywood's game might argue the opposite, that the personnel of studios is largely made up of highly intelligent and personally ethical individuals. Most business affairs executives are trained lawyers, who often practiced some form of law outside of entertainment before starting their studio careers. Likewise, many development executives also have law degrees or MBAs. Whatever attitudes one might have about such "suits," those who control the purse strings of the business are not unlike decision makers in any other industry; their chief concern is the bottom line. And they are always on the lookout for a moneymaker.

In turn, a cutthroat mentality has naturally developed in Hollywood's high-stakes game. "Nobody objects to rough behavior in business or in art. Anyone who thinks the art world is genteel never read about it," says Thom Mount, producer of *Bull Durham* and *Frantic*. "When you think about Picasso and Matisse and Braque and the boys slugging it out in Paris in the 1920s, it was not exactly a lovefest over there.

These guys were none too gentle with each other, critics were none too gentle with them, and there were money and reputations at stake.

"On the business side of that equation—because motion pictures both put so much money at risk and have such great potential earnings—things tend to get strangely rougher," Mount continues. "In a weird way, the further you are away from the center of the creative process, the rougher you are able to be, so that agents and lawyers and studio people frequently hammer it out."

"It's the 'honor among thieves,' " says *Good Will Hunting* coproducer Chris Moore. "We all know we're trying to rip each other off. But if we all play by the same rules, then we may have a good time. It's like playground basketball. There's no referees there, but everybody has a good time."

Another suitable sports analogy for the movie business is the game of ice hockey, where it's common to see fights break out that will occasionally provoke benches of players to rush onto the rink and throw off their gloves; such team spirit is equally embraced in the filmmaking maelstrom. While screenwriter Nancy Dowd's spec script for 1977's *Slap Shot* was inspired by her brother's experiences as an amateur hockey player, it may as well have also been a metaphor for his subsequent experiences as a movie producer.

Notwithstanding, Hollywood players, with a combination of egomania and paranoia, are constantly running scared of losing their jobs. "I don't know why they think that, because do any of these people ever go away?" says *Courage Under Fire* screenwriter Patrick Duncan of the musical chairs that studio execs seem to play. "Unless you go and destroy your body, or you commit suicide, you could have a career forever in this town.

"What can you do to get yourself kicked out of a studio? Very little," says Duncan, who discovered screenwriting at the age of thirty, then moved out from Michigan to land various industry jobs before making his mark as a screenwriter. "You can be found guilty of a crime and still get a deal, right? You can be forced to go for drug rehab and still run a studio, or a company."

Los Angeles, a town built on the kinds of corruption immortalized in Robert Towne's script for 1974's *Chinatown,* serves as a ripe territory for con artists among a land of dreamers. Studio legend is filled with tales of deception. The lure of easy money prompted Chicago hoodlum turned International Alliance of Theatrical Stage Employees

(IATSE) racketeer Willie Bioff, an accessory of Al Capone mobster Frank Nitti, to extort MGM's overlord Nicholas Schenck in 1941. To keep Hollywood's studio machinery running, Bioff often had little trouble attaining a steady flow of $50,000 cash bundles, of which very little went to union members.

Bioff and IATSE puppet leader George Browne were eventually brought to trial by October 1941, charged with tax evasion, racketeering, and conspiracy. After two years into a ten-year sentence at Alcatraz, Bioff chose to turn state's witness against Nitti, who (contrary to the movie version in *The Untouchables* in which he is thrown from a roof) responded by downing a bottle of liquor while firing his .32-caliber pistol wildly along the Illinois Central Railroad tracks. Then Nitti put his last bullet into his head. Twelve years later, an in-hiding Bioff exited his suburban Phoenix home to start his pickup truck. The resulting explosion flung Bioff's body over twenty-five feet from the wreckage in a still unsolved murder.

Schenck's brother Joe, who like Bioff was an impoverished immigrant from Russia, served only a three-year prison term for tax evasion resulting from his connections with the Chicago mob scheme. Schenck served just four months and five days before receiving a presidential pardon and lived happily in a Beverly Hills hotel penthouse on his fortunes until his death in 1961, leaving an estate of $3.5 million. From Hollywood's start, it appears that crime does pay, so long as you're on the studio side of the exchange.

The Begelman scandal shook up Hollywood during that certain period when "the big deal" became a more salient topic of discussion than its movies. As well as garnering a reputation as a dynamic deal maker, David Begelman had a habit of stretching the truth. An agent turned executive (who ran MGM and Columbia Pictures), Begelman's charismatic personal charms reflected the motion picture business notion that perception is reality. While running Columbia Pictures, Begelman claimed to have a Yale law degree; in fact, he had attended an air force training program in New Haven, Connecticut, and never earned a college degree.

Begelman's reality began to crumble February 25, 1977, when the Internal Revenue Service notified actor Cliff Robertson of a $10,000 check, drawn at Begelman's request in his position as president of Columbia Pictures, which the actor failed to claim on his taxes. Upon discovering a forgery, Robertson (son-in-law of E. F. Hutton and a former client of Begelman's) pursued its roots, opening up a remarkable scandal: Begelman's bosses discovered another check forgery to director Martin Ritt and two embezzlements. Once the crimes became public, the scandal sent a shockwave through the civilian business environment, then keen on getting in bed with its Hollywood counterparts.

The Washington Post and *The Wall Street Journal* covered the embezzlement scandal with wide eyes, but the movie kingdom's players were more apt to look the other way in determining blame. Begelman remained in his post until public pressure caused Columbia's Wall Street overseers to replace him. In true Hollywood fashion, he soon returned to run MGM and subsequently Columbia again. Despite being the victim, Cliff Robertson was considered to have suffered the career setback from being shunned by the industry as the whistle blower.

Times may have changed a bit since Bioff's and Begelman's vices were discovered, and the overriding corporate mentality in Hollywood today brings about a more aboveboard image to its business practices. After Begelman committed suicide by a gunshot to the head in a Century Plaza Hotel room on August 7, 1995, *Variety* editor Peter Bart eulogized the former studio chieftain as representing both the best and worst of Hollywood: a combination of charisma and a taste for the high life, with hidden agendas and a propensity for self-destruction.

LAWS IN THE LAND OF OUTLAWS

Everybody entering the Hollywood Game should prepare for its climate, and "anybody who can get burned in a deal is toast," says Jacques Haitkin, the cinematographer of *Nightmare on Elm Street* and *The Hidden* who got a taste of hardball tactics when he set up a script at one of the majors. "When a studio acquires a project, they have a business affairs department whose job it is to acquire that property for the cheapest amount. If you've got coproducers and hangers-on, who are really not part of the chain of title, they look around the table and go, 'He's toast, he's toast, he's toast. Out of here. Cowriter? He's not registered at the Writers Guild, gone, boom, out of there.'

"Every deal starts with a piece of literary content. That is at the core of the deal," Haitkin continues, regarding the intangible yet real value placed on a spec script. "That's why writers have a very strong position.

They are *owners*. They are not just authors, they are owners, and cited as such in contracts. They need to protect that ownership and never give up that ownership until they get in return what is fair."

"Most writers can't read a contract and refuse to," screenwriter Patrick Duncan contends. "So every time they get screwed, I tell them, 'I don't want to hear about it.' 'I had points and I got fucked.' I say, 'Points of what? Whose net?' And they answer, 'I don't know.'

"I am a businessman," Duncan continues. "I read the trades, I follow the films, I do my research. When you write a spec script, you have the power to say yes or no. That's important for new writers. Writers otherwise have very little power. But if you write a spec script, then all of the sudden you have some power. You have to use it judiciously."

Oftentimes, new screenwriters anxiously jump into a deal without considering its future consequences. "One thing that a writer should be aware of is that once they sell their script, they *sell* their script. It's no longer theirs," says APA agent Justen Dardis. "It can revert to them in seven years, according to the Writers Guild, because once you sell a script to the studios you automatically come into the Writers Guild. But once they say 'sold,' then you lose control over that script."

To protect yourself at the gate, you should be familiar with copyright laws, an area known as intellectual property. Technically, any idea is free. If you talk about your ideas, then anybody can use them. Once you write them on paper, or commit them to a "tangible medium," then no one can copy the ideas as they were expressed.

Copyright litigators can then consider whether or not the use of a similarly expressed idea is an infringement of your rights. The idea may be "free," but the way you express your idea is protected by copyright laws. Marking work with a copyright symbol, a date, and the name of the author indicates that it's protected. Further protection can be obtained by submitting the work to the U.S. copyright office, although this is rarely done with scripts.

A more expedient method than the copyright office is registration with the Writers Guild. For a fee of $20 to nonmembers, the WGA registers a work for a period of five years. Registering with the WGA can also protect a writer should their credibility be attacked.

"When you get sued, you better have your paper trail of when you registered everything," says Dan Sullivan, the cowriter of *While You Were Sleeping,* who went through the process. "Believe me, every movie gets sued. *Junior* got sued. *The Air Up There* got sued. *Higher Learning* got sued. *Rookie of the Year* got sued. *Regarding Henry* got sued by everybody with a brain story. *When a Man Loves a Woman* got sued by everybody with an alcohol problem. *Pretty Woman* got sued, the list is endless. Register the script so when you get sued, you'll be able to say, 'This is when I had the idea . . .' so you can prove to people you had the idea before they did. I recommend registering all things, even if you have an idea, even if you haven't written the script. If you have a one-page treatment, go register it."

Those within the industry, on both the writer and studio side, tend to agree that "idea theft" is in most cases not a deliberate and willful act, but rather an inherent consequence of a process that continually searches for a variety of premises, then shapes them through an amalgam of individuals who are all, at one time or another, exposed to the same material.

Similarities are more likely to result from an unconscious attempt to make pictures that are broadly appealing. Unfortunately, the burden of defending oneself often rests on the writer-creator's shoulders, when in fact they are the ones most driven by their original visions and desires. The germination of any particular picture can be rooted in some idea somebody else once had, yet each screenwriter displays their talent through the unique execution of such ideas.

As a product of the studio development process, motion pictures are often quite different from their original genesis. Because distinct premises are few and far between, and the studios are all looking for product, one idea can often give rise to a number of different creations. Remember in 1984 when *The River, Places in the Heart,* and *Country* —all female-driven pictures about saving the farm—were released? More recently, *Dante's Peak* versus *Volcano, Deep Impact* versus *Armageddon,* and *Antz* versus *A Bug's Life* all had the same premise.

Then there was that one-year period where *18 Again!; Like Father, Like Son;* and *Big*—all identical concepts—reached the screen. It was only the last of the three pictures, *Big,* that garnered any box office or critical acclaim, proving that in Hollywood, it's not concept but execution that ultimately matters.

NET PROFITS MEAN NO PROFITS

One need only pick up a studio contract and look at the standard definition of "net profits" to get a good laugh. An incomprehensible document, the average contract is completely inscrutable without the help of costly legal counsel and, consequently, is almost impossible to challenge. Thus, the idea of "net profits" has spawned considerable cynicism within the writing community. On projects with a number of "gross-profit" participants involved—those who take money off the top—such pictures will likely never see any net profit.

The standard definition of net profits is so controversial and mired in legal battles that most writers equate net profits with no profits. So, they look to other alternatives. "You can go into the independent world where your net or your adjusted gross can actually mean something, if you do it right," says Above the Line agent Rima Greer. Agents have responded to studio net profit trickery by making clever deals with studios, such as negotiating a "trigger bonus" that kicks in when an undervalued writer's motion picture becomes a surprise hit.

"A pretty standard practice for the past few years that I've gotten for a lot of clients—and other agent friends of mine get this as well—you get advances against net based on the grosses reported in *Variety*," Greer continues. "So on Tuesday, I open *Variety* and I see my movie's made $40 million and I send the studio a bill for $50,000. There's no accounting, and there's no hiding money. It's a bonus that's an advance against their net profits, which don't exist."

"Occasionally in a hit movie—and it's only in a hit movie that we ever discuss anything—there will be an audit done by one of three accounting firms who specialize in auditing," says Leonard Goldberg, former president of 20th Century–Fox under Barry Diller, of a major insight into Hollywood's financial quagmire. "It's a big enough business that people actually specialize in it."

When a producer who feels short-shrifted wages a battle over being treated unfairly, his accounting firm audits the picture's costs and receipts, then meets with the studio. "They show them their audit report, the studio goes, 'Oh my God, this is all wrong, you're wrong, you're right, you're wrong, you're right,' and in most cases a negotiation is held and some compromise is reached," Goldberg continues. "And by the way, the same auditor and the same studio people are meeting the next week on two other projects.

"Maybe it's just my cynical nature," Goldberg smiles, "but I always had a thought that since these guys deal together all the time, the studio would see to it that the auditor was at least paid for the cost of the audit, and something above that so he could say to his client, 'It didn't cost you anything, and I made you some money.' In return for which the auditor never *really* said to the studio, 'Well, we're going to the district attorney.' But that's the way it works."

When the studio process was simpler, net profit contracts were straightforward, and often participants would see pots of gold at the end of the box office rainbow. Today's pictures rarely see net profits, according to provisions prescribed by the studios' standard definitions, so challenges are few and far between. "First of all, we're only dealing with hit movies, and most of the provisions are applied accurately by these studios," Goldberg explains. "There can be disputes, because in many cases the contracts are not perfectly drawn, in which case, you have your audit, you have your studio, and they usually compromise. Some studios are harsher than others in the sense that they won't compromise until you're on the steps of a courtroom for a lawsuit. Others are a little more lenient. Some haggle faster, some haggle slower. But it isn't as if they cheated everybody in a hit picture out of a lot of money.

"Most of the time, they go, 'Wait a minute, how is it possible that a film that cost this, that *grossed* this, is still at a loss?' Well, *Sleeping with the Enemy* is still at a loss," says Goldberg of a film he produced that grossed $173 million globally. "Now, we had our audit report done, and we're meeting with the studio. They have already agreed that one provision was applied inaccurately. Not a *major* one, but to some amount of money. Okay, so let them go on with their process. I'm certain we'll pay for the audit, and maybe get some money.

"It's not as bad as everybody thinks," Goldberg concludes. "People who are represented by attorneys and business managers, by lawyers, by agents, they sign contracts. To a large extent, when a picture becomes a big hit, they complain about the very contract they signed. Most of it is applied properly. That's a fact of life. Now you may say in retrospect, 'It's not fair.' That's fine, don't sign the contract, don't make the deal. Many of the provisions are 'not fair,' but that's in the eye of the beholder, of the negotiator."

While those outside of Hollywood might be surprised to hear that blockbusters of late such as *Forrest Gump* and *Batman* have yet to return a net profit, these and other hit motion pictures like them will pay off their writers in future bonuses and more writing assignments.

"I can't fault the studios for believing that by investing their money they deserve the largest return; they do," says producer Jonathan Sanger. "It is, after all, a business. It's only objectionable when there's an attempt to create loopholes for everything and to create legal dodges to get around their obligations, and that happens."

With an original budget of $4.2 million, 1979's *The Elephant Man* was structured independently of the studio, making a modest return in every market and a huge success in Japan and earning about $75 million around the world. "The negative was owned by [Mel Brooks's] Brooksfilms, not by Paramount," says Sanger, "so it was the cleanest profit you could imagine because there was no way to tack on any studio charges beyond their normal distribution fees. Everyone who was connected to the movie, the writers—for whom it was their first movie—myself, the director David Lynch, and the actors all received net-profit participation, and all have received a considerable amount of money from the success of the movie. It was one of those classic, lucky cases."

In Hollywood today, studios are unlikely to structure such potentially favorable deals through a studio release. Yet the independent world is filled with just as many horror stories. "Actually, in my experience you're more likely to get screwed by a smaller company," says Wes Craven, director of *Scream*. "Unfortunately, I have not had a big hit with a big studio, but I seem to get regular smaller checks from the films I've done for studios." Craven feels the years and years of creative bookkeeping by studio lawyers and accountants make everyone leery of the system.

"I think that is initially why stars wanted up-front money," says Craven, indicating another insight into how studios create their own nemesis. "They just figure, 'These people are such incredible cheats. I'm never going to see any of the back end no matter how much the picture makes, so I just take it all up front.' I mean, it's the only way you can do business with that kind of a person."

SKULDUGGERY IN THE SPEC WORLD

Heaven help the studio executive overheard in the hallways of a studio shouting, "Get that goddamn writer to make his characters more sympathetic, or *fire* him!" Yet in Hollywood, being direct is generally considered a better virtue than being polite. How such bad behavior affects the writer is largely due to the degree the writer wishes to be involved in the game.

Some screenwriters prefer keeping as great a distance as possible from the whirlpool of industry politics. They might move as far away as Hawaii or the South of France, buy a fax machine, and talk to their agents only when necessary. Others go nearby to Santa Fe or San Francisco, where they can be in Los Angeles within the hour for a meeting and still play in the game without getting too dirty. For those who love to jump into the fray, landing an office on a studio lot is a sign of arrival. But the studio environment is just as unscrupulous and vindictive within as it is toward those on the outside. It's an industry atmosphere known for eating its own.

"The spec market is now filling the role that the studio development people used to do. They can't develop new ideas anymore," according to one screenwriter. "What happens is you get the MBAs coming in [to the studios], and I see a trend that [they] tend to hire people they can browbeat—people who don't threaten their position—because the jobs change so much, you don't want the guy beneath you taking your job.

"You can maneuver around and manipulate who's not as smart as you," he continues. "But the problem is, you get fired anyway. And that person gets promoted because he does the same thing you do. I have found that the reality of people running the show—and the pool's getting smaller and smaller—they are getting more and more focused on the numbers and the built-in markets, and all of that stuff."

Given the massive influx of material to studios, it's more than common for buyers to see a script similar to something already being developed and purchase it to avoid competition. Writers who are removed from the process will likely be disappointed to find their script eventually buried in development hell, an unavoidable consequence of playing the game. The buyers then have the best of both worlds because they can then enjoy the option of switching courses if the new acquisition makes more sense than their original project.

Wes Craven and Neve Campbell on the set of *Scream*.
(© Miramax Films; photo by Kimberly Wright)

John Travolta (*left*) and director Quentin Tarantino (*right*) on
the set of *Pulp Fiction*.
(© Miramax Films; photo by Linda R. Chen)

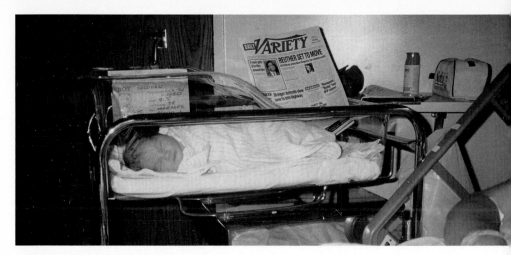

Writer Dan Sullivan's little boy, Thomas Patrick, born the day of his father's
first spec sale, which became *While You Were Sleeping*.
(Patricia Sullivan)

Sandra Bullock, producer Arthur Sarkissan, and Bill Pullman on
the set of *While You Were Sleeping*.

(*from left*) Writers Eric Bergen and Chris DeVore, producer Jonathan Sanger, and director David Lynch under the billboard on Sunset Boulevard for their movie, *The Elephant Man*.

Producer George Litto (*left*) with director Brian De Palma (*right*) on the set of *Obsession*.
(*Agenzia Fotografica Partenope, Via Chiatamone, 29, Napoli*)

Legendary agent Evartz "Ziggy" Ziegler.
(*Courtesy of Hal Ross*)

Director Steven Soderbergh on the set of *Out of Sight*.

Director John McTiernan (*left*) with Samuel Jackson (*center*) and Bruce Willis on the set of *Die Hard with a Vengeance*.

Cary Brokaw (*left*) with director and cowriter David Winkler (*right*) on the set of *Finding Graceland*. *(John Bramley)*

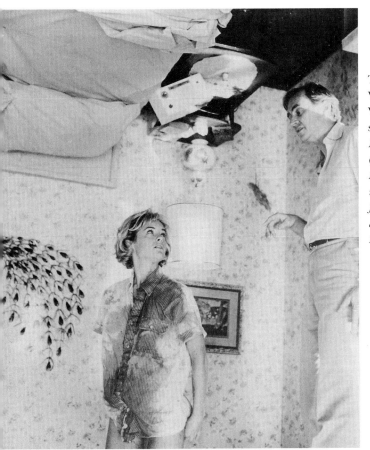

Tina Gray (Amanda Wyss) and director Wes Craven on the set of *Nightmare on Elm Street.*
(Copyright © 1984 by New Line Productions, Inc. All rights reserved. Photo by Joyce Rudolph. Photo appears courtesy of New Line Productions, Inc.)

Director David Fincher on the set of *Seven.*
(Copyright © 1995 by New Line Productions, Inc. All rights reserved. Photo by Peter Sorel. Photo appears courtesy of New Line Productions, Inc.)

Writer Shane Black on the
set of *The Pornographer*.
(Sheri Lane)

Mike Medavoy, chairman of Phoenix Pictures.
(Alia Mohsenin)

Andrew Licht, producer of *Waterworld* and *The Cable Guy*.

Ben Affleck (*left*) and Matt Damon in Gus Van Sant's *Good Will Hunting*. (© *Miramax Films; photo by George Kraychyk*)

John Lee Hancock, screenwriter of *A Perfect World* and *Midnight in the Garden of Good and Evil*. (*Jenafer Gillingham*)

Zak Penn (*left*) and Adam Leff, the writers who first conceived of *Last Action Hero*. *(Bart Bartholomew/NYT Pictures)*

Shane Black (*left*) and David Arnott, two of the many writers brought in on *Last Action Hero* rewrites. *(Bart Bartholomew/NYT Pictures)*

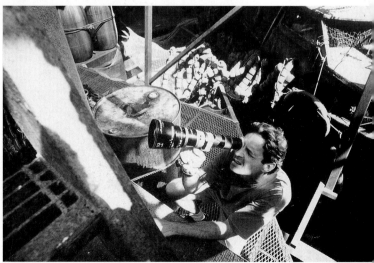

Director Kevin Reynolds on the set of *Waterworld*. *(Ben Glass. Copyright © 1999 by Universal Studios, Inc. Courtesy of Universal Studios Publishing Rights, Division of Universal Studios Licensing, Inc. All rights reserved.)*

Other practices can be less than on the level, originating on both the studio and agency sides. "Certain high-level executives will place bids on a spec script that aren't real in order to drive up the price and force some of their other counterparts to pay more for it," says one studio executive turned producer. "That kind of stuff happens *all* the time, especially at the level when deals are worth one and two and three million. Ten percent of one of those deals is $300,000.

"An agent will convince the studio executive to put a certain bid on the script, even though the studio has no intention of buying it. The agent will make a deal and they'll say, 'We will not hold you to it, but I want you to make an official bid so that everybody else will start getting into the bidding war. We will not hold you to your bid if it's the highest bid.'

"So-and-so will call so-and-so and will put in a bid of $300,000 against $800,000 for a spec *just* in order to drive the price up as a favor to the agent. Then that favor will be returned on the other end. So [in reciprocating the artificial bid] the studio executives can actually make money off a script that is not even purchased by his studio. That's a pretty wiry one."

Agents will occasionally bluff that a bid is on its way to spur interest, and "there's some outright lying that occasionally goes on. If somebody says, 'Okay, we've got an offer,' you'll say, 'Okay, do you have a money offer on table?' 'Well, we don't have a money offer on the table, but I promise that business affairs will be calling.' Technically, they don't have an offer until business affairs calls," according to another studio executive.

"I've heard rumors of kickbacks and things. I would doubt that happens much of the time. I'm sure that kind of stuff occasionally goes on, as it goes on in any business—but what, you're going to make $50,000 and if it's actually discovered, you probably don't have a career? Or who knows, maybe a couple studio heads will just go after you. And they'll say, 'This guy will do whatever it takes.' *That's* the scary part."

Studios will occasionally only purchase a script because of who is attached to it. If a certain director is attached to the project but they want him for one of their other projects, the studio makes a pay-or-play deal (meaning the filmmaker will be paid whether or not the project moves forward) and then kills the project. And yet they are still contractually bound to make another deal with that director, now for a project of their choosing.

Much studio skulduggery is rooted in the nature of the spec market itself. "It's such a perverse dynamic . . . there's just no secret in the fact that it's no way to produce art. There's no way it even produces enjoyable popular films," says one studio-based producer. "When a script gets out into a spec apparatus, all of the decisions are made for bad reasons [and] all of the decisions are pushed down to the very youngest people in the process [the trackers] who have the least knowledge of what's really good and what's bad.

"A tracker's only business is to track what's coming up and try to get it. Trackers are anticompetitive in that they talk to each other all day long, probably in violation of the Sherman Anti-Trust Act, and they make decisions largely based on whether or not their friends are in. So if one of their tracker friends is in, they're all in. If there's a tracker who says no, then they're all out, so you wind up with insecure young children with no real guts protecting their jobs. . . . In the late eighties, groups of development executives would get together once a week and literally put in a pick to decide what they're going to go for that weekend. They were first meeting once a week at Hugo's [a popular West Hollywood industry restaurant], representing about seven of the major spec deals at each studio."

The executives figured the problem wasn't the price of a script going up; after all, that just added to its value, which in turn made the executive they worked for look better. The problem was an inability to recommend to their bosses the hot spec script of the week. Thus a collusive "cover-your-ass" approach developed from a conglomeratized group of executives. It drove the price of the winner up, costing the studios more money, and therefore pushing the likely bids on other sales down.

"Once a script has been 'dinged' in that market, it's excruciatingly difficult to interest people in it, because it's been seen, it's been covered, it's 'been there and done that,' and you're on to the next thing. It's like brushfire. You're just lighting fires, burning it up, and hundreds of very good scripts, which could make very good movies for one reason or another, just don't ignite at this junior level. It's just no way to make movies. And once the investment's been done that way, then the studio's into it for a million dollars.

"It's just a bizarre mechanism that operates in all of us, almost without exception," the producer concludes. "The minute they pay a million dollars for something, the very next day the decision is how to completely rewrite and retool what you just paid a million dollars for. It's like buyer's remorse, or this self-loathing thing after a one-night stand, where the very next morning they have to negate everything they just did."

MAKING THE FINAL CUT

Most directors, and perhaps every screenwriter, despise the thought of a bunch of gangly teenagers in Canoga Park deciding how their movies should end, but as Richard Grant's character in *The Player* taught us, "*that's* reality." L.A.–based National Research Group, Inc. (NRG) takes the primary role in an activity that might be making Cecil B. DeMille roll over in his grave. Its founder and chairman, Ron Farrell, oversees the test screening of near-finished pictures, a process that can severely alter the final cut. Farrell's organization provides helpful gauges for the studios' marketing departments and ultimately can determine whether or not a studio will scrap a film's release altogether.

Since, in William Goldman's immortal words, "nobody knows anything" in Hollywood, the studios are eager to take a look into Ron Farrell's crystal ball. After Farrell attended Harvard Law School, he worked in political poll taking and moved to Los Angeles in 1977 to apply his research tactics to the entertainment field.

Although it may come as a surprise to film purists, it was director Francis Ford Coppola who put Farrell's NRG on the map by asking him to help with the marketing plans for 1979's *Apocalypse Now*. Studios have always test-screened movies; even Billy Wilder changed his opening to *Sunset Boulevard* because the original opener of Joe Gillis's talking corpse narrating the story test-screened to giggling reactions. The process was then a benefit for the filmmaker at a time when studios didn't have marketing directors guiding the course of a motion picture's content.

Flash forward to today: If you wander around Old Town Pasadena, Westwood, or a Sherman Oaks shopping mall, an overanxious peddler with a clipboard is likely to approach you with free movie tickets. Invitations to test screenings make a fun (and cheap) date, so NRG and its competitors never have a problem filling theaters. Viewers are provided with a simple questionnaire asking them to rate the picture—usually in a rough-cut form without titles or credits—on an excellent-to-poor scale. Specifically, attendees are also asked what characters or scenes they liked or disliked, and these responses can then lead to changes in the editing room.

Of course, the logic applied can sometimes irritate the creative community. For instance, if a "bit player" is brilliant at being just that, and the audience responds favorably, then the studio might go back and add numerous scenes until that character's charm wears off. Too much of a good thing can dull the senses, which ultimately means a weaker box office when the research might predict otherwise. The results aren't iron-clad indicators. Some rough cuts, such as for *Seven,* scored poorly but performed remarkably well in their release. In fact, test screenings for box office sensation *Pulp Fiction* resulted in a number of audience members actually storming out of the theater.

What might be the most valuable indicator the test screenings provide the studios is who their target audiences will be. A test should garner at least 65 percent favorable opinion to get the studio's faith. Wes Anderson's clever *Bottle Rocket* yielded a score in the low fortieth percentile, prompting Columbia Pictures to slash the movie's marketing budget by two thirds, and it grossed less than $500,000. *Back to the Future* tested phenomenally well and performed likewise in release.

Notably high scores for 1996's *Mrs. Winterbourne* prompted TriStar to feel they had a winner, but the film bombed in its release. In 1982, test screenings predicted that *The Best Little Whorehouse in Texas* would out-gross *E.T.* It didn't. Early screenings for 1986's *Howard the Duck* anticipated an upbeat commercial life, while *The Godfather* was met coolly, and Scorsese's *Goodfellas* caused a mini-exodus at preview screenings. *Fatal Attraction* altered its ending after audiences weren't pleased when Glenn Close's character took her own life in the original cut.

Distribution strategies play a huge part in a motion picture's success, and sometimes odd and brilliant movies such as *Rocky Horror Picture Show* and *The Wicker Man* (both dead-on-arrival in theaters) found eventual audiences as cult classics. The question of how effective studios, by nature, are in releasing the "special" movies they used to (like *Lilies of the Field*) creates an area of debate. When Mike Medavoy ran TriStar, Danny DeVito brought him Quentin Tarantino's script for *Pulp*

Fiction, and Medavoy passed (Tarantino labeled his submission "Last Draft" to indicate his desire to make his film as written). Yet if that studio had made and released the movie, veteran distributors contend that *Pulp Fiction* might have made $30 to $40 million and fizzled.

"That's true," says Jack Lechner of Miramax, the company that wound up backing the movie. Tarantino, after all, wouldn't have been able to make the project he wished under the normal studio constraints. Moreover, would a studio know how to market such a film? Miramax, known for its savvy distribution of specialty material, released *Pulp Fiction* internationally before coming to America, and the film harnessed a lot of heat by nabbing the Cannes Festival's Palme d'Or before American audiences had a chance to see it.

"It was the biggest thing for Miramax, and Miramax pushed the hell out of it. Sold it very cleverly," says Lechner. "I learned this when I was at Columbia Pictures years ago: There are movies that are too small or too odd for a studio to know what to do with."

Turning down *Pulp Fiction,* says Medavoy, was more of a personal decision. "Quite frankly, I was really derelict in my duty, because if I knew that that picture was going to do business I should have made the movie. I put up the money to develop it, and I knew it was going to do well."

But after having fought with then boss Peter Guber to make *Philadelphia* and *Sleepless in Seattle,* Medavoy didn't want to enter another battle with the studio. "I also felt it was unduly violent. If that's the case, I felt it would be better at *my* age that I didn't have to make that movie. I've done enough movies to justify that action," says Medavoy. "Maybe in retrospect I should have, but I don't feel any remorse about it. I always thought it was a great script, I told him that. And by the way, nobody wanted to do it except Harvey [Weinstein], and probably in part it had to do with the violence."

Miramax ran into similar good fortune with *The English Patient,* says Lechner. "A studio could've made it, and in fact a studio almost did. It's a very similar situation to *Pulp Fiction. The English Patient* was developed [by producer Saul Zaentz], and Fox was going to make it; and they pulled out at the last minute because they wanted Demi Moore instead of Kristen Scott Thomas. We came in and picked up the whole thing." Distributors often point to 1986's *Platoon* as the ideal release pattern for an independent. It played in art houses and built a strong word of mouth, because a conventional release could have killed it. *The Crying Game* utilized its "mystery factor" to make it a must-see on a wide basis; studios might have scratched their heads as to whether to release it at all.

"As a rabid independent these days, I'm very, very interested in exploiting the places where studios are weak. Thank God there are lots of them," says *Night Falls on Manhattan* producer Thom Mount. "We don't try to make *Die Hard* because frankly, a Warner Brothers does that better than we do, and Fox does that better than we do. But Fox and Warner Brothers can't begin to figure out how to make *The Indian Runner*. They can't begin to figure out how to make *Death and the Maiden*. They can't begin to figure out how to make even *Bull Durham*. These are all pictures derived from real authorship sources. They are pictures that take—within the context of the Hollywood system—a considerable risk. All of those pictures at least break even. Some of them don't make money, and some of them make a lot of money. But they all at least break even because they're managed well."

"Ultimately every film succeeds or fails on word of mouth, no matter what size," says Avenue's Cary Brokaw. "You can fool a national audience for an opening weekend, but by the second weekend the word of mouth is in effect. These days, word of mouth is in effect by Sunday. If you open Friday, and you see a movie that's a fooler, however great the [TV] spots are, if the movie's not there, you can chart the business Friday to Sunday and see where it's going, and how much dropoff you're going to get in week two. Whether it's *Forrest Gump* or *Jurassic Park* or *Pulp Fiction* or *sex, lies and videotape*, ultimately it's word of mouth that makes that film successful." With the media more prone to leak reactions of preview audiences and test screenings, the word of mouth moves faster than ever before.

"The release plan is how you manipulate the timing and availability of the picture so as to hopefully 'peak' at the time when the demand is greatest for that particular movie," Brokaw concludes. "And that is an art form."

MAYBE IT'S NOT PERFECT, BUT IT'S THE BEST HOLLYWOOD WE'VE GOT

The structure of the business would be different if people actually did try to participate in their own successes and failures, according to agent Rima Greer. "And that includes the studios themselves, because they just seem to be endlessly traded by a thousand other corporations.

"If anybody really knew what a successful film was, everybody would do it, so everybody's frantically looking for a secret formula that doesn't exist," says Greer. "I always feel bad for studio executives because they're faced with this impossible task that can't be done. I don't think anything they do is evil. It's more like they're floundering because of the nature of what they *have* to do. And when people are flailing around, the people standing around them get hurt."

Says producer Jonathan Sanger, "It's almost institutionalized. . . . The studio is the government, and [the executives] may be taking over the government, but they're not going to change the government. When Harry Truman came into the White House, the process of creating the atomic bomb that he was going to drop on Hiroshima was already in place, and maybe he could've dismantled that, but not as easily as one might think. You're dealing with a situation where it's unclear whether or not the next executive will be able to do a tremendous amount to change these processes that have been built up over generations. [The studios] don't change that much, and the accounting practices are not only nebulous, but venal in some ways."

"It's very difficult to fit in to that studio system," director George Huang says. "I know that even knowing what the drill is . . . I honestly don't know if [the current system] is the best way to make a movie. Ideally, what I'd like is to see what the budget is: 'I promise I will deliver it to you within that budget, just *please* leave me alone.' But studios are very nervous about that."

Shane Black experienced differences with Warner Bros. over the direction of the *Lethal Weapon* series after he turned in a *Lethal Weapon 2* draft with a climax the studio hadn't anticipated. "At the end Mel Gibson's character died. I thought it was a very interesting setup for his death scene, and they didn't want to use that one." Perhaps the studio's desire to some day make a *Lethal Weapon 17* eventually overruled Black's tragic ending.

"I was sending away the bread truck," Black says. "Remember, this is me at, like, twenty-four or twenty-five, but I offered to give the money back for the script because I didn't like what they were doing." Shane has no idea how his agent got word, but within five minutes he called from his car phone and after an ear-ringing conversation convinced the writer to take the check. "So, I didn't give the money back. I read it again recently; it's the best script I've ever written.

"To think that at the time I was so caught up in pleasing people that I offered to return money on the best script I had ever written, it makes me laugh. It's just this silly-ass idea because *Lethal Weapon 2* made a great deal of money," Black continues. "If it had been the script that I'm talking about, I think it would have still made a great deal of money. But the studios have traditionally been afraid of that darkness, certainly of killing off the main character.

"I kind of sand-bagged them in *The Long Kiss Goodnight.* I made it impossible for the main character *not* to be killed at the end, Sam Jackson's character. He *has* to die; it's the way the story goes," says Black. "The chemistry is so fun between him and Geena [Davis]. They're so good together, they're going to think, 'Well, couldn't we figure out a way that maybe he didn't die?' There was a lot of talk about *Thelma & Louise 2* for a while. People would say, 'How could we do it? How could we do it?' You can't!"

After New Line test-screened Black's desired ending of *The Long Kiss Goodnight,* they in fact changed the ending after all; Sam Jackson's character survives, and Black reluctantly went along with it. Unlike the hit *Lethal Weapon 2* turned into for Warners, *The Long Kiss Goodnight* became a box office dud, and we'll never know how Black's desired ending would have played.

Kvetching about Hollywood gets most people working in the industry through their day. It's a business that's only glamorous from the outside, and motion pictures about the perplexing realities of filmmaking, from Preston Sturges's *Sullivan's Travels* to Billy Wilder's *Sunset Boulevard* to Barry Primus's *Mistress* to George Huang's *Swimming with Sharks* to Robert Altman's *The Player,* have enjoyed poking fun at the trappings of a less than ordinary way to spend a life. Yet as much as people bitch and moan about the inadequacies of an unchangeable system, that's often where the story ends.

"Whatever is wrong with Hollywood, there's so much more that's right with it," says producer George Litto. "It still represents great opportunity for people to work in an interesting profession, whether they're writers, directors, agents, executives, actors. It's more fascinating than making cans of beans, right? The reward is great if you can survive the competition.

"It's a medium where you can express yourself," Litto continues. "If you have the perseverance, you can write, or direct, or make a film that makes a statement. I have in the past, and other people have, and more people will in the future. I think there's a tremendous amount of things that are right with Hollywood. But of course, you know, we like to pick on everything about it. And everybody outside of Hollywood wants to be in Hollywood, so naturally the people who are in Hollywood have to pick on it."

Development Heaven or Development Hell

While the paradox of the development process is often the bane of a screenwriter's existence, benefits can come out of the process. It's perhaps a reactionary notion to condemn development fully, categorically labeling it "script vandalism." Certainly, development has hurt some projects, but this all depends on the particular talents of the executives and producers dealing with the project.

"There are two kinds of people in the buyer world," says Fox 2000 executive Chris Vogler. "One is the kind of person who wants to know 'Does anybody else want this, and does it have economic value because it's in demand?' That kind of person may buy something and then turn to the other type of person who can evaluate it creatively and say, 'Okay, you bought this for $350,000, is it any good, what have we bought?'

"I'm on the creative end, often coming in after that decision has been made and then saying, 'All right, I assume that we're gonna do this,' " says Vogler. "It's irrelevant to say, 'It stinks.' It's too late to say, 'It's no good,' we've already spent half a million dollars on it. So you change your focus to 'How do we make it work?' given what is there. You begin by trying to project how to fix it, whether you need to bring in a new writer, or reconceive the idea around the core." Often studios bring on a whole tier of development people to throw in their two cents; for instance, director Stephen Sommers once received Disney story notes that exceeded the number of pages of his entire screenplay.

"The development process is not well designed," says Zak

Penn, original cowriter of *Last Action Hero.* "You can't give notes by committee. There should be at most one person, or two people, giving notes. Preferably it should be the director or someone working on the movie, but to have a whole staff write notes for something is absurd. It definitely shows in a lot of movies, but I think that's been a problem for a while.

"What's so absurd about the whole thing is that after you do all the work and after you rewrite the thing a hundred times, they hire a director, and then he needs to rewrite it," Penn continues. "Then the actor comes on and he needs to rewrite it." One reason for this process is that many more independent companies are putting movies together themselves and then selling them. In other words, with autocratic control of studio moguls like L. B. Mayer a thing of the past, the creative thrust has become naturally diluted.

"I think the studios are increasingly going to become the distribution outlets, and that their staffs will be reduced and a lot of the jobs that have been created in this boom market will go away," Penn continues. "The studios will say, 'Okay, Mr. Big Producer, what movies do you have for us this month?' And he says, 'Well, I have got this packaging, which has this writer and this director, and this is when we're shooting it, and here's the budget, and this one with this . . .' The truth is that at the end of the day, the people who actually must make the movie are the creative personnel. I think it saps a lot of the life out of movies when they're not that way."

Writing instructor John Truby feels that because any form of art deals with very ethereal terms, such terms can become so general they are meaningless. "When people don't really know what they're talking about—as most writers, executives, and so on do not—then they'll throw these words around and not know what they mean. . . . For example, they say, 'Well, I didn't identify with the character.' You ask most people what does that mean; they don't have any idea what it really means. Another one is, 'The character didn't develop.' What does that mean?

"These are all buzzwords that they use to make it sound like they know what they're talking about, that they're actually giving you criticism," Truby continues. "It's worthless. It doesn't tell a writer anything. Yet that's how most writers and most executives operate.

"People think, 'We'll fix it in the rewrites.' A favorite meaningless line that everybody uses, 'Writing is rewriting.' Well, yeah, you've gotta rewrite because it's a craft and you've gotta improve it. But what that line leads to is the idea that we can improve everything by simply rewriting it, either with the original writer or somebody new.

"Well, is building a house rebuilding a house? Because that's what you're doing," adds Truby. "Yeah, we can rewrite, we'll rip the whole first script down. But then maybe we need to rewrite that too, so we'll rip that down and rewrite it. It's a completely wasteful system. What I always say to people is, if you basically didn't get it right in the first draft, it's not gonna get better. So what I always try to do is teach people how to get it basically right in the first draft, instead of saying, 'Oh, I'll just put it down and then fix it later.' The more drafts that are written, the harder it is to fix.

"When you get development comments so often they are completely contradictory, it's just ridiculous," says John Truby. "I have seen that *many* times, where the comments—if you actually put them into effect—would make the script decidedly worse, and yet they don't *know* that. *You* don't know that. If *you* don't know how to distinguish the good comments from the bad, then you're going to be in big trouble. And you're going to try to please everybody and you're going to end up with trash that everybody says, 'No, this thing sucks, let's get rid of it' or 'This writer sucks, let's get rid of him,' and that's how a lot of the business is done."

Each studio is known for a distinct process of development. "Warner Brothers seems to be maybe even 'development happy,' meaning that they have a lot of projects in development," says Chris Vogler. "They have the capital to invest in sort of a long term of working projects along, as opposed to a smaller outfit that is looking to buy a script that's ready to make, somebody like Vidmark or Trimark. Those smaller companies pretty much need to streamline the development process as much as they can.

"Disney certainly was known as a 'note happy' studio, one that had a lot of staff who had the time to work over a project and give a lot of notes," says Vogler, who cut his teeth at the Mouse Factory. "There was a whole system developed there under Katzenberg, who is a very systematic thinker, and they came up with this system of collecting notes from several people, maybe the producer, maybe the vice president and creative executive and maybe even Katzenberg himself, and then having a creative executive sanitize those notes and make them diplomatic so they could be handed to the producer and the writer in a way that wasn't offensive.

"This is a lot of the problem, communicating the wishes and desires of the studio through the producer to the writer," Vogler adds. "As a story analyst, you usually are just coldly, brutally telling the truth and laying it out with all the sharp edges on it. As an executive, you have to smooth it over a little bit, or else you get a defensive reaction from the writer, they take offense, and you have to find a diplomatic voice. Often what happens with the specs is that right away you have to take a deep breath and say, 'What have I bought and what are the problems? What is it gonna take to make it work?' And find a way to communicate that properly."

Development hell is the fate of many projects, while purgatory remains as an alternative for screenwriters powerful enough to defend their original intentions. To get to development heaven, a screenwriter must ultimately convince or force all of his or her story's meddlers to back off.

"Nobody knows what makes each film great," says *Mr. Holland's Opus* writer Patrick Duncan. "My biggest problem with the studios is that [they feel a need to change everything]. If you read a script and it moves you, shoot it. If it makes you laugh, if it makes you cry, whatever it does, shoot it. Don't mess with it, you're not going to make it any better. Very rarely does the process make it any better.

"Nobody knows how to make you care about a character, make him sympathetic or empathetic, and want to take a ride with him. That's what movies are really about," says Duncan. "Everybody can fuck around with the plot, and you see these cookie-cutter movies, right? You can see the studios' handprints all over them. Most of the films that really, really break through and succeed are the ones that nobody would make.

"*Pulp Fiction* breaks every rule the studio could think of—and a few more that they couldn't," says Duncan. "You have [in the studio process] what I would call amateurs; they really don't know what makes a film great. If they did, they'd be running the studio, and it would be the most successful studio in town. They're diddling with this stuff because that's their *job*. The best executives I have worked with are the ones who gave me the fewest instructions and let me try to figure it out for myself."

10

When Big Guns Conspire

THE POLEMICAL PASSAGE OF *EXTREMELY VIOLENT,*
THE CABOOSE THAT DROVE *LAST ACTION HERO*
BY ZAK PENN AND ADAM LEFF
Rewritten by Shane Black and David Arnott; rewrite by
William Goldman

Purchased by Columbia Pictures
MPAA Rating: PG-13
Director: John McTiernan

A young boy, Danny Madigan, escapes to the fantasy world of his local theater to avoid the painful realities of growing up in New York City. But when Danny literally sets foot in his favorite action movie, he helps his cinematic hero, Jack Slater, partake in capturing the villains of his current pursuit.

CAST OF CHARACTERS

Chris Moore, agent at InterTalent Agency
Chris Lee, VP at TriStar Pictures
Bill Block, David Greenblatt and *Tom Strickler,* partners at Inter-
    Talent Agency
Stephen Roth, Columbia Pictures–based producer
Mark Canton, Columbia chairman
Barry Josephson, executive VP, Columbia Pictures

EVEN YEARS AFTER the release of *Last Action Hero,* executives bristle a bit at the mention of it—whether or not they were involved. Was this an action picture to end all action pictures? Was it a spoof? Was it a fairy tale? Or was it a studio's hopeful solution to the next *Back to the Future* franchise? Perhaps this film could provide a bold and thoughtful commentary on that magical line—the fourth wall—that separates the hero onscreen from that kid in that audience. Or maybe it was just a train wreck waiting to happen.

The script's sale is legendary: Two novice writers fresh out of Wesleyan University orchestrated an industry assault with their whimsical spec, then titled *Extremely Violent,* which their friends in the lower ranks of show business helped promote. The script landed Zak Penn and Adam Leff with the agent of their choice, led to a bidding war pitting colleague against colleague, and became a priority-event movie for Sony-owned Columbia Pictures.

"We thought it would get a lot of attention, particularly when Arnold Schwarzenegger signed on, but certainly I never expected that we'd get all the negative attention," says Penn. "Even considering how annoyed I was with the way we were treated on the movie . . . I think you see some of this backlash. A friend of my mom's is a film critic in New York who actually liked it, you know? I disagree; I don't really like the movie. I think it's pretty hard to sit through. But a lot of people *do* [like it] because they feel, like, at least it's an unusual movie. It's, like, a weird movie. Particularly the way they did it, it was *really* weird."

Last Action Hero misfired on its opening weekend after being shrouded in last-minute drama of round-the-clock editing sessions, misinformation about a poorly received "phantom test screening" (severing relations between Columbia and *The Los Angeles Times*), emblazoning of the movie's logo on a Conestoga Rocket to be sent into outer space (the flight was later canceled), a $20 million promotion with Burger King and tie-ins with other corporations, public protests in front of Sony Studios by PTA leaders who decried the anticipated violence of a "kid's film," and finally a gala premiere topped with a gigantic blow-up doll of Arnold Schwarzenegger, after which its audience uncomfortably stared at each other as Columbia executives braced for an onslaught of media hoopla about the studio's "Big Ticket for '93." The surreal atmosphere of the Westwood gala was augmented by the previous day's arrest of the Hollywood madam, Heidi Fleiss, whose links to *Last Action Hero* producer Steve Roth and a number of attendees added to the general discomfort.

At Wesleyan, Chicagoan Adam Leff was New York–native Penn's film class teaching assistant, and as movie buffs, the two started writing screenplays together once they moved to L.A. *Last Action Hero* began with Zak's idea that a kid should be sucked into a movie screen, says Leff, and the writers decided the movie-in-the-movie would be an action picture. "You go to an action movie these days and there's nothing new that's under the sun. They're reaching these baroque, gothic buddy genres, retellings of themselves again and again, and it had therefore reached a humorous level.

"You know everything that goes on in these action pictures, but you enjoy them anyway," Leff continues. "What if we send this kid in there who knows every turn in the action and says, 'Hey, don't go through the front door, idiot. There's a back door to these places. Go through there' or 'You don't have to blast 150 people to get the girl back' or 'You can't go check on your old CIA buddy right now because they're going to kidnap your wife, don't you know that?' And making fun of the structure of the genre.

"We created the story of this disillusioned kid knocking around New York," says Leff, describing the main character Danny Madigan. "His father died and he turned to the movies obviously for his fantasy life and fulfillment of the kind of powerlessness that he feels in New York, being beat up by thugs and what not. One thing I would've liked to have seen is that they kept it with a seventeen-year-old kid, who's more sophisticated and has a wish fulfillment on a more subtle level than a screeching twelve-year-old saying, 'I'm in a movie! I'm in a movie!'"

Penn recalls when the idea of a kid who knows everything about action movies being sucked into one came into his head fully formed. "It was a pretty easy concept to flesh out. The funny thing was, most people I told it to thought it was a really stupid idea . . . even *Adam* wasn't so big on it, but I was pretty sure. My friends said, 'That's a really stupid idea,' so I had this little file on my computer that says, 'This is a really stupid idea' and I stored it there. The minute I had that idea, I was totally 100 percent sure that it would turn out."

Penn went to his Dictaphone to record the original concept. "I just sat down and brainstormed the story. The beginning should be like *Taxi Driver* set in New York City, a harsh reality of this kid's life—*Taxi Driver* as more of a visual [setting]. Then 'the movie' portion should be candy-colored. Originally we wrote that 'the movie' was in a different color stock than the rest." Akin to Dorothy's Land of Oz, or *Roger Rabbit*'s Toon Town, this device would differentiate Danny's two worlds of fantasy and reality.

When not playing tennis together or writing, Penn and Leff both read scripts for Quincy Jones (musician and producer of *The Color Purple*) and created their own work assignment to evaluate the action genre by viewing over forty movies with a checklist; they didn't consider it work at all. "We made up question sheets like 'Who is the second-most-evil bad guy?' In every one of these action movies, there's the bad guy, then there's the second-most-evil bad guy, and one of the little rules is: *That* guy always dies last. You would think the main bad guy would die last. But no, it's always the henchman who dies last. We had all these other little rules like 'Why is it personal?' and 'At what point does it become personal?' 'Who's his partner?' 'His friend who betrays him . . .' "

They started writing *Extremely Violent* in March 1991 and two months later showed it to some friends for feedback, then spent another two months rewriting. "While it meant a lot to us, it didn't take up that much of our time," says Penn. For [our follow-up movie] *P.C.U.,* we spent two years writing with all the drafts the studio made us do. So the irony of it was that Shane Black and all these guys tore their hearts and hair out much more over the script itself than we ever did.

"People were surprised at the intense critical backlash, and I think most of that came from the studio's endless hyping of it," says Zak Penn. "The incredible irony of the whole situation—and I'm surprised it isn't brought up more—is that we literally were parodying Shane Black when we wrote this script in his writing style. We made fun of his writing style, and then they hired the guy we were parodying to rewrite us. There is something perverse about that."

BACKING UP THE BLITZ

At the now defunct InterTalent Agency, agent Chris Moore developed somewhat of a rep as a Hollywood Golden Boy with plenty of connections to the town's up-and-coming executives and producers. Unbeknownst to Moore, Penn and Leff made him the center of an intricate plan to elevate themselves from their low-level work for Quincy Jones's Burbank-based company.

"Now I had this whole philosophy, which I give [InterTalent partner] David Greenblatt full credit for," says Moore, "which is, if anybody takes the time to tell you that something's worth reading—whether it's a bum off the street, your mom back at home, or whatever—read it. That takes effort, and you never know. That's how David Greenblatt found Shane Black."

In late October 1991 Wendy Rose, then an assistant at TriStar-based Jersey Films, wanted to help out Penn and Leff. Moore, a Maryland native and understudy to fellow Harvard alumnus Tom Strickler, had met Rose while making his studio rounds, and Wendy called him to say she had some friends who had written a script that Jersey was considering buying. "She thought I'd be a good agent for them," says Moore. "So I thought, 'Sure, I'll read it.' But you have a ton of other stuff to do as an agent, working through this maze, trying to make my bosses happy."

Then Michael Goldman, an agent trainee at InterTalent who was also part of Penn and Leff's blitzkrieg strategy, approached Moore. "Michael came running into my office saying, 'Listen, this thing is genius, and it's starting to happen' and 'You got to read this thing 'cause they need help.' Michael had a way of exaggerating.

"What do you mean? Is the deal going to close tomorrow and I should read it right now?" Moore asked.

"Well, I'm not saying the deal's going to close tomorrow, but what I'm saying is that people really like this script," Goldman replied.

Goldman dropped *Extremely Violent* on Moore's desk. Not a big fan of spoofs, Moore figured it would be an over-the-top Leslie Nielsen satire of action movies, so on his desk it remained. Then another agency employee who knew Penn and Leff also pleaded that the agent give it a look.

"One day went by where I told everybody I was going to read it," Moore recalls. "It was a Wednesday, something else came up, and I'd left it at home. The next day, Goldman walks in with *another* copy of the script."

"Listen, you *have* to read this script before the weekend," Goldman told Moore. "There's too many people reading it. . . . Other people are reading it. Don't be a moron here. I'm trying to help you out."

"And I wasn't trying to be a moron; I was just busy and usually it's hyped at a certain level [of agent above me]," says Moore. But respecting Wendy's and Michael's opinions, Moore intended to eventually get to it. "Then completely randomly, that day my lunch canceled and I was just sitting there. I had nothing to do. So I ordered some food and I sat there and read it. By page forty-five, I loved the movie. Then I got totally nervous; if I had this reaction, I could literally see it going. I cannot wait to sell this movie, and if anybody else was reading it right now, they'd be having that same reaction or they're stupid."

Moore got on the phone to set a meeting with the writers. "He was our age, he went to Harvard, he's supposed to be a really nice guy, likes action films, might be looking for young clients—it all seemed to fit," says Adam Leff. "Somewhere around lunch, to have all of these people call him within a space of five minutes saying, 'You've got to read this script, it's hilarious, just came across my desk' . . . basically no agent in Hollywood is going to take this as coincidence. But it was, I think, reasonable enough support for this thing."

InterTalent's Tom Strickler also got excited about the script. "I can't remember exactly how it got to UTA, but Jeremy Zimmer had read it there," Leff recalls. "That weekend, we started to field phone calls from [InterTalent's] Bill Block, who was calling personally to say how InterTalent's going to be giving us the team tackle. Then we're getting the call from Jeremy Zimmer telling us, 'The cream floats to the top, don't go with the scum,' and these incredible pitches. These were only giant names to us at that point, and it was damn exciting."

Zak Penn was twenty-two at the time; Adam Leff was twenty-three. They signed with InterTalent and their script sold within a week, but not before some furious deal-making drama to rival any in spec history. "I was very flattered that they actually decided through word of mouth the *other* way that I was a good guy to represent the script," says Moore, who had only been an agent for nine months. "There was also the part where if they're going to take you, you might as well do the work and see if you like it." Moore finished the script that night and entered Block's office the following morning to say, "Bill, I guarantee you, this movie is going to sell for a ton of money."

Moore pitched it as a nineties version of *Wizard of Oz* and believes it would have been a gigantic success had it been made that way. "It's what I fell in love with when I read the script. . . . When my parents got divorced, or life was hard, I would find myself in a movie theater sitting in the dark, thinking about my life, wondering what I'm supposed to go do, and hoping that one of those guys on the screen would just look out at me for five seconds and say, 'Hey, you're gonna be all right.' That sounds really cheesy to admit that, but that definitely happened to me. When I read the script, *that's* what this little kid was. And the script was a lot more about the little kid."

Regarding the wacky, energy-charged Zucker-Abrams-Zucker (*Airplane!, Naked Gun*) humor that inspired their script, Adam Leff says, "The 'movie-within-the-movie' was very ZAZ [and the rest] was very dark. Intentionally, the first fifteen pages read like a really gritty, shitty neighborhood life for a seventeen-year-old kid who's got no real parenting, living in Hell's Kitchen in New York" who found movies a release of emotion.

Moore found three aspects in the script: "You had the theme of saying to all the people out there, 'Listen, movies are just movies, these guys are just heroes, don't put so much weight.' On the other hand they're saying, for all of you who *do* go into the movie theater when you're upset or angry, 'Wouldn't it be fun if you could actually get a magic ticket and go *into* the movie and help your friend out?' Because after watching a movie, sometimes you know the hero as well as anybody else, and I loved those two ideas." (The third was parody; the *Hamlet* "coming attraction" sequence, in which Danny Madigan fantasizes about his action hero rewriting Shakespeare's words, was the only scene in Penn and Leff's draft that stayed fully intact throughout the rewrites.)

Penn and Leff wrote the villain as Mr. Id, whose bandaged head masked the scars from the time Slater threw him into a vat of acid. His two henchmen, Jules and Jim (the Lumiere brothers), were two Belgian troublemakers who pirouette through all their dastardly deeds. In the finale, the bandages come off Mr. Id and—like bread crumbs—lead Danny back to a burning theater where the villain reveals himself to be the projectionist.

"Most everybody felt the first sixty to sixty-five pages were really, really good, and then once the kid was in the movie, the rules got a little twisted," Moore recalls of the need to develop what happened once the hero and kid become friends, besides just spoofing the movie. But Moore also felt that the script's intriguing action provided a stellar casting opportunity. "You have this wonderful chance for a big action star, whoever it is, to be much more heartwarming because he's partnered with the kid. And not in the way that *Kindergarten Cop* or *Don't Stop or My Mom Will Shoot* were, [but where] there's actually a real action movie, such as how *Indiana Jones* had that little kid in the second movie, where the lead could be tender but still is the action hero."

In the following months, the very locomotives *Last Action Hero* required to get pushed over the movie mountain were also by their nature causing the project to become a mishmash of different and incompatible ideas. As a first course, InterTalent had to sell Penn and Leff's script.

TAILORING THE TEAM TACKLE

Last Action Hero was the chosen title after Penn and Leff ran a list of alternates by InterTalent. Moore cites Chris Lee, a rising executive at Sony-owned TriStar Pictures, as the script's prime mover. "Chris, I haven't really done this before," Moore told Lee. "I've sold a couple little things, but I have this action movie that I think is the next generation action movie. It makes fun of the Sylvester Stallone straight-on action movies, but it has all that action; so it's the best of both worlds. But it also has some heart, and I really love it."

Moore informed Lee that the other agents were reading it over the weekend, and he wouldn't send it out to anybody else. "Just take a look and let me know if you think I'm insane. Let me know if you think you guys would be interested."

"Of course, whenever you do that, you are partially selling it," Moore explains, "but you are also partially taking a temperature reading on it: 'Am I insane? Or is this thing as good as I think?' "

InterTalent indeed *was* about to give Penn and Leff the team tackle. The agency felt rushed, however, to position *Last Action Hero* with specified producers to submit to competing studios; they had learned that the script had been slipped around town, and they didn't want producers making submissions without their knowledge. Since Steve Roth, a former agent with a deal on the Columbia lot, had close ties to Mark Canton's predecessor Frank Price, Roth was about the only producer from Columbia not invited to a welcoming party Canton held at Morton's restaurant that Friday afternoon. Thus Roth was able to officially submit the script to Columbia Pictures for the weekend.

Bill Block told Moore that a million-dollar offer wasn't likely to come in quickly, but expected a sale. So Chris got on the phone to Zak and Adam, "Well, someone's going to buy your script. Things look very good. You should come hang around the office on Monday and we'll see what happens."

Adam Leff recalls that it was slipped to someone at Carolco who considered it treasonous to action films, that it was propaganda to somehow end the genre. "They were going to 'kill it,' was the word. At our age, and with our experience in Hollywood, if someone at Carolco's going to kill your script, it's killed. I mean, we didn't know," says Leff. "What this caused was a sort of a quick spurt-out of the scripts to about twelve different producers. Who knows, maybe the slap-dash approach helped create heat on the thing that it might not have ordinarily had."

That weekend, Chris Moore held a big barbecue at his house in Venice. At about five o'clock, TriStar executive Chris Lee phoned, luring Moore from the festivities. "I just called Bill Block," Lee told Moore, "and I just called [TriStar chairman] Mike Medavoy. I told him I loved the script, you're 100 percent right. I think Mike is going to offer you a million-dollar preemptive bid tomorrow to just take this off the market, on Sunday. . . . I don't know what's going to happen. But I wanted to tell you that we really appreciate it, and we're going to buy this movie."

"Well, of course at that point Bill [Block] was *wide awake* and paying full attention," Moore laughs. "Greenblatt was then involved, and then Strickler had the idea of maybe sending it to Shane Black. At one point, we thought of sending it to Shane and [comedy screenwriter] Pat Proft, who we both represented. It would just be one of those funny things, 'from the guy who brought you *Lethal Weapon* and the guy who brought you [*Hot Shots!*], here's the *Last Action Hero*.' "

As Mike Medavoy recalls that frenetic week, "Chris Lee came to me, he read it and thought it was terrific. Of course Mark Canton, because of his relationship with [then Sony Studios chairman Peter] Guber, got it. Then it just got out of hand. . . . We put a bid in, but I don't think we got into a bidding war. Internally we said, 'Look, this is what we're willing to pay. If they want to sell it to us, fine. If not, give it to Columbia.' "

TriStar obviously *didn't* come in to offer a million-dollar preemptive bid, Moore confirms, but they made an offer with Kathleen Summers (partnered with actor Dennis Quaid at a TriStar-based company). "Monday morning, we were still talking about it. There was this whole thing about 'Should we get Shane? We got to wait and see what Shane says.' Because if he's involved then it's a much bigger deal. David Greenblatt obviously has a great relationship with Joel Silver [selling him Shane Black's original *Lethal Weapon* and other projects]. He had sent it to Joel, and Joel wasn't a fan of it the way TriStar was."

Meanwhile, Steve Roth fought hard to make the deal at Columbia. "I learned a lot from watching, or at least now remembering, what Steve did as a producer," says Moore. But the script had also been slipped to Schwarzenegger's then agent at ICM, Lou Pitt, before the deal closed.

Whether or not the action hero was written for Schwarzenegger is open to interpretation. Named "Arno Slater" in the original script, he speaks with a Teutonic accent, but was also spoofing Schwarzenegger's personae. For Arnold to parody himself would be both difficult and potentially harmful to that image.

"It was such a crazy long shot, we never believed that he'd really do it," says writer Adam Leff. "You expected, once it had been bought, maybe this thing could get made with Van Damme and it would still be funny. . . . At that time, Arnold was the biggest box office star in the world. It would have been lunacy to suppose that he would really do it. The stars were in alignment or something, because it worked out." With Arnold's inclusion, the character's name changed to "Jack Slater."

"We thought it would be made with Dolph Lundgren, you know, mocking Arnold . . . but really?" Zak recalls. "I mean, we thought that was the realistic thing. But we were *hoping* we would get Arnold.

"Arnold's character, in our script, was a parody of the character *he* plays, which is a kind of hulking menace, the 'without edges' character, like the superhero almost," Penn says. "Now *The Simpsons* does a really good parody of him . . . much more of this big lummox who's constantly shooting people and asking questions later." (At the time he signed on to *Last Action Hero,* Arnold had already killed an estimated 275 people onscreen, and his agents and lawyers were looking to soften that image.)

Zak Penn felt the original script's theme—and one of the things that some people didn't like about it—was the point that action movies were mindlessly violent. "Hollywood action movies were serving as a replacement for a kid's anger. This kid's father died of cancer and there's this big scene, which I thought was pretty good, where he talks about how he's always had this anger, and he always wanted to do something to make up for his father's death.

"At the point that the Arnold character finally comes around, he says, 'Look, there's nothing you can do about that, that's just *life,*' that not every situation requires violence, and for the most part, violence just begets more violence," says Penn. "It doesn't make you feel better. So at the end of the movie, the kid learns to stop projecting himself into action movies, which is a very cynical and negative thing to say about Hollywood movies. We *knew* that wouldn't make it in. . . . In fact, apparently, there are a lot of people who didn't like our take on it. I heard Carolco hated our script because of that."

THE CULVER CITY CLASH

With a chance to close their deal, the writers had to decide on TriStar's offer. Adam Leff recalls a phone call from Tom Strickler: " 'TriStar's bidding $150,000, what do you guys want to do?' It was around 10:30 A.M. on Monday and we're going pretty crazy at this point, and we say, 'I don't know, what should we do?' " In the era of "the million-dollar spec," the writers felt they should hold out, though they were damn happy to get anything. "When InterTalent suggested that we go for more, we were pretty much behind them."

It was Barry Josephson's first week at Columbia and also his first stint as an executive on the studio side, so he was eager to buy a script right away to announce to the town that he was ready to do business. Josephson, known for his talent in attracting actors to projects, became the script's champion.

The Sony edict was for their studios to make bigger pictures, one of the reasons they brought Josephson over from Joel Silver's company (known for its action movies such as 1988's *Die Hard,* as well as the 1991 clunker *Hudson Hawk*). The project offered potential marketing tie-ins of every sort, such as a huge merchandising line of Jack Slater toys, *Last Action Hero* video games, and a hip, heavy-metal soundtrack.

On Monday, InterTalent submitted to more buyers. "MGM/UA called up, was going to make a bid, Fox was going to make a bid," says Moore. "We were actually *real* close with Touchstone [but] it was probably too big of an action movie." Meanwhile, the TriStar and Columbia bids were gradually going up.

"I believe we ended on Wednesday night at 500 against 750 [thousand dollars]," says Leff, "but nothing had been closed." At about 7 P.M., Steve Roth phoned from his white BMW to check on the deal's status; he was told TriStar would get the project for Summers-Quaid.

Angered, and then only a few blocks from InterTalent's Beverly Hills' office, Roth stormed into the agency, passing Penn and Leff, who were playing Ping-Pong in the agency's side room. Chris Moore was then on the phone to TriStar's Chris Lee, and Steve physically cut off the call.

"Look, I fought for you, I battled for you, I pitched for you," the producer shouted, raising ears and eyebrows throughout the agency. The enthusiasm and theatrics Steve Roth showed impressed not only the writers but also the InterTalent agents, who huddled with Zak and Adam. Their consensus: "This was the kind of producing we needed."

As the TriStar and Columbia bids escalated, Moore recalls, "somebody at the higher level at Sony realized they were bidding against each other, and that they were going to lose half a million dollars just because of that." The writers, especially at their age, were ecstatic to watch the bidding skyrocket on their first sale. But the corporate heads at Sony's Culver City studios were not.

"That night, Mark Canton discovered he had been bidding this whole time against Mike Medavoy, and I'm sure the shit hits the ceiling over there," says Adam Leff. "TriStar dropped out of the bidding, and Columbia came back the next day at $100,000 against $350,000. Now this was sort of a bigger deal for the InterTalent Agency than it was for Zak and me, because we were just two clients who had been screwed by the massive corporate arm of Sony pictures. It would have been a forgotten incident."

Bill Block, however, was furious that Columbia reneged, effectively dropping their sale from $500,000 to one fifth of that. "Columbia's claim was that if someone else wants to step up and pay more, they can," Leff says. "So when they were the only bidder, they had no competitor. No other studio stepped in, so they could close it at that point. It was a matter of breaching an ethical oral agreement, which is the way this town operates. But they didn't care, because at that point InterTalent didn't have the sway to make a fuss. . . . You know, you would never think of doing this to a CAA or an ICM. So it became a huge issue for Bill Block, who I know personally drove down and interrupted Peter Guber's dinner and threw a fit in his dining room."

That TriStar was able to match Columbia's bid but not top it incensed all of the InterTalent agents, "because theoretically that's illegal, or it's against the rules anyway. You don't make an offer and then change it," says Chris Moore, recalling the bitter pill served that Wednesday night. "We spent a day desperately trying to get these other studios that were circling around it, who had made smaller offers, to come up."

Chris Lee urged InterTalent to make the deal with TriStar, since they were the first to show interest. "Either place could get Arnold, it wasn't about that," says Moore, who figured that Bill Block knew the inside scoop that Medavoy would soon be leaving TriStar. "[Block] felt Columbia was going to make the movie and TriStar might not. Then having Arnold involved; it was going to happen. *Also*, Shane Black had at that point come into the game, and so that made a guy like Canton just get *all* excited. TriStar's thinking, 'Jeezus, that's another big production fee.' At that time, Shane wasn't writing it, he'd just come in to produce. But it was becoming a $5 million deal all together."

For the sake of getting the picture made, everybody was now keen on getting Arnold Schwarzenegger to commit. "What finally came out of it for us was a provision in our contract so that if Arnold signed on," says Adam Leff, "Columbia would make good on their original five-hundred-grand bid. So when he did sign on, we each got a quarter million dollars in the mail. That kind of more than made up for any spilt milk."

On November 8, 1991, *Daily Variety* reported that Columbia acquired Penn and Leff's script for $100,000 against $350,000. Moore feels that while InterTalent exhausted all their avenues, Columbia had an edge throughout. But because a number of other projects competed for Schwarzenegger's attention, Columbia had to move fast to secure his interest. The studio was even competing with itself (with Norman Lear's *Sweet Tooth,* to feature Arnold wearing a tutu and playing the Tooth Fairy). *Last Action Hero* was considered a dark horse among the dozen or so studio projects Arnold could have accepted at the time, five of them with directors already attached. Even TriStar had a Woody Allen spoof about Freud and Jung that Arnold was considering.

"If Arnold had attached himself [to *Last Action Hero*] and it was a free-for-all, we could have had all kinds of people bidding on it, Warner Brothers, everybody might have come back to get Arnold," Moore says. "Having met Lou Pitt and worked at ICM, I asked him about it one time. I think Arnold or Lou had kind of filtered out, no overt thing, but that Arnold was only going to do it at Columbia. So with that, there was no reason for anybody else to buy it. But I think Arnold had kind of stepped forward, or his lawyers, or somebody, or just the intimation alone. It's just the honor among thieves. Of course, had I been at ICM at the time [of brokering the script], Arnold probably would have gone anywhere and jacked the price to a million bucks for the script!"

At the time, Schwarzenegger was carefully balancing his roles between hard action and soft comedy fare. It became a juggling act for Columbia to hold his interest. "In defense of the people who were working on *Last Action Hero*," says Adam Leff, "I think the reason why this turned out the way it did is because everyone was running scared making sure that Arnold doesn't walk from the picture. 'Give him what he wants, it doesn't matter.' 'He's the biggest box office star in the world, if we shoot him sitting on the toilet, we'll make $150 million,' that was the thinking. That's why things got so frantic."

Because Canton's team at Columbia put the deal together, Chris Moore felt they deserved to get the project. "Which, in a way now, I respect. It's too bad for Zak and Adam and for me that I couldn't get somebody else to buy it. But the truth of the matter is, without Arnold, the movie might not have ever gotten *made*."

THE TURNOVER

Not only did *Last Action Hero* need a director, it also required rewriting of the script, and the rush to keep Arnold onboard meant fast action. While the stars did align to bring Schwarzenegger to this massive production, harmonic convergence wasn't exactly heading in Penn and Leff's direction. It all began with a January 1992 meeting designed to smooth over the deal at Arnold's offices above his Schatzi Restaurant in Venice. Among its attendees were Mark Canton, Barry Josephson, Lou Pitt, Michael Nathanson, Zak Penn and Adam Leff, and Shane Black.

Shane's role was then as a producer. Having written the first two *Lethal Weapon* scripts, Black had a great track record with Mark Canton (who oversaw their production at Warner Bros.). Black was also friends with Arnold after working together on *Predator,* in which Shane Black acted; his character was the first of Arnold's commando team to get slimed by that nasty alien headhunter.

"Shane said to us, 'I'm gonna help you guys, you're gonna work with me on it,' et cetera. We had one discussion about it," Zak Penn recalls. "He did call us again, but basically he didn't tell us for a month, and then we found out, he had already started rewriting the script. So we were thinking, 'Okay, I guess that's down the drain.' But we tried to be helpful; we actually said to him, 'We're going to bring you all our notes, all our jokes, all our earlier drafts. Anything we can do to help, let us know,' because we just wanted to be involved. For a couple weeks he let us be involved, but then he started to really resent us even asking questions."

Black was in fact apprehensive about *Last Action Hero* to begin with, a feeling that continued to return as the train pushed forward. "Everyone was trying to convince Shane to write," Chris Moore explains. "He didn't want to, because Shane had never rewritten anybody before, and he doesn't ever want to be rewritten. He was thinking, 'There's something wrong with this.' "

"I liked the idea. I liked some of the writing a lot, but I didn't want to take an assignment," Black confirms. "The truth is, I get very upset when people rewrite me. The truth is, if I'm handed a script, the first thing I do is I read the whole thing . . . I have to do it my way, it's now my job. I'll apologize for doing it, and if someone does it to me, I hope they apologize to me; but I got the script and knew how I wanted to do it. I felt so bad about what we were going to end up changing, I said to [Zak and Adam], 'Look, I would like to keep you in the process, I don't want to kick you out. If you have suggestions call me up. I'll show you the script. You can tell me things you like, or don't like.' "

To resolve the issue, a decision was reached to bring writer David Arnott into the mix. "David is the funniest guy I know, always has the newest jokes," says Black. A buddy of Shane's from their UCLA days together—part of a social circle known as the "Pad o' Guys," who lived in a Westwood fraternity-like environment—Arnott was also a client of David Greenblatt's. He had never written on his own, but collaborated on such projects as Renny Harlin's *The Adventures of Ford Fairlane* and later a *Tales of the Crypt* episode (both Joel Silver productions).

Bearing some resemblance to John Belushi, Arnott makes his living largely as a comic TV actor and looks back fondly on the ideas he and Shane developed in the rewrite process. The deal at that point wasn't defined—simply a concerted effort to get the picture made—and Shane's stature as a writer added cachet. "He was essentially there to shepherd me," Arnott explains, "and in all fairness, no one would have hired me without him. I wasn't anyone that anybody was willing to bank this movie on."

Arnott recalls that in February, "Shane called me and said, 'David, they're really interested in this script; they're interested in me maybe doing a rewrite on it, and I don't really want to do it. But I would love to sort of keep my fingers in, because there's something here. Would *you* be interested?' At the time, I was interested. Shane and I had always talked about working on something." Arnott then gave *Last Action Hero* a look. Black and Arnott realized an opportunity to spoof action movies *and* illustrate the love affair the kid has with those movies.

"All of a sudden it dawned on us that we really had a chance to make the *Wizard of Oz* of action movies, the *E.T.* of action movies. What if an action movie wasn't about any of the action?" says Arnott. "Adventure movies are really what they are. A lot of times people forget that, they substitute action for adventure. So we basically said, 'Well, let's do it. Let's do this job.' "

It was only when Schwarzenegger got involved that Black and Arnott were convinced that he could be the powerful icon to make the film work. "It wouldn't be just a love affair with some guy you never recognized. It would be the icon that sells the thematic material that we're trying to express." For Black it was also a lesson in what was good about taking an assignment, "which was all the excitement I felt toward the material. What was bad was the, 'Well, there's some *money* in it.' Because unless the excitement is everything, the money won't follow. . . . I learned to ignore the pressures of 'This is a big picture' and just think in terms of story. Even if that's not the way the film turned out, I learned that I was on the right track to be thinking about story, not 'summer picture.' To this day, I will never go into a movie thinking, 'This is a big summer release.' I'll think, 'Do the movie first, *then* worry about where it gets released.' "

The concept of a real-life character breaking the fourth wall and entering the screen world wasn't particularly original, seen as far back as 1924's Buster Keaton classic *Sherlock, Jr.* Woody Allen more recently reversed the process in 1985 with his period piece, *Purple Rose of Cairo,* in which Jeff Daniels's character walks out of the screen and into a movie fan's life. But what caught people's interest in Zak Penn and Adam Leff's take was how the *Last Action Hero* became a replacement "father" to Danny Madigan, perhaps reflecting a sign of modern times.

Despite their differences of opinion, the Black-Arnott team was in sync with Penn and Leff on that note. On several others they would disagree, causing a nasty severance between the two writing teams. Penn and Leff failed in urging Columbia to hire *Back to the Future* writer Bob Gale to maintain their original script's fanciful tone and contractually took a pass at rewriting. Since they knew the train had left the station without them, they went on to set up Fox's *P.C.U.* with producer Paul Schiff.

David Arnott didn't even see *Extremely Violent* until months after he and Shane completed their script and recalls Zak and Adam's "Was it a dream? Or was it not a dream?" take on the script's ending. "The villain *within* the movie turns out to be the projectionist in the theater," Arnott recalls, "and he's always in shadow or wearing a mask." Black and Arnott concentrated on changing the "one-joke premise" of knowing all the movie clichés and set act three in the *real* world, when Slater comes out of the movie, and all devices he used in the movies *don't* work.

"More important, *that* was where the movie was going to become the *E.T.* of action movies, or the *Wizard of Oz* of action movies, in that, 'What if this character starts to realize about what his life is?' A speech that got rewritten so many times by everyone—initially it was Shane's speech—was a wonderful speech about the main character all of a sudden realizing, 'Wait a minute, you think you've got problems. I'm a fictional character. I have two kids, I might have had three but someone ran out of typewriter ribbon.' And 'Your four-year-old kid, we're gonna kill him off because it's interesting. It doesn't matter how it affects me.' It's that weird fantasy world where, as a writer, you don't think of your characters as caring one way or another."

In Black and Arnott's approach, Danny's father's acting career comprised of one scene "where he plays the sad hero who gets shot right away. It's one line," says Black, who loved the notion of the kid contacting his dad through the screen for one brief moment. "It was really touching to me. But it was considered a tangent. We wanted to do a film that was more about the kid and his transformation . . . and that was all grist. It didn't really involve Arnold as the principle. This is not, by the way, Arnold's input. This was the people making the movie, designing it for him.

"The sense was, 'No, this is an Arnold summer picture,' [meaning] that everything that was 'out there' was now a tangent," says Black. "I wish there were less fear in the process of making movies for that kind

of money. I wish they were still willing—even at that monetary level—
to try things and experiment."

STOKING THE COALS

Subsequent drafts focused more on Jack Slater, not an unusual change
once a star signs on. In Penn and Leff's original draft, they deliberately
wrote the hero as one-dimensional until the end, when he realizes that
violence serves no purpose in a civilized world. In the rewrites, Black
and Arnott provided the hero with more traditional backstory, including an ex-wife, a daughter, and a dead son, thus adding character
dimension.

In Penn and Leff's version, the kid takes up guns inside the movie
because of invincibility from the fact he is actually human, while the
characters in the movie are celluloid creatures. "Therefore, the kid's
actually *stronger* in their world," says Leff regarding the kid's transformation. "It's Arnold who has to stop him, bring him back, and therefore
teach himself a lesson that the cycle of blood and violence and revenge
will never end and never solve anything."

David and Shane sat down to hash out a bunch of ideas and threw
a bunch out. One scene had Slater and the kid trapped at the dead
end of an alley after Slater shot all his bullets. Throughout the sequence
the bad guys approach, and the writers put a little hair on the screen.
"You know, that might irritate you in the audience," says Arnott. "All
of a sudden the Slater character goes, 'Wait a minute' and reaches up
and grabs the hair and pulls it down. Where in *his* world, because it's
the same size, it's like nine feet long. He skewers three guys with it,
and he and the kid make their escape.

"There are certain things you can do in movies," says Arnott, citing
as examples the Uma Thurman box from Jack Rabbit Slim's scene in
Pulp Fiction or Woody Allen pulling Marshall McLuhan out of a movie
theater line in *Annie Hall.* "You *can* do things that really don't make
sense as long as they work. . . . There were *so* many ways to go it was
almost scary. What if the bad guy held New York hostage and wanted
$10 million? Well, what does he want money for—he's fictitious? What
if he wants to be real? If you burn a print of a movie do the characters
die? Or do you have to burn all the prints? Or go back to where the
negative was?"

At one point, the villain let loose King Kong on New York again. Other ideas were to create a *Ghostbusters* ending with the Stay-Puff Marshmallow Man and to let "Death" out of the *Seventh Seal.* "It's still in the final part," Arnott says of the sequence where Ingmar Bergman's Death enters the theater. "It's a perfect example of how, in rewriting a script, certain things stay that don't make sense anymore. But where it's set up properly, you would understand a moment where Death comes into the theater, Danny pulls the gun, and he says, 'Forget it, I've had it up to here with you, Mister, who stays and who goes. Well, I'm telling you this one stays,' meaning, 'You took my dad, but you're not going to take [my surrogate father].' That could have been a real moment. As it is, it's in the movie, it's not anything. It's just there."

The two writers set up their new ending, where, in the real world, if the Slater character dies, he really dies. So Danny goes to the theater to help Slater get back into the screen. Nick (the projectionist) then reveals himself to be the Devil. In addition to setting up a number of known movie props and characters, Black and Arnott created "the Ripper," Slater's villain who had killed his son. When Slater faces off with the Ripper, Nick stands in the way, holding the sword from *Gunga Din.* "Nick's got all these weird movie props—the phone from *Dial M for Murder*—he's got this sword and Danny goes, 'What's this?' He says, 'This is the sword from *Gunga Din.*' The kid goes, 'What's *Gunga Din?*' Nick says, 'You don't know? *Gunga Din* is, like, the first action movie, one of the best movies. . . .' 'Get out of the way, Nick,' says the kid. 'You know, you gotta get by me, kid.' Throughout the movie the kid has never fired a gun.

"But he's got Slater's gun," says Arnott, and Nick tries getting Danny to shoot him under the guise that if he does, then Nick's got his soul. "Whose better soul to steal than these young kids who sneak into R-rated movies and live for the violence? So he's basically going to do it. Nick is goading the kid by making fun of his dad. . . . We were really writing a movie about a 'real-world kid' who's got no real-world father, meeting up with a 'fictitious father' who loses his fictitious son. The two of them find surrogates in each other, but they obviously can't stay together because they're from different worlds."

Once Danny's about to fire the gun at Nick, Slater puts his hand on the kid's wrist. "Don't do it, don't fire that gun," the hero says. "That's what he wants you to do." Then Shane got an idea for the ending, where the kid looks at Nick, then puts the gun down. "Nick, the Devil, says, 'What are you gonna do, kid? Your friend is dying, you're not gonna help him? C'mon,' sensing that he's losing," says Arnott. "The kid says, 'Nick, when I was younger and my dad was around, my dad and I used to play cowboys and Indians. All I ever really needed was this.' And he clicks his finger in a fake gun, and he sort of looks at it, and there's a pause. The kid aims his finger at Nick and just says the word 'BANG!' and a thick hole blows in him. He goes 'BANG!' Another hole. Nick's saying, 'What the . . . ?' And the kid goes 'guh-guh-guh-guh-guh . . .' and all these holes blow in him. Not to sound really corny, but he essentially kills him with his *imagination.* . . . And we thought, 'God, that's good.' It's almost as if you want to write a movie around that scene—just so you can write that scene."

Black and Arnott's overall approach wasn't a send-up, but rather a fantasy-adventure intending to put the action genre to bed—literally, the last one. The rewriters once met with Zak Penn and Adam Leff to pitch their ideas. "We wanted them to know the way we were going, thinking, mind you, foolishly, that these guys were going to say, 'Wow, you guys are great! You've taken our script and made it so much better.' I'll never forget it. They just looked at us," Arnott recalls. "I understand now why a lot of guys who rewrite other people don't want to meet them. It's a very uncomfortable moment, because for them it was their spec. It was their baby, and it got taken from them. There are only two things they can do. They can either be really depressed and despondent about it, or they can be just the opposite. More often than not, they're not going to be the opposite.

"It's just such a subjective medium that there's always going to be validation from somebody," says Arnott, who realized that others in town obviously liked Penn and Leff's script. "I'm sure there are people who were telling Zak and Adam, 'You guys got screwed. God, you wrote such a great script and I can't believe they brought these guys in to rewrite you.' Those people weren't necessarily saying that to be Machiavellian, or manipulative—they really felt that way. I mean, I don't feel that way. Maybe this sounds arrogant, but I think Shane and I made *Last Action Hero* a much better movie, a much better script, than what Zak and Adam wrote. But what am I gonna say?"

The first time Shane showed Zak and Adam pages, he literally thought they were going to throw things. "Zak had expressed such anger that I was taking things in the wrong direction than he had wanted, and I apologized," says Black. "I realized that I had made a mistake in trying to involve them in the process, because I knew I was going to change everything. Rather than pretending we're still going to be buddies, I had to accept at the onset, 'You know what? If someone did this to me, we probably wouldn't be buddies.'

"I should have just said, 'Zak, I apologize but now that I'm on the project you're not going to like what I'm doing. So maybe we should not talk about something that's just going to prove upsetting to us. It's now in the realm of business so there's nothing I can do about preserving any friendship here over the script. I am going to change your words, and not just a couple of them.' And I did, I changed a whole hell of a lot, and David changed the rest of it."

The reasons the original writers disagreed with the rewrites became quickly apparent. "Think of the first scene: It's a horrible, scarred serial killer chucking a kid off the roof of the building," says Penn of the opening sequence of *Last Action Hero*. "It's not even an exciting action scene. It's just this awful, horrible scene. In fact, I got a lot of shit from people. My friend's brother, who has four little kids, is saying to me, 'That movie shouldn't have been so frightening.' It's, like, 'I didn't write that scene.' That's way too large for little kids to see that."

Penn and Leff opened their version with a softer touch, without the Ripper character or Slater's kid, but rather a comical action scene at the Beverly Center shopping mall. "This woman has her kid in a baby carriage, she's pushing it along, and the bad guys are coming one way toward an escalator. Slater's going the other, and the baby goes flying through the air and he catches it and shoots the bad guy with the other hand. Slater runs into the parking lot, and he runs out of bullets. But he has one of those guns with the laser scope on it," Penn recalls.

"He's sitting there and he doesn't know what to do. There's guys coming at him from all directions. He puts some gum in his ears, and he takes the gun and he fans it out over the parking lot with his laser scope. There's a brief moment, a pause, and then all the car alarms in the lot go off at the same time. The bad guys all fall to their knees with their ears in pain, and [Slater] runs out of there. Then you pull back and you realize you were just watching a trailer."

Zak felt that the Shane-David team shifted the parody of the hero to much more of the Mel Gibson–Bruce Willis archetype, "the wisecracking, angry, down-on-his-luck cop, which is a pretty enormous change and pretty much pervades every line of Arnold's dialogue. I think, frankly, that it hurts the movie tremendously, because the whole point of the movie was the counterpoint between the kid who's smart and who's like us, and this other character who's a fantasy character, who's an idiot . . . who's literally one-dimensional.

"Instead, the Arnold character [in the final movie] doesn't seem any less real than the kid's character," Penn explains. "They both have backstories, it's just that Arnold lives in a separate world. The second key change would be that the kid and the hero come back into the real world, which we don't do until the very end.

"I'd say the third [change] is the addition of the mobsters. They're taking the movie out of the strict action movie genre and trying to make it a parody of many different kinds of movies. Some of it's a parody of James Bond movies, some of it's a parody of action movies, and some of it's a parody of buddy camp noirish movies. It's pretty astounding to see how badly they screwed it up," says Penn, breaking into laughter at the thought of a film he can't sit through.

It was harder for Zak Penn to laugh about it when it happened. "Could you come up with a better crash course in Hollywood?" he wonders. "From how we got an agent, and that whole thing, which was a very extreme Hollywood agent story . . . to the sale, which was an insane roller coaster, which was crazy. To the movie itself, which is going to go down in history as an all-time case study.

"It very quickly opened my eyes to both the incredible excess, and also the incredible cynicism [of today's Hollywood]," Penn says. "It would be like working on the O. J. Simpson trial for your first case—on the prosecution side, not on the defense." But the learning curve wasn't limited to Zak and Adam.

"Here's what was frustrating," says David Arnott. "We *got* Arnold Schwarzenegger. He *signed* to do the movie. If you buy into the marketing of that, it ensures that people are going to see it, more so than if you got [B-movie action hero] Jeff Speakman or one of those guys. So you don't *have* to necessarily give people what they expect to see, because they're already going to come. Who better to cast in a movie in which you can maybe take some chances?"

While the original writers did not continue speaking to Black and Arnott, they received occasional revisions as they would go to executives. "These were always locked-down scripts with your number on it, printed over," Leff recalls, "with direct orders you had to sign off, that you would not pass this to your grandmother." Steve Roth, who wasn't at first privy to the rewrites, had to read them while sitting in Mark Canton's office.

"Honestly, you couldn't really tell from the script if this would work or not," Leff continues. "I wouldn't say that we were walking around going, 'Oh God, we're heading for a train wreck.' I'd say that we were a little baffled, but who knew? 'Maybe this will work,' was our feeling, and 'Hey, that was a good idea. Maybe he should come out of the movie earlier and go back into the movie in the end. Yeah, that's true, that's a good turn.' We were learning from masters. But that was a fairly minor slice of our lives at the time . . . we were on to pitching our next movie."

Shane Black was equally disappointed with the outcome of *Last Action Hero*. "This is supposed to be a kid who's very wise, and wry," says Black of Danny's character. "We wrote him as a little older. The kid was in high school. And [the studio] chose to play the kid as a darling. I thought he should be kind of a wise-ass kid, like Anthony Michael Hall from *Sixteen Candles* . . . but it was wrongly instructed by the process, by the studio, by everybody to be *cute*. I hated *Home Alone*. I don't like cute. I like *real kids*. You know what real kids are like. They're not precious, they're not darling, they're assholes.

"It should have been a movie about wonder and sadness. It was instead a movie about crowd-pleasing moments where little boys are just screaming, '*Yeahh,*' like we were supposed to cheer. Satisfying an audience and making them cheer are two different things. One you can try, and then you hope they're satisfied enough that they cheer. The other, if you *try* to make them cheer, well, good luck with presenting a movie that is so charming that it's *aware* that it's charming.

"Tell the story first, and if you're a good writer, we'll be charmed out of our socks," Black continues. "But if you keep pushing into people's faces when the tears come and try to milk it, it's not going to happen. So the studio was so afraid to leave any avenue unmilked, I think, that in *Last Action Hero* they made this very obvious movie that tried to please everyone and ended up pleasing essentially no one. Our way wasn't necessarily the only way [the movie could take]. But I do know that, for the time we were in that room, we weren't writing the big hit studio movie. We were writing the best, fun, most interesting version.

"It's like two comedy writers throwing a ball back and forth, trying to come up with a routine for Garry Shandling," Black says. "We just sat there and did jokes all day and pitched things and threw paper balls back and forth and we would get excited. While we were getting excited, the studio was going to market it and would get clinical. They were assessing if things worked for women, or worked for old people, or worked for cats and dogs. Pretty soon I realized we were getting all excited trying to do something that may be breaking some ground or is a little out there. No one wants to be 'out there.' They want to say, 'There's a formula that we have.' "

Like telemarketing a consumer product, "if you start getting creative, you'll lose your sale. That's what they were thinking. Stick to the pitch. Audiences want 'Spielberg-meets-this-meets-that.' On the first day's meeting, I brought up a scene and one of the executives laughed and said, 'Gee, but that's not a scene in a movie that makes $200 million.' I realized we were sunk. That's what the studio's goal was from day one. You can't set out to make a picture that makes $200 million. That's like a guy who steps up to the plate and takes one of those home run swings and whiffs. You just have to meet the *ball*."

BRINGING IN THE CONDUCTOR

With Black and Arnott's rewrite completed, it was time to find a director to take charge of the train. Scripts had gone out to such A-list filmmakers as Richard Donner (*Superman, Lethal Weapon*), Penny Marshall (*Awakenings, Big*), Garry Marshall (*Pretty Woman*), Larry Kasdan (*The Big Chill*), Joel Schumacher (*The Lost Boys, Dying Young*), and the Zucker brothers.

John McTiernan, who's had the fortune of previously working with such icons as Sean Connery (*Hunt for Red October, Medicine Man*), Bruce Willis (*Die Hard, Die Hard III*), and Arnold Schwarzenegger himself (*Predator*),was not initially solicited. While the Black-Arnott draft attracted some interest, and Larry Kasdan was very close to committing, nobody came onboard.

McTiernan, who ushered in the modern era of action pictures with 1988's *Die Hard,* would appear quite comfortable in his own "movie world" sitting around a poker table downing whiskey shots with The Terminator, James Bond, and John McClane by his side. Although not known for softer material, the Juilliard-trained McTiernan first aspired to be a theater director but then stumbled into action pictures after his small movie with Pierce Brosnan, *Nomads,* caught the attention of Joel Silver. Silver hired McTiernan in 1986 to direct *Predator.*

McTiernan was at first wary of *Last Action Hero* because of all the hype associated with the project. "In general, hype for me is counter-productive," says McTiernan. "I sort of shy away from things if there's a *lot* of hype involved, just because it is very hard to tell what's real from what's nonsense in a situation like that. People tend to talk themselves into all sorts of foolish things. So perhaps that may have been why I shied away from *Last Action Hero* the first time; there was just too much noise about it."

But always interested in branching out, McTiernan committed in mid-July 1992, reuniting the *Predator* team once again. "Shane and David and I, *and* Arnold, really did still view it as a fairy tale, as the *Wizard of Oz* or *Cinderella.* I read it as a fairy godfather story, sort of a *Cinderella* for boys. Whether it was that when it hit the movie theaters, I don't know."

McTiernan feels that the principal difficulties with *Last Action Hero* were its advertising, "and to some extent it was sold as something it wasn't, and what it was never intended to be. The sense of it being a great action movie, the selling of it as a great action movie, was really what the studio generated. There was, not a unanimity on every bit of how we do X, Y, and Z on the creative team, but a general fairly solid agreement that just stayed right through, about what was the nature of this piece and where is its heart. I still believe in the piece, and I think the original idea was a great one."

Columbia executives Mark Canton and Peter Guber could now go to Japan and say, "We've brought you Arnold for the summer" to their bosses at the Sony headquarters. Everything looked exciting as *Last Action Hero* was being talked up around town. McTiernan liked Black and Arnott's ending with the imaginary gun, but then things got a little scrambled.

"The studio all of a sudden realized that the message might be re-interpreted as 'Hollywood is the Devil, and we're bad.' I think they got scared," David Arnott recalls, regarding the Nick-as-the-Devil take on the ending. "*The Exorcist* was a big hit years ago, and it's not like they don't make movies that have that kind of religious thing. But it still surprises me to this day that for anything with some slightly religious overtone, people say, 'Well, maybe we should rethink this.' It is still one of the few taboo grounds."

Thus, more rewriting. "At the very end, after everyone was gone, which we, the movie viewer, saw but no one else did, Nick wasn't in fact the Devil but an Angel," says Arnott. "He was Danny's dead dad who came back to Earth to save his son. We wrote that to appease everybody, and everyone looked at it and went, 'Ahhh, it's *sooo* Hollywood and corny.' It just wasn't right. We weren't thrilled with it, but we wrote it. It's the equivalent of a dream scene where you wake up and go, 'Oh, it was all a dream.' It's like everything that we set up was wrong, but it still allowed us to keep the Devil aspect of it. In retrospect, who's to say? Maybe that version of the movie might have been a huge, huge hit. I mean, you don't know. But I understand why people got scared.

"Not to keep harping [or] sound too lofty or arrogant, but if you're trying to make the *Wizard of Oz* of action movies, it means you're probably going to shoot something that's a little unconventional and a little out there," Arnott continues. "Someone's got to take a chance. It's not our money, we're not spending the $40 to $80 million. So if the guys writing the big checks say, 'I'd rather do this,' you ultimately have to go, 'Well, I understand. It's your call to make.'"

The darkness of tone in Black and Arnott's rewrite had some executives worried that they weren't making another *Back to the Future;* they were making something that couldn't be released as a PG-13 movie.

FINDING THE FORMULA

The mingling of so many differing ideas from experienced Hollywood figures clouded the project's vision. Would it be an action movie or a comedy? "You had *so* many eight-hundred-pound gorillas as part of that movie," says Chris Moore, "that nobody actually took responsibility to look at the dailies and say, 'You know what? This is all over the place.' Listen, I just watched the movie, I didn't work on it. But from the original script to what it became, there was no one single vision. Most movies that are good are because of a guy who says, 'I know the movie I want to make,' and everybody comes on his train and they make a great movie. Because you had Shane Black writing it, Arnold Schwarzenegger starring in it, and John McTiernan directing it, and they were all trying to be so polite and courteous and respectful of each other's opinions, nobody stepped up and said, 'Listen, this movie to me is *this*, this is what we should do.' "

The Columbia executives also differed in their interpretations. "So one of them is out there talking about it, 'Well, I love the way it spoofs all action movies,' so you have all those spoof scenes thrown in there," Moore says. "Then somebody else is saying, 'Wait a minute, this is like a nineties *Wizard of Oz:* You have the kid, his father just died, he's walking into a movie, got some heart in it, it's a relationship between Arnold and the kid and then his mom comes in.' Then you got the other kind who says, 'Listen, I don't care about *any* of that stuff; this is just a giant Arnold Schwarzenegger action movie. We've got to blow some shit up, we've got to have some bad guys, we've got to have a dude running around with a marble in his eye,' playing with all that. Then no one says, 'Well, they can't all fit together,' you know what I mean? Okay then, make two movies."

As Columbia execs grew more concerned that the Black and Arnott rewrite might be hanging on too many "inside jokes," they began looking for a new approach. Now if it was perverse that the studio hired the writer of whom the original writers were making a parody, Shane Black and David Arnott were then taken off the project by the screenwriter to whom they were paying a tribute in *their* version. The *Gunga Din* homage "was actually really our personal nod to William Goldman, before Goldman was even brought on the project," says Arnott. "Goldman describes *Gunga Din* as one of the original action movies."

Goldman took the rewrite job after at first declining. But a million dollars for a few weeks' work brought him in to give this project some heart. Goldman streamlined the existing draft, making Danny younger and changing the demonic projectionist into the kid's best friend. In the finished version of *Last Action Hero,* the gangster activity centered around the funeral of a flatulent mobster, "Leo the Fart," and his Sicilian foe Vivaldi, who mis-spouts clichés.

Prepping for a start date in November 1992 to meet Columbia's summer release plan, everybody was writing pages. "*Last Action Hero* was a perfect example of moviemaking by committee. It became everybody's version of 'the Bear,' what they thought the movie was about. In the process it became nobody's movie," says George Huang, whose job at the time was to keep all the pages organized between the rewrites, including writing by McTiernan as well. "Everyone was writing it. Hell, I even think I threw a few pages in."

Columbia's marketing plans were on as similar a fast track as the movie, conflicting somewhat with the creative team. "That's on the line of somehow selling it so broadly, or in so many directions, in so many ways, that you do blur 'What have you got here?' The initial intention came from the guys, from Zak and Adam, and carried right through with David and Shane's work, and Bill Goldman's, that this was a fairy tale," says McTiernan. "That was followed with original studio decisions about what is the rating of this movie." The studio designed it as PG-13 right from the beginning, shooting for a younger audience. Therefore, the picture couldn't concentrate on violence.

"I do remember somewhere near the end [of the movie], one of the principal disagreements, if you will, was having the kid resolve his problems with a gun in his hand," McTiernan explains of a scene that several found inappropriate. They reached a compromise that Danny could hold the gun, and wave the gun, but it could only be at a non-person. "So he can do it at the Death out of the Bergman movie, but he shouldn't be going around to real people; because you really don't want to have that in three thousand theaters across the country all through the summer saying, 'Kids, here's how you resolve your problems in life.' "

Shane and David were brought back during the last month and a half of filming to try putting the runaway train on course. "This sounds like I'm tooting my own horn, but it's really a sign of frustration," Black says, "because I worked so hard to make what I felt would be a good movie and then watched everyone seem to like it but make changes anyway for commerce, thinking they were smart. Now, my movie, David's movie, might have bombed anyway. We'll never know. That's the part that bothers me. We'll never *know*. Now when someone says, 'I think it should be this way, I'm changing your work,' even if the movie flops, you still can't say I was right. Because you'll never know what would have happened the other way. They wouldn't let you find out.

"*Last Action Hero* was an exercise in just that," says Black. "Not being able to find out if our sort of 'out there ideas' would have worked, because they were reined in and disregarded and rewritten to fit a more universal formula by my favorite writer, as a matter of fact, William Goldman, who I still think is a brilliant writer. I just think on this one he was sort of told what to do and did his job."

At one point Black met with Goldman to say how much he envied him. Asked why, Shane said that it was because Goldman worked on movies in the 1970s, when *The Exorcist, The French Connection,* and *Dirty Harry* (some of Black's favorites) were produced. To Shane, that period was the heyday of studio filmmaking, and Goldman agreed.

FOURTH-DOWN SCRAMBLE WITH SUDDEN DEATH LOOMING

On November 2, 1992, about a year after Penn and Leff's spec script sold, *Last Action Hero* began production. The picture shot around L.A. and in Times Square, New York. The project that started with more producers than desired essentially ended up having none. Because he didn't have any time at night, McTiernan spent his lunches catching up on sleep. Steve Roth was largely pushed out of the way by the studio brass.

Penn feels that since he and Adam were closer to the studio's target audience, their role should have been given greater consideration. "Look, we're not only the original writers, but we're also the main character," says Penn. "That's us ten years ago, not Shane. He had a very different childhood. Most important, we are the target audience. At the time, everyone else was in their thirties and Arnold in his forties. Everyone else working on the project was removed. They were the people who had made the movies that we grew up on. But we were thinking, 'We're the ones who were the fans here, so we're the closest to understanding what we want to see in this movie.' That's what was so ironic about it. It was just like a bunch of people trying to parody themselves.

"It's just strange," says Penn of the studio's decision to bring in Shane and David. "I think people get confused between a satirical sense of humor and other forms. I mean, Shane definitely writes great—what Adam and I used to call 'deadpan tough talk.' He's great at writing *that.*

"Shane made five times as much money as we did," Penn continues. "I don't feel compelled to do the same things he did. I mean, the idea that someone would come to me with *their* original idea as their first script that's going to make their name in Hollywood. Then to take that credit from them, *even* if I did all the work—even if it was all rewritten by me—I don't think I could live with myself. . . . It would be so easy for them to have just been understanding, appreciative, and helpful, because the truth is, they all made a lot of money off our idea."

"Zak and Adam had just finished writing it not long ago, you have to understand. Then I came on and started rewriting," says Black. "They sold it pretty quick. So that within a month of a sale to have it being changed, you're not far from the day when you typed 'The End' and thought, 'There, we're done, and we're so proud.' I think they were still very attached to the material. But the drafts exist. If someone wants to read the drafts and decide who was an asshole, they can read their draft; they can read my draft. They can see why the kids chose theirs; they can see why I chose to change what they selected. I will stand by whatever choices I made, and I can only feel bad that feelings were hurt if they were and apologize for not having a solution. But there is no solution."

In an age where studios routinely hire "script doctors" onto existing productions and pay them small fortunes to tweak characters, punch up the humor, or add a line or two, it's no wonder that the general rule is "never to rewrite a friend's script." Perhaps there is no solution to the battles that go on every day between writers and rewriters of their work. *Last Action Hero* may have been a cautionary tale for all involved. For Shane Black it meant a return to spec scripts, subsequently writing *The Long Kiss Goodnight*.

As original writers, Penn and Leff were disappointed by not receiving "Screenplay by" credit for the movie (reduced to "Story by"). "We were not happy about that, even though in retrospect, sometimes I'm relieved that we didn't get credit," says Penn. "It's just typical Hollywood bullshit. The whole credit system is absurd, if you ask me. It doesn't even have to say, 'Original screenplay by.' It could just say, 'Based on an original screenplay by . . . and written by Shane Black . . . ' I mean, if I wrote a book, that's exactly what it would say, even if they threw out every single thing in the book. It lets people know the source material is 'this,' and then was rewritten. What was difficult, in fact, was that the story was the thing we *didn't* write, because that's one of the things they changed.

"We wrote a lot of the scenes, and a lot of the jokes that are in the movie, and we came up with the premise," says Penn. "But the story, I consider to be the plot, the structure of the movie. . . . It's just such an inaccurate thing to provide a 'story' credit. We lost a lot of money because of it." At the Schatzi restaurant meeting, Zak and Adam understood that they were not having their screenwriting credit taken away. Yet Black and Arnott filed for WGA arbitration, considering the great extent of their changes, and won. William Goldman did not receive credit on the picture, nor did he want any.

At the initial point Penn and Leff were removed from the process, Chris Moore fought for his clients to get a shot at writing for Schwarzenegger and McTiernan, but couldn't overcome the powers that be. "Zak and Adam had a definite point of view, which I respect, and I think that's the way creative people should be. Unfortunately, they were in the 'jungle,' right? They were basically starting to give their guides hassles. It reaches a point where the guides would say, 'All right, forget it' and leave, and these guys are just stuck in the middle of the jungle.

"There was some heart to it, that original draft, that I don't even think Zak and Adam admit to themselves," says Moore. "I think that part of it to them was just kind of plot-point. They really were just writing the jokes. What's interesting about it, to me, is how Steve Roth and Arnold had fallen in love with the story."

Aside from the crazy-making development phase, everybody involved felt the project's incredibly short postproduction period definitely hurt the process. "We definitely suffered from trying to make a release date," says David Arnott. "Certainly postmortem, but even during, they all said, 'What are we doing? This is insane.' But they had already agreed to do it. The train had left the station at that point, so all you could do was get on it." But Columbia was determined to release *Last Action Hero* on its assigned June 18, 1993, opening, fearing that postponing would be a sign that something was rotten in Culver City. An editing team worked around the clock, creating undue pressure. The picture opened to $15.2 million (the studio had projected $20 million) against the *Jurassic Park* second week of $38 million, and *Last Action Hero* dropped by 47 percent to $8 million for a low, fourth-place second weekend.

"No one else was stupid enough to open against *Jurassic Park,*" says Penn. "People were saying, 'Who could have expected it?' I'm thinking, 'Well, Spielberg did make *E.T.* He did, three times in the past, make a movie that shattered all box office records, so it's not [surprising]. The idea that everyone was so shocked that *Jurassic Park* did well? Okay, it was an enormous best-seller, great idea, done by the number one commercial director of all time: It doesn't take a brain scientist to figure that out.

"*Last Action Hero*—and I think *Waterworld* is an even more annoying example—with both of these movies the media attacks them because they sunk all this money," says Penn. "Imagine if AT&T was building a new phone line, and it blew up, for example. And so they had to spend a hundred million dollars on it. You wouldn't see mocking articles saying, 'Can you believe AT&T lost all this money?' *Waterworld*, their set sunk! That's not their fault. . . . Here's the key thing—both *Last Action Hero* and *Waterworld* are not just like run-of-the-mill sequels, they're not just some incredibly callous attempt to wring money out of people. I mean, they are somewhat that. But at least with *Last Action Hero,* it was an original movie that was unlike other movies."

This historic studio debacle all began with a clever thought Zak Penn considered trashing in the first place. To many in the industry, the problems of *Last Action Hero* were attributed to karmic retribution to a studio flagrantly burning up lots of yen from its Japanese parent corporation, which seemed to have little clue to how its motion picture division was run. *Last Action Hero* was the climax of many embarrassing flops that finally caught Sony's attention.

FEAR, FRUSTRATION, AND FALSEHOOD

The media's reporting of *Last Action Hero* reflected very much of what those in the industry felt. However, one craw that stuck out for Columbia was when a *Los Angeles Times* freelance writer, Jeffrey Wells, reported on a bogus preview screening that gave *Last Action Hero* awful reviews. Whether or not that screening actually happened (no participants were ever located), it led to a war between Columbia and Los Angeles's major publication. The studio was outraged and threatened in a letter to ban reporters from future studio screenings unless Wells was removed from ever writing about Columbia projects. The newspaper shrugged, standing by its story.

Perhaps some people in the business "had it in" for the film, but *why* they did is a more intriguing question. Was it due to the fact that everybody in the industry has an adverse reaction toward the process of movies "made by committee," the exact fate of *Last Action Hero*? Despite that, they can become rather hypocritical over the subject when it comes to *their* studio's movies.

The great economist Adam Smith once said, "People of the same trade seldom meet together, even for merriment and diversion, but the conversation ends in a conspiracy against the public." Of course, this was long before the origin of Hollywood's business as usual. Nonetheless, *Last Action Hero* failed to live up to Columbia's expectations. "It's possible that that's a function of all the original hype," says McTiernan. "If you get so much nonsense and false aspiration built up around something, then it gets a life of its own. You're continually dealing with the ghost of something that never was real."

The movie sold better around the world than in the United States, perhaps a result of both Arnold's global star power and the lack of such press scrutiny overseas. "I think that initial vision was clouded by its high profile, probably," says McTiernan, who met Zak Penn and Adam Leff on one occasion but never had the opportunity to work with them. "It had been sold so aggressively that it had to appear to be too many things to too many people. That's not a very good creative environment, it's damaging. Too much of a circus is damaging.

"One of the most dangerous things is being involved in a corporate situation where there . . . are so many interests, where a whole corporation may have bet its future on the damn thing," adds McTiernan. "From the moment I saw the 'Big Ticket of '93' in the first test-ad copy for the particular ad campaign, I anticipated that that would provoke a negative reaction, that it was just arrogant. Several of us said that to the studio."

According to Shane Black, his and David's version might have also failed to meet audience expectations. "Just because of the gods of film, you never know. My frustrations lie with not being able to try things because of fear. The biggest problem a writer in the spec market will have is to sell their spec script for precisely the uniqueness of it, only to have *fear* enter the picture—almost immediately—to start canceling out one by one the very things that made it sell.

"I don't hold anything against the people who tried so hard to make that movie work," Black continues. "John McTiernan tried his *best,* we tried, *Goldman* tried. The studio was afraid. I guess that's the only thing I have problems with—it's fear. I don't like people who start changing things out of fear and flinching."

PICKING UP THE PIECES

In the final analysis, Columbia grossed $121.2 million worldwide off its mega-production, a dollar-for-dollar tally comparable to the same year's (but not equally hyped) Sylvester Stallone vehicle *Demolition Man.* Thus, *Last Action Hero* became more of an emotional bomb than financial, and one would be hard-pressed to come across anybody involved in the picture who looks back with pride. Yet in a strange way, all of the participants—except for the writers—fulfilled their initial expectations.

Columbia's Barry Josephson delivered a movie when all the odds were against him. All the agents involved made plenty of money from their clients' earnings. Mark Canton continued to hold a powerful position at Columbia until exiting his post on Friday, September 13, 1996, with a reported $10 million settlement (and returning to a producing deal at Warner Bros.). Some of the pictures he backed at Columbia, such as *Air Force One* and *Men in Black,* made a fortune for the Sony studio the following year. Josephson moved on to run a production company with *Men in Black* director Barry Sonnenfeld, Michael Nathanson presides over MGM, and Peter Guber chairs Mandalay. (Showbiz veteran John Calley now runs Columbia's new regime.)

Mike Medavoy abruptly lost his job at TriStar in January 1994. Having failed in the studio's *Last Action Hero* bid, he went on to make *Philadelphia,* directed by Jonathan Demme, and *Sleepless in Seattle,* a modern romance directed by Nora Ephron. *Sleepless* was a sleeper smash, grossing $228 million worldwide and boosting the careers of Tom Hanks and Meg Ryan. *Philadelphia* reined in $202 million around the globe and also brought Hanks an Academy Award.

InterTalent closed its doors in October 1992. Its agents dispersed, some later forming Endeavor, which quickly became a dominant Hollywood agency with a stellar list of clients. Chris Moore walked away from agenting to produce such movies as *Glory Daze* and *Good Will Hunting.* Bill Block, after a stint running ICM's motion picture department, became a top exec at Artisan Entertainment. And Jersey Films, where Wendy Rose had started the whole *Last Action Hero* engine, went on to make the edgy $8 million budgeted *Pulp Fiction,* which earned over $213 million around the world.

Whatever can be said of *Last Action Hero,* its concept provided a foundation that could have gone a million different ways. It started Zak and Adam's careers, although they now write separately. Penn sold his spec script, *Suspect Zero,* to Universal for $750,000 against $1 million, and he keeps busy with production rewrites on such movies as *Mighty Joe Young, Men in Black,* and *Small Soldiers.* Leff cowrote the story for Pauly Shore's *Bio-Dome* among several other projects. But their first break in Hollywood turned into a project from which they would prefer to distance themselves.

Chris Moore, reflecting on the "*Wizard of Oz* fairy tale" at the heart of *Last Action Hero,* sums up the feelings of almost everybody involved in its making. "For me, it was a life-changing experience. I went for another couple years where that happened a few more times. But it was definitely one of those things where—to this day—it still makes me so sad that I'll have to be fifty years old to go back and remake that movie the way it should be made. You can't just say, 'Okay, we fucked that up. Let's do it the right way now.' Because people will remember. They're not going to spend the money again. They're not going to do the whole deal.

"To me it was a core idea that I think had all the opportunity to stay right up there with *Jurassic Park,* and they would have each made $300 million at the bank, or stand the test of time," says Moore. "It was going *into* the Hollywood movie and being with your hero, and what that's like when you actually know about the real world but you're only twelve years old. There's all this stuff to play with. You can make fun of movies while doing that, but really, you're making fun of life in general.

"It was a sad experience in that sense," Moore concludes. "Going to the premiere was one of the things that was great. It was a big deal. Everybody was very nice to me and said things, and it was this *huge* ordeal. But you know, the movie wasn't good. It's not a good feeling to stand around a giant premiere when they spend $200,000 on a blow-up doll of Arnold and feel, 'Wow, it's just not that good, you know?' And it's sad, everybody knew it. Every single person knew. We were all just sitting there, walking around, having free sodas, and just looking at each other. Everybody smiling and shaking each other's hands."

Circumventing the Hollywood System

There are many inroads to a screenwriting career outside Hollywood's conventional spec market. In the rival world of screenwriting, it's only fitting to find an abundance of formal competitions, designed to judge scripts on their merit rather than heat. Merit is also subjective, or as *Deep Impact* scribe Michael Tolkin said, "As with most writers, I have mixed feelings about prizes unless I win them." Such competitions have nonetheless become a common way for the unknown writer to suddenly become known.

The Academy of Motion Picture Arts and Sciences oversees the highly regarded Nicholl Fellowship, which receives as many as five thousand submissions and offers up to five fellowships of $25,000 each year to writers without previous professional credits. Past winners have written such features as *Air Force One, Excess Baggage,* and *Speed 2,* and the major agencies now read every quarter-, semi-, and finalist in the Nicholl competition, looking for new talent. By winning the first Nicholl Fellowship in 1986, indie filmmaker Allison Anders was able to get off welfare and go on to write and direct *Gas Food Lodging* and *Mi Vida Loca.*

The Los Angeles–based Chesterfield Writer's Film Project and the Walt Disney Studios Fellowship offer wonderful opportunities, and outside of L.A., opportunities have grown. With local competitions sprouting throughout the country, writers have numerous places outside the realm of Southern California to get their material considered. For instance, Sundance Institute in Park City, Utah, also offers a five-day Screenwriters Lab. Serving as a judge for a screenwriting contest sponsored by the governor of Virginia, *Rain Man* producer Mark Johnson stumbled upon a script that launched writer Vince Gilligan's career and Johnson ultimately produced.

"I judged twelve scripts," Johnson recalls, "eleven not very good, and then one was *Home Fries*" (made into a 1998 Warner release). Gilligan's victory earned him only a small monetary prize, but was a solid entree to Hollywood without having to leave Virginia. "You certainly know within thirty pages that you're reading somebody who is able to complete the world in which their characters take place," says Johnson. "I wanted Vince to stay in

Virginia, in Richmond, because I was afraid he would lose the uniqueness of his voice if he came here and started writing what other Southern California screenwriters write about.

"He recently moved to Los Angeles because he's on *The X-Files*," says Johnson, "which he's enjoying and is actually a great experience for him. But Vince's material is very geographically fit. He writes of the South, but not the kind of South that we know from movies and literature. It's not the Deep South . . . but actually a fairly idiosyncratic South, with a humor that you don't associate with the characters."

Modern technology has allowed writers to remain in their indigenous environments. And because Hollywood loves what's unattainable, being further from the center of heat can add to a screenwriter's fire. "I've got several clients who *do* live out of town," says Gage Group agent Jon Westover. "I have one I've never even met. We have great phone rapport, though. Theoretically none of us really have to be here."

Filmmaking's Feeder Ponds

> HOW NOVEL IDEAS PIQUED HOLLYWOOD'S LATEST FRENZIES.
> TV OR NOT TV, THAT IS AN EXECUTIVE'S FIRST QUESTION.

Having your book turned into a movie is like seeing your oxen become bouillon cubes.

—JOHN LE CARRÉ

I'm delighted with television, because it used to be that films were the lowest form of art. Now we've got something else to look down upon.

—BILLY WILDER

AS TWENTIETH-CENTURY filmmaking flourished, novelists turned to Hollywood. To free Nathanael West from the drudgery of scriptwriting for RKO, a profession providing him $350 a week, when at the time an average newspaper reporter earned about $50, he wrote his biting Hollywood 1939 tale, *The Day of the Locust*. Among those to praise West's novel were Dashiell Hammett, F. Scott Fitzgerald, and Edmund Wilson. Yet it originally sold only 1,464 copies, making West's incomes from four novels total $1,280, or less than a month's work from writing screenplays.

Early motion pictures were often based on novels, and the list of novelists who traveled west for Hollywood's riches has been well documented. Fitzgerald's battles with drink while living in the San Fernando Valley are legendary, while Thomas Mann discovered paradise in the Pacific Palisades and brought out his brother Heinrich, who found work as a screenwriter at Warner Bros. After watching new-to-the-town Russian expatriate Ayn Rand stare at him in his open roadster outside his studio, Cecil B. DeMille hired her, first as an extra, then as a writer. She would later author her 1943 novel, *The Fountainhead*, after many up-and-down years as a junior screenwriter.

But then the best-selling books of the sixties and seventies, such as *The Other Side of Midnight* and Judith Krantz novels, didn't necessarily translate into features. Perhaps the lure of an underdeveloped market prompted novelists to pursue high-concept books, or those driven by heroic characters and thrilling action sequences. Today some novelists even write movie treatments simultaneously with their book proposals, and studios look for material far upstream, more eager than ever to get their hands on unpublished manuscripts and unproduced plays.

Books from best-selling authors carry a presold weight. A reported $10 million was paid for Michael Crichton's *Airframe*, and $6 million was paid to John Grisham for *The Rainmaker* and $8 million for *The Runaway Jury*. Scott Turow secured a multimillion-dollar deal with his unfinished *Laws of Our Fathers* from Universal, the studio that also paid Grisham $3.75 million for *The Chamber* before he had even written a word. As a follow-up to *Waiting to Exhale*, Terry McMillan's *How Stella Got Her Groove Back* sold in less than forty-eight hours to Fox for $1.5 million.

While it helps to have a *New York Times* best-seller, emerging novelists can just as easily find the film rights to their books going for the same astronomical numbers as spec scripts. Kenneth Atchity, a former comparative literature professor turned movie producer, proved this point when he took on a manuscript that thirty competing agencies had already rejected. The result was the sale of *Meg*, written by thirty-seven-year-old first-time novelist Steve Alten, who Atchity had not even met at the time.

When he had $48 in his account and lost his job at a wholesale meat plant, Alten was banking on the publication of his story about a treacherous seventy-foot-long, big-toothed shark that had mysteriously descended from the prehistoric Carcharodon megalodon. What if, through a freak of nature, this mammoth mega-monster lay trapped in the seven-mile-deep Mariana trench off Guam and rose up to terrorize

Hawaiian shores? Atchity was blown over by the concept when he read Alten's letter.

"Melville says in *Moby-Dick*, to write a mighty book you must have a mighty theme, and that's what I could see in Steve's query," says Atchity. "Very marketable, I saw it as *Jaws* meets *Jurassic Park*. But it needed a lot of work, which we did with him between March and September. And then we ran out of development money and said, 'Let's see if we can sell this.' "

Atchity sent the manuscript to producer Warren Zide who "went nuts over it." Only the first hundred pages went over to Disney, where Zide had a first-look deal, for the weekend read. Executives Allison Brecker and Jeff Bynum brought Alten's pages to the attention of Walt Disney Pictures president David Vogel. "They made us an offer on Monday morning," Atchity recalls. "ICM was then prepared to go out with it to everybody, but by the end of the day, Disney had doubled the offer they made early in the morning."

Alten accepted Disney's $700,000 bid, faced with the possibility that competitors might pass if they went wide looking for more money. "You know, you could do worse than being in business with Walt Disney Pictures," Atchity told Alten. "They're very serious about it, they're making you a solid offer on an unpublished book, it's only one hundred pages of an unpublished book." With movie rights in place, Atchity back-pedaled a $2.1 million two-book deal for Alten, then sold foreign book rights for another $1.4 million.

"People are looking for stories with beginnings, middles, and ends," says Atchity of *The Old Man and the Sea* meets *Moby-Dick* tale at the center of *Meg*. "There's a long tradition of 'big fish' stories that go back to the beginning of time. . . . So there's that mythic element in *Meg* that really makes it work." While skeptics were critical of its literary merit, the strategy of selling the film rights before the book deal benefited both the writer and the Disney studio, who would have had to pay more if the huge publishing deal had come first.

Like Alten's *Meg*, *Absolute Power* was a debut novel. It landed David Baldacci a whopping $2 million publishing advance before Castle Rock paid another million for rights to make the Clint Eastwood film. Relative newcomer Lorenzo Carcaterra carted away $2 million from Warner Bros. for his novel *Sleepers*, which became a 1996 Barry Levinson release.

Another bidding war that rocked the studios was Hollywood Pictures' acquisition of Nicholas Evans's first novel, *The Horse Whisperer,* which was made into a 1998 Robert Redford film. The heat generated from Evans's £350,000 U.K. book rights sale at the Frankfurt Book Fair led to a forty-eight-hour whirlwind bidding war once studios caught word, with Scott Rudin tossing in an initial $200,000 bid against a $1 million production bonus. Evans, an overnight success after years of trying his hand at screenwriting, watched with excitement as Sydney Pollack, Jon Peters, and Peter Guber jumped into the fray. Ultimately, Redford's commitment to star in the picture sweetened the final $3 million deal for what was then a 215-page manuscript.

After a cooling period of Hollywood's attention to novels during the 1980s, interest in purchasing film rights has been clearly revived. "You have more novelists who are writing almost directly for the screenplay form," says producer Jonathan Sanger. "You know exactly how it's going to be adapted, and when you look at the Grisham and Clancy books, they're perfect blueprints for movies. They were meant to be movies when they were conceived and they were written as novels as kind of a marketing tool. And they are."

Best-selling novels have obvious built-in marketing advantages. "Books are more frequently a source of motion pictures than they used to be," says producer Thom Mount. "But the downside is that [publishers] can generate a best-seller if they're clever about it. Particularly when there are only three or four chain bookstores that count and *The New York Times* best-seller list can be penetrated with a sale of fifty thousand hardback copies. If you're clever about marketing the book, you can pretty much drive it into the best-seller list, and from that you can begin to generate a film sale."

Mount feels more consideration should be given to selecting novels with compelling possibilities for film, rather than only looking at books that sell well. "No one can be faulted for making money by considering the books based on Scott Turow or John Grisham, or any of the other big-selling authors. And in the same way, you can't fight the James Bond series derived from Ian Fleming. What can you say? It's its own phenomena. But for each Grisham or Turow or Fleming, there should be a role of ours, on the part of the filmmakers, to embrace a more diverse kind of novel."

Comic Fred Allen once asked why any individual would take a year or two to write a novel when somebody could easily buy a book at the local store for just a few bucks. Historically novels have been paths to literary acclaim, but the money—and notice—often took years to follow. After all, Edgar Allan Poe, who craved fame and ultimately achieved it when the *New York Mirror* published 1845's "The Raven," a poem that was widely republished, waited a year to receive his paltry $10 fee from the newspaper.

The book market has changed, possibly as the result of the movie market, says Manifest's Janet Yang. "Books in Hollywood are always read as a basis for a potential film. It skews the whole literary industry. It's unfortunate, but it's just a fact of life. Everybody wants to make a buck."

WRITING THE GREAT AMERICAN ADAPTATION

What turns a novel into a satisfying motion picture is as mysterious as the spec market itself. "I tend to feel very strongly that good novels usually make bad movies," says Miramax's Jack Lechner. "The best movies that are adapted from novels tend to be from not very great novels: *The Godfather* or *Jaws*. . . . I don't think anyone would say *The Godfather* was one of the great novels of the twentieth century, but most people would say *The Godfather* is one of the great movies of the century.

"Partly it's because nobody minds very much if you change huge sections if it's not a great book to begin with," Lechner continues. "When you've got a really great novel, one of the things that makes it great is it tends to be unique to the literary form. It's something that really gets into the minds of the characters. It's inventive on the page. It does things that don't translate [to film] necessarily.

"Nine times out of ten, or more often, I read a novel and think, 'This is a really good novel, I see no reason why it should be a movie,'" says Lechner, who cites Anthony Minghella's adaptation of *The English Patient* as a rare exception. "It's a trap that development people fall into. You fall in love with something [and] as a result, you confuse that with thinking there's a reason that that's a movie, where in fact all it *really* is is some ego thing where you want to feel you have a piece of the thing you love."

As long as novels provide great characters and the seed of an idea that filmmakers can work with, they need not have perfect story structure, according to Spyglass's Jon Glickman. "If there is a huge marketable book and you get the sense that, like John Grisham, it has a built-in commerciality, you know they're going to sell the hell out of it. So you get involved because you have a lot of presold value, just on the title itself. Otherwise I think it's the same things you look for in a screenplay, just a good idea."

Because of that aggressive search for the good ideas in manuscripts, several producers have established New York offices simply to mine the literary material that can become that next big thing on screen. Scott Rudin, already a fixture in Manhattan's literary world, jumped into the game early on and was quickly followed by producers Arnold Kopelson, Danny DeVito, Richard and Lili Zanuck, and others.

As *Clockers* writer Richard Price once observed, "Writing a screenplay from your own novel is like a cannibal eating his own foot," so a studio often brings in a screenwriter to adapt the work.

"When the studios get a manuscript, they've got a goldmine there, not just the vein," says literary manager Ken Atchity. "When they pay for an original script, or when they commission an original script based on a treatment, a proposal, or a pitch, what they're getting is *hoping* they will get a vein of gold, but they don't have that whole mine to go back in to look at."

This is the primary reason why unpublished works can have such a great allure in Hollywood. "With an unpublished manuscript, if it's a good story, it's a good story," says Atchity. "Then [the book] comes out and extraneous concerns start entering into the picture like, 'How well did the book do?' 'How well is the book reviewed?'

"Even if you read a book and see a good story, any executive doing his homework has got to ask those other questions," Atchity concludes. "If they don't blow you away, then they go, 'I don't know if I should do this. Yeah, it's a good story, but how come it didn't do well?' And there are a million reasons why a book doesn't do well, from bad distribution to timing. A manuscript has that kind of virginal quality about it, nobody's seen it yet . . . and the executive could make a pitch for his boss to buy it at a good price. If it helps launch the book, then the executive is proved right."

While book authors are no doubt excited by the possibility of a big paycheck for their literary gifts, media critics fear the merging of the literary and visual worlds dilutes the possibility for wonderful literature to emerge in an impatient, money-hungry society.

"As Hollywood has grown more corporate, so has publishing," says

Miramax's Jack Lechner, "and there isn't the kind of patience for more literary novels. A lot of the people working in publishing want their novels predigested the way people in Hollywood want their movies predigested; and I don't think that always leads to what the audience wants, because the audience doesn't know what it wants until it sees it.

"The public usually has more interesting taste than the people who work in the studios, and the literary public has *far* more interesting taste than the people who are working in publishing right now," says Lechner. "Some of the novels that have made the best movies are not the novels that were best-sellers, or even novels that anyone particularly noticed. *Il Postino* comes from a novel, and one that the studios might overlook, but Miramax and producer Gianni Nunnari turned it into a surprise hit.

"It's true that in the distribution pattern, the whole market is more driven by best-sellers than ever before, and the reason for that is that there's focused distribution down to the airport gift shop," says Ken Atchity. "We're living in a world of global advertising and marketing, and what people are looking for are brand names. Grisham automatically sells hundreds of thousands of copies, so does Clancy, so does Stephen King.

"It's almost a religious experience that they're even selling the other books," says Atchity of bookstore chains that carry a wider variety. "Hollywood is just a story factory, just as the publishing industry is in New York, and everybody is looking for stories. Books deliver stories, and I don't think there's anything new in that relationship." But what is new is the studios' interest in unpublished manuscripts. Sellers need not disguise the fact that it hasn't been submitted to a publisher. That fact can make the work more desirable.

TV OR NOT TV

Often derided as the bastard child of moviemaking, necessary only as a stepping stone to features, television suffers under the perception that it is a lesser medium than film. The elitism makes little sense. No one argues that the very prolific writer Rod Serling was a lesser artist because he spent most of his career writing for the small screen. He not only created quality television with *Twilight Zone,* but also made a tremendous fortune from it.

Not only have acting and directing talent emerged from television, many studio heads today started at the networks. Fox's chairman Peter Chernin oversaw Fox Broadcasting before taking the feature reins of their Century City studio. Bob Daly ran CBS before moving to head up Warner Bros. Disney's Michael Eisner started as an ABC programmer, and Barry Diller, perhaps the godfather of them all, launched the Fox network from scratch while chairman of 20th Century–Fox.

A lucrative and immediate business, television provides programming wherein long-running series such as *Who's the Boss?* and *The Simpsons* can be more appealing in the accounting books than a box office smash. Because of packaging fees and syndication value, it can also benefit the agencies: ICM credits a large chunk of its early success to *Taxi* and, more recently, *Friends,* as does the William Morris Agency to *Cosby* and *Roseanne,* Creative Artists Agency to *ER* and *Beverly Hills 90210,* and the United Talent Agency to *Mad About You* and *Married . . . with Children.*

Likewise, the list of feature talents who got their start in TV is so long that it could fill this entire book. Television served as a break for Steven Spielberg, who directed episodes of *Night Gallery, Columbo,* and the TV movie *Duel* before getting his first feature, *The Sugarland Express.* Richard Donner also started on the small screen, directing *Gilligan's Island* and *The Twilight Zone* before his feature debut, *X-15.* And the list continues with producers Jim Brooks, Carl Reiner, and Garry Marshall; writers Lowell Ganz and Babaloo Mandel; actors Tom Hanks, Meg Ryan, Tom Berenger, Demi Moore, John Travolta, and, more recently, the cast of *Friends,* all breaking into features through TV.

Because TV is a writer's medium, feature writers often enjoy making the shift back to television, or staying in it altogether. Shortly before his death in 1997, former Paramount chairman Brandon Tartikoff commented that part of the reason Paramount hired him after running NBC was to make an effort to bring the writer more respect in features. "[But] I was really climbing uphill there because a lot of people still believe to this minute that it's really the director that's the straw that stirs the drink, whereas in television it's the writer-producer. I mean, it's Steven Bochco in TV, and Steven Spielberg in features. And therein lies the difference."

The cinematic quality of the long-running series *Homicide* was rooted in European film styles. While Barry Levinson always designed *Homicide* as a TV show, he was inspired by the French New Wave film styles of Jean-Luc Godard and François Truffaut and recruited Paul Attanasio to script the pilot.

"I said, 'Okay, let's do it,' because I was frustrated," Attanasio recalls. "I couldn't get a movie off the ground. It was just taking so long." While Attanasio's screenplays for *Quiz Show* and *Donnie Brasco* ultimately became features, he loved the comparable immediacy of *Homicide* as a series, while born out of a style and language primarily seen only in films. "The film values now were possible because you could shoot [*Homicide*] fast, you could shoot it without movie stars, and you could shoot it for not a lot of money. *All* the things that have made films less like films.

"*Seven* is basically like a fabulous episode of *Homicide,*" says Attanasio. "Movies just take so long, and they become such elephants. [Television] is organized differently so that the writer is king. And as a result, I think you have better dramatic writing, and certainly better comic writing on TV, because it is valued. In movies, the writer is number three, behind the movie stars and the directors. Actually in a lot of movies, the writer's number four—behind the movie stars and the directors and the special effects supervisor."

For a writer, the chances of getting a script developed for a TV movie are significantly better than in features. "The development-to-production ratio in a feature company is somewhere between ten-to-one and twenty-to-one, and they bring in multiple writers to rewrite whatever they're working on, as opposed to the development of a network where the development-to-production ratio is about two-to-one," says J. J. Jamieson of Avenue Pictures TV. "A lot of writers in the feature world come back to television or go into television because they're sick of writing and never having their work produced."

Television movies tend to fit into a certain criteria, however, and thus "disease-of-the-week" dramas were often pegged right away for the small screen. "True-crime" stories, from *Helter Skelter* to *The Gary Gilmore Story,* have continued to bring in huge ratings for the networks and will always find their niche on television. But as network tastes have broadened, there is a greater thematic crossover.

"[In TV] you need an accessible quality," Jamieson continues. "It's worth acknowledging that TV movies, now as much as ever, do every genre under the sun: horror, science fiction, western, period pieces, family dramas, Christmas specials, cop dramas, murder mysteries, thrillers, character pieces, and World War II pieces, you name it. We've developed them, and they make them. You can find a home for just about any genre."

Writing television movies "can be very rewarding and very immediate, touching the lives of millions of more people than you ever get as a journalist or even as a motion picture maker," says Pat Faulstich of Broder-Kurland-Webb-Uffner, an agency known for its TV strengths. "But it's also a game of inches, financially, not yards. The networks will spend only so much, and a network movie will return only so much from foreign distribution, which is the profit center for the producers and suppliers. It can end up being more about execution, pure inspiration, and creativity for a writer."

"With maybe four, five, or six exceptions in the feature world," says J. J. Jamieson, "your average television movie for one screening is seen by *millions* of more people than your average feature. That's an important part, especially if you've got an issue piece, or even if you just like people to watch your work.

"*Gulliver's Travels*—fifty million people watched," Jamieson adds. "If each of those viewers had bought a $7 ticket, that's a $350 million movie in one night. . . . And there are more and more television movies being made. When there were only three networks making TV movies, each one was doing thirty some-odd movies; that's a hundred TV movies. Now that figure [with cable included] is probably up above 250."

DISCOVERING THE VIEWERS' TASTES

Because word of mouth is ineffective, television movies are primarily driven by concept. "If you watch a great television movie tonight, and you call me the next day to say what a great television movie you watched, I've got to wait two and a half years and look for it in the summer during repeats," says Avenue TV's Jamieson. "That doesn't do the network any good.

"It's all about selling it quickly and concisely with a nice high concept," Jamieson continues, "with a graspable concept that you can sell in *TV Guide,* in your press release, and most important, in your on-air promo. If you've only got thirty seconds at the most to sell it, it's got to be pretty simple. You've got to get people to tune in based on the concept alone. Reviews make a difference, probably, but not as much as promos."

Spec scripts sold directly for movies of the week (MOWs) are often smaller budgeted features that provide a "showcase" role for TV actors when freed from their series' production schedules. "Very rarely is a script bought by a network without having the inclusion of some actor or actress excited about getting involved," says agent Lew Weitzman, a partner at Preferred Artists.

"The network telefilm market used to focus almost exclusively on women twenty-five to thirty as their audience," says BKWU agent Pat Faulstich. "So their selection of stories, their development of stars and cast for those movies, even their physical execution of those movies was focused on that [demographic]. Now the target has moved down; you can see this from the preponderance of [*Beverly Hills*] *90210* and *Melrose Place* cast members who are now the lead actors in network movies, which was never the case before."

Generally, movies of the week are not built by script submission in the way features are, but rather by taking a particular idea to a producer, who in turn pitches the story and the writer to the networks. The TV producer's role is perhaps even more vital than in the feature world; the network needs to know they can deliver within a time frame, whereas studios can always bring on other producers. As they say in TV, the messenger (the producer) is all crucial.

"We did buy finished scripts occasionally . . . either in turnaround from another network, or a feature that we bought and rewrote for our television needs," says J. J. Jamieson about his previous tenure as NBC's director of development, citing as the perfect example 1995's *The Beast,* based on Peter Benchley's best-seller. "Structurally it's like *Jaws* with a gigantic squid. Before it aired, they had just found a couple of these off of New Zealand, which was good timing for the network."

Universal Pictures optioned the original novel *The Beast* and developed two scripts for a feature. When nothing happened, the book rights went back to Peter Benchley, but Universal still owned the scripts. When a TV producer came across the book, he went to Benchley and optioned the book rights. "But then instead of pitching just the book to NBC, he said, 'Okay, bird in the hand is better than coming in with just that book again.' So he went back to Universal and said, 'This is exactly what NBC needs, even if you're making twenty-five cents on the dollar for the money you've spent on a very expensive feature script, get the twenty-five cents on the dollar because you're never getting it elsewhere.'

"Universal was smart enough to say that makes sense," Jamieson adds. The producer then presented NBC with ideas to turn the 135-page feature script into a 210-page miniseries script. "Sold. Instantly. Within eighteen months, it went from that idea to being on the air during May sweeps."

In TV today, "you're trying to bring to the tube a segment of the audience that wasn't the most important of the larger whole, historically," Pat Faulstich says. "You can't use a *Murder She Wrote* production approach for an audience whose preference is informed by MTV and Nike commercials, so now the indulgence in directors, and really strongly visually oriented cinematographers, is higher and higher and higher. Because of its requirements, the TV movie market will probably always remain an executive producers' market, but there's a new generation of executive producers who are coming up. They're a little more answerable to those same sort of creative impulses and appreciation of their generation. I think they are cultivating more adventurous and interesting projects. I mean, you could have made sixty network movies for the cost of *Waterworld*.

"Working writers in [TV movies] end up acquiring a set of technical skills that are rather specialized," Faulstich continues. "They're able to work under pressure. They're able to work from outlines. And because so many projects produced as network movies have originated from a record of fact, the writers must have the skills at adapting the factual stories."

It's no surprise that "real" people or events usually provide the basis for most TV movies, and big audiences often tune in for them. After all, such movies are generally already "headline news." While some filmmakers consider true-life stories legal minefields, docudramas rarely present problems, largely because rights to privacy for "public figures" differ from the average Joe. Despite this safeguard, wise producers can't be too cautious in seeing that their films present no legal complications.

"There's a certain cynicism in defining what makes a public figure," says entertainment lawyer Steven Rohde, "because to the extent that somebody is seized upon by the media—and subsequently in [TV movies or] motion pictures—the media may bootstrap itself into creating a public figure out of an otherwise private person." Rohde had to find answers to this area's most trying questions when representing the producers of 1983's *Silkwood,* a project ABC chose to produce as a feature, about a Texas woman exposed to nuclear radiation by her employer, the Kerr-McGee corporation.

Silkwood, directed by Mike Nichols and starring Meryl Streep, Cher, and Kurt Russell, is a textbook example of a carefully portrayed true-life story. "This script was virtually footnoted in terms of accuracy and source material," says Rohde, an essential exercise when writing true-life films, whether the subject is a public figure or not. "Just because someone is a public figure doesn't allow for conscious or deliberate false depiction. They haven't lost all their rights to protect their reputation. Nobody goes to the 'court of public figures' to get a certificate. A producer makes a judgment, and it can prove faulty."

Writing a script about true-life events is no easy task, but even inexperienced writers and producers can acquire rights to a story that can then translate not only into a high value in the network marketplace, but also can secure the writer's first shot at the script. "What I've found with people holding rights to a particular life story is that it's based entirely upon establishing a credible, personal relationship with that person," says Gordon Freedman, a former ABC newsman who produced the *Baby M* miniseries. "I think if a producer—no matter what his credentials are—establishes a real sincerity in doing a project and can work hard on it, *that* has the most influence in the end.

"When somebody's worrying about how his life story's going to be told," Freedman concludes, "he's going to go with the person he considers the most sincere and honest in telling the story."

Just as with writing specs in the feature world, honesty is the best policy. A screenplay is really about identity, and the ability to tell a sincere and engaging tale is what the buyers most desire.

Television Goes to the Movies

"Even if you have the best of ambitions of selling the script for $500,000 and it didn't happen in the feature market, it helps you get a job in the television world where somebody's willing to pay you, albeit $50,000, to write a two-hour, unless you've got something better to do," says J. J. Jamieson. "You should be so lucky to say, 'Oh, I only have to work for $50,000.' It gives you another spec script, it gives you the chance to go through the process, and for a lot of people with a produced television credit, it helps them along their career. It helps them go back to the feature world.''

Feature filmmaker Michael Mann, who got his start in television by creating *Vegas* and *Miami Vice,* originally wrote the 1995 feature *Heat* as a television pilot. Frank Darabont made USA cable movies before *Shawshank Redemption,* and David Burton Morris, indie director of *Patti Rocks,* has gone on to make distinctive television movies. Originally, Michael Crichton wrote *ER* as a feature in 1974. Twenty years later, after updating the script ten times, Crichton showed *ER* to CAA agent Tony Krantz, who in turn sold it to NBC for a series. Such crossover in the market has opened up the field tremendously.

"Certainly a lot of [projects written as features] could have been television movies," says Jamieson. "For example, *The Juror* is a television movie at heart. *An Eye for an Eye* could have been a television movie. . . . *Mr. Holland's Opus* could've been a Family Channel movie, or a Hallmark Hall of Fame."

What formerly defined a feature film versus a television movie has changed and blurred, according to Avenue's Cary Brokaw, "so a movie like *A Trip to Bountiful,* which I did at Island in 1985 and was made for $1.4 million, that's a Hallmark Hall of Fame movie today. That film doesn't get made as a feature film anymore. But it can have a very full and real life with a tremendous audience on television.

"We've taken a couple feature scripts and reconfigured them for television, and they've made terrific television movies," says Brokaw, who feels fortunate that networks see individuals with feature backgrounds as likely to break the creative boundaries of conventional TV movies. "It's a great change and luxury to be able to deliver a script to a network and have it on air in four months. The pace and the process of television are such a different timeframe than features. In the time that I'm waiting for a rewrite on a feature film, I can commence development, produce, and broadcast a television movie. Being able to do both is terrific. It's also true that the discipline of shooting a movie on a nineteen- or twenty-day schedule for television has [provided me with] a lot of tricks that as a producer I've been able to bring to bear in feature production."

Most television movies are executed on an eighteen- to twenty-one-day schedule for between $2.5 and $3.25 million, often with heavy above-the-line fees for actors, says agent Pat Faulstich ("above-the-line" refers to producer, director, and star budgeting). "That total is about a quarter of the cost that it takes to just *promote* a studio theatrical motion picture these days. [In features] you want to see what they've never seen before and sell that to the audience. But in television, there isn't the time or the money just to do the research, if it were possible to execute the concept on a very economical basis, so that a lot of the elements are pretty circumscribed.

"Unfortunately, the network film community and the truly independent film community are very separate communities," says Faulstich. "An independent filmmaker who's lucky enough to have $2 million to make a movie might have waivered his whole cast and crew and spent most of the money on equipment rentals and stock. A producer in the network movies, having the same money, has probably had to spend $250,000 for his lead actor, because that's where the market is, and $100,000 to get a decent script [and] pay between $85,000 and $160,000 for a director. That's why these end up being eighteen-day shoots. The independent filmmaker with $2 million might easily shoot thirty-five to forty days."

Studios and independent financiers are more often calling on network movie production companies to join with independent film projects because TV movies are an enterprise known for getting the most from the production dollar. "If the [TV movie] director has historically been treated too much like a 'traffic cop,' directors are becoming more and more of the essence of the moviemaking venture," Faulstich concludes. "So I think you'll start to see—and I think you do already—more and more visually interesting network movies."

Putting a current TV star in a movie has the obvious advantage of the public's familiarity with that talent. The same reasoning explains why so many television series, from *Lost in Space* to *The X-Files,* are being made into movies today, whereas in the past, movies such as *M*A*S*H* and *The Odd Couple* instead became the springboard for subsequent television series. That perennially lovable dolphin named *Flipper* first spawned on celluloid in a 1963 feature; during a successful run as a TV series [from 1964 to 1968], *Flipper* was remade into another 1996 movie starring Paul Hogan. Now it's even another TV series that lenses off the Australian shores.

On the studio development slates are such former TV series as *Adam 12, American Gladiators, Bewitched, Bonanza, Bullwinkle, Charlie's Angels, Coffee Talk, Combat, Dudley Do-Right, F Troop, Father Knows Best, Felix the Cat, Gentle Ben, Gigantor, Gilligan's Island, Gomer Pyle U.S.M.C., Green Acres, Green Hornet, Hans and Franz, Have Gun Will Travel, Hawaii Five-O, Highway Patrol, Hogan's Heroes, Honey West, I Dream of Jeannie, I Spy, It Takes a Thief, Johnnie Quest, Land of the Giants, Mr. Ed, Scooby Doo, Secret Agent Man, Speed Racer, The A-Team, The Ghost and Mrs. Muir, The Honeymooners, The Incredible Hulk, The Jetsons, The Lone Ranger, The Love Boat, The Man from U.N.C.L.E., The Monkees, The Munsters, The Partridge Family, The Prisoner, The Rifleman, The Six-Million-Dollar Man, The State, Wanted: Dead or Alive, Wonder Woman,* and *X Men.* And don't touch that dial, because there's likely many more to come.

Humble Beginnings

THE INDEPENDENT WORLD—A COMMON WAY
FOR A FILMMAKER TO START A CAREER—SEARCHES
FOR THE NEW VISIONARIES WHO KNOW WHAT IT TAKES
TO THINK SMALL AND BIG AT THE SAME TIME.

Go to the ant, thou sluggard; consider her ways, and be wise.

—PROVERBS 6: 6

A professional writer is an amateur who didn't quit.

—RICHARD BACH

HOLLYWOOD LOVES THOSE who do it on their own—but of course, only after they've done it. Nike's "Just Do It" slogan might have originally come from the inner voice of some frustrated filmmaker who couldn't get Hollywood financing. Many talents continue to go unnoticed because they don't take the steps to just make the films they feel should get made. The role of an independent today is as much a professional fund-raiser as it is filmmaker, but the payoff can be a quick path to Hollywood's megabucks.

The modern era's indie forefather, Steven Soderbergh, first witnessed Hollywood's trend of scouring festivals for the next original voice after he received both the Cannes and the U.S. Film Festival (later known as Sundance) awards for his 1989 debut *sex, lies, and videotape*. But what was even more remarkable in Hollywood's eyes, Soderbergh's film was one of the first independents, outside the horror genre, that did so extremely well at the box office (on a budget of $1.2 million, the movie grossed $25 million domestically), setting him apart from those who preceded.

Soderbergh, like many others labeled as "independents," doesn't really give credence to the sharp distinction of identifying films or their makers as either indie or studio types. "What a given filmmaker wants to do with him or herself and wants to make and under what circumstances is a very personal decision," says Soderbergh. "If I have a film in mind, I just try to think, 'Where's the best home for this? What's the best way for this to be made? What are my options, and how long a period of time am I giving myself to try to get this thing set up? How much control will I have, and do I care?' It's a complex decision, and I make it on a film-by-film basis."

Perhaps the real difference between studio and independent is the manner in which the audience perceives the picture. A "studio" movie, indie filmmakers like to explain, often has *too much* money and time to develop projects, while "independents" might *never have enough of either.* Yet many "studio" producers, such as Jim Cameron, Michael Douglas, James Robinson, Mike Medavoy, Arnold Kopelson, or Arnon Milchan, by the nature of their deals operate rather independently within the studio structure.

Studio projects languish in development for years, and even once made may sit on a shelf if deemed unreleasable. An independent project, on the other hand, will begin rolling once the money's in place, even though the filmmakers might tacitly agree that the script's not yet ready. There's too much of a chance for the money or a key actor to fall out, so independents promptly work with what they have. Sometimes their coarse effort will at least catapult them into gaining Hollywood's notice.

"I would encourage any young writer to focus on just getting their movies made, to getting the recognition, or to getting people interested in making their *next* script for more money," says writer's manager Peter Scott. "If you can't get the attention, you will be like many of the artists we talk about. When you go back to historical times, I don't know if Raphael got the appreciation he deserved, or van Gogh the appreciation he deserved, but we would tend to say no. Marc Chagall died before his material was really recognized as brilliant. It's the same thing for artists today. You have to get the recognition first."

For instance, had Robert Rodriguez come to Los Angeles with his screenplay for 1992's *El Mariachi* determined to make a Spanish language film with no stars in it, doors would have slammed left and right. Maintaining that strategy, he would never have completed the action-packed movie that quickly had every executive and agent in Hollywood talking. Rodriguez instead had a very modest goal: make something for the Mexican video market so he could gather some money to make another movie. To his pleasant surprise, Columbia Pictures picked up his first undertaking.

Fortunately Rodriguez had an ally in ICM's Robert Newman, a former Miramax executive who's paved the way for the "who's who" of independent and foreign filmmakers, including Mike Figgis, Danny Boyle, Baz Luhrmann, Ed Burns, Alex Proyas, Lee Tamahori, and Jean-Pierre Jeunet, just as the timing was perfect for studios to seek out such new visions. Newman sent an *El Mariachi* trailer that Rodriguez put together to Stephanie Allain, then at Columbia, whose little child happened to watch it and loved its fast-paced action; talk about a test screening. Rodriguez now considers that if he had dealt with traditional Hollywood from the start, rather than just making his own movies, he would never have survived.

Today's studios have improved channels of distribution, something that the independent market lacks, so this has led to couplings of major studios with independent distributors. "That's why the Miramaxes of the world are focused on acquisitions," says Peter Scott. "They're basically saying, 'Okay, independents, come to us and we will get your films out there to the world and get them seen. It won't just be a labor of love. You won't just be an artist who dies and then becomes famous.' But you're also seeing [Disney-owned] Miramax turn into Gramercy [Universal] turn into Fox Searchlight [20th Century–Fox], and all of a sudden it's becoming big business. The independent world has become a big business and they start to wonder, what is the *new* outlet for the actual independent film? You see everyone becoming part of a bigger financial entity. It's getting big, to win big, that's what it boils down to. So being at the forefront of that kind of industry, that, to me, is the solution to making it in this business."

DEPENDENCE AMONG THE INDEPENDENTS

The distinction of what separates a "studio" from an "independent" production company isn't a question of limited finance, since many so-called independents in fact have deep pockets. And major studios often create "negative pick-up" deals that allow filmmakers to go off and make a movie, rolling costs over to a third-party financier, such as a bank, thereby making such movies "independently." Such movies can then side-step union requirements and thus lower production costs.

What Hollywood has realized is that most inventive filmmaking comes out of financial limitations. Richard Linklater broke traditional formats with 1991's *Slacker,* a $27,000 film made in his hometown of Austin, Texas, that delightfully meanders from beginning to end. Robert Townsend shot for the moon with credit cards to finance his breakthrough *Hollywood Shuffle.* Declining generous offers to include bigger-named thespians in *Swingers,* actor-writer Jon Favreau cast his friends who had participated in staged readings, and not only found a more lucrative return (a $250,000 investment that Miramax picked up for $5 million), but also launched careers for Vince Vaughn, Heather Graham, and director Doug Liman.

There are so many variables that determine an indie film's success, says Steven Soderbergh, "that it's very impossible to predict—even with hindsight—and come up with a template for someone to follow, because it has to do with the movie, it has to do with timing, it has to do with the filmmakers themselves in terms of what they want to do with that movie, and what they're trying to do after that movie. [It's] who they are personally and what they want to achieve, and what career they want for themselves.

"It's all so individualized, and it changes so quickly," Soderbergh continues. "A movie comes out of nowhere and really changes everybody's ideas about this stuff, whether it be *Stranger Than Paradise* or *She's Gotta Have It* or *sex, lies . . .* or *Pulp Fiction.* Every few years something pops up and people go, 'Oh, so that's possible now.' That's what's great about it.

"You never know where it's going to go," says Soderbergh. "Whenever anybody comes out of 'the dirt' and emerges, the studios are going to be interested because they are talent driven—and that will never change. Your knowledge of how to make a movie, and how to make a movie in a specific place, gives you a shape that you can dictate, that you can work within. Using *sex, lies . . .* and *Schizopolis* as examples, the things that are most interesting to me about those films have nothing to do with their cost or size. They're ideas that—because they don't cost a lot—you can get away with trying in a way that you could never get away with in making it for a studio."

According to producer-director Jonathan Sanger, "the variables are all about what you can market, and the hardest things in the studio process are the original, unmarketed, untested material, which is where the independent market has grown in the last several years."

The independent market is "the area where material comes in from the bottom, that nobody knows about: the small book, the unheralded writer, the unknown director, the newer actors that studios don't want to take the risk on, maybe a Miramax will take a risk on and maybe a New Line would take a risk on," says Sanger, cofounder of the Chanticleer-Discovery Program. "It's a constantly evolving process, so that those smaller companies are becoming bigger companies. Now Miramax wants stars, and New Line wants stars, so you have to go a step below them." (Sanger and producer Jana Memel originally designed Chanticleer, under David Puttnam's 1987 Columbia regime, to provide half-hour directing debuts for writers, editors, cinematographers, and others who had proven talent but had not otherwise earned a shot at directing.)

Distributors ignore the majority of independent attempts; the Sundance Festival receives up to one thousand finished films for the one hundred-plus vacancies, and not all of those accepted get any distribution at all. Sometimes filmmakers will four-wall their movies (rent out theaters for screenings) to prove they have an audience, such as 1974's *Benji.* Tom Laughlin's *Billy Jack* used the technique in 1971; Warner Bros. ended up distributing it to the tune of over $37 million. Gus Van Sant's *Drugstore Cowboy* originally four-walled at L.A.'s NuArt Theater. Director Henry Jaglom (*Eating*) prefers this approach to build profile and visibility since exhibitors today too often yank movies before they can find an audience.

When it comes to the script, Avenue's Cary Brokaw contends that the independent market is in certain ways not that different from the studio market, yet in other ways appreciably different. "A particular script, because of subject matter and tone, and maybe elements of the filmmaker, you would submit to Miramax and Fox Searchlight and

Gramercy and Fine Line, just as you might submit another project to Fox, Universal, and Paramount. So it's horses for courses. Is this that kind of movie?

"Everyone in this industry is always fueled by the gold at the end of the rainbow—the potential success and upside of a small, sleeper picture catching on—and they happen just enough to fuel each year's slate of movies financed in that fashion," Brokaw continues. "It affords the industry new talent, and new opportunities in a way that you wouldn't get otherwise.

"One has to wonder if you really sit back and took all those films and all the financing what the economic ramifications are, if you take it collectively," Brokaw concludes. "It's probably not very good. But the burden's spread enough so that the doctors and dentists who lose money on one film this year, their colleagues are back with another film next year."

BIGGER FISHING IN SMALLER PONDS

After working in Hollywood for several producers and executives, George Huang discovered that the filmmaker was the actual driving force behind a motion picture now more than ever. "I never really had the courage or the wherewithal to *do* that, until . . . I became a good friend with Robert Rodriguez, almost solely as a fluke. Here was this kid from Texas, and he was a good old boy. All the executives and producers were wining and dining him at all these chi-chi fancy places, and he was eating stuff that he couldn't even pronounce." Rodriguez asked Huang, then working for Columbia when *El Mariachi* was acquired, where to get a good burger and the two forged a fast friendship.

On Rodriguez's encouragement, Huang quit working for the studios to write and direct *Swimming with Sharks,* a dark tale of ambition in Hollywood that soon had the town on its ear. After collecting various war stories from beleaguered assistants in the studio machine, Huang holed himself up in a snowbound cabin at Sundance in Utah, a place he found conducive, and wrote the original draft in three weeks. "There were only three Mormon channels on TV, so it was either *write* or *convert,*" Huang laughs.

But getting his movie made was again a separate task. An old boss from Lucasfilm gathered money to make it "guerrilla-style," but once

Variety got hold of the script (then called *The Buddy Factor*) it became the talk around town. "I went from a wannabe filmmaker to a promising, budding filmmaker without having done *anything,* just solely on the basis of the heat alone, of what the studios were talking about, what everyone was reading about the script. All of a sudden, I had this great potential and every agency in the world was out to sign me." A major studio wanted to make the movie, but Huang soon found that his vision would be drastically altered.

"They wanted to turn it into a *Secret of My Success.* 'Can we have a happy ending?' 'Can we cut out the paper-cut scene,' and 'Can we one-up the boss?' So we just clearly didn't see eye to eye," says Huang, who returned his check and instead gathered some money from Wall Street investors. "I was writing it for Kevin Spacey and Frank Whaley, and not in years did I think I'd get the cast I wanted. . . . I got my first choice of actors, they came onboard, and two weeks after Kevin Spacey said 'I'll do it,' we were shooting."

Then the real fun began. "The first day, we had no film. Second day, the transportation coordinator got run over by one of his own trucks. Third day, the art truck blew up, and we lost all our props," says Huang. "Okay, nothing worse could *possibly* happen to this film, we're over the hump, it can only get easier from here. Then the big Northridge earthquake happened and the actors took it as a sign from God that they should not be involved in this project. Nonetheless they stuck it out, and we were able to get it done."

Kevin Spacey gave a sparkling performance as an unctuous studio executive with an undercurrent of evil to outdo Keyser Soze. Frank Whaley, as a bright-eyed Hollywood newcomer who nimbly reinvents himself as a modern-day Sammy Glick, depicted a very accurate baptism into the wicked behavior underlying studio politics. Ultimately, the $900,000 film benefited Huang in ways the studio system would never allow. "It was more sort of a test of fire than anything else. So that was the most valuable part of it. . . . After I finished directing *Swimming with Sharks,* I told myself I'm never going to direct again. It falls into the 'Life's too short' category. Fortunately I've had two years to let the wounds heal.

"Nowadays, to make your mark, especially on the independent side, you have to have a gimmick, the story," says Huang. "Like Robert Rodriguez had the $7,000 [after selling his body to science], Quentin Tarantino was a video clerk, Kevin Smith worked at a convenience store and did *Clerks* for $30,000, Ed Burns was a production assistant on *Entertainment Tonight*—everyone has to have a great backstory.

"Now, I was an *assistant* to a Hollywood executive, and I knew that playing that up helped sell it, even though *Swimming with Sharks* could have been set in advertising, fashion, Wall Street, or any other business," Huang continues. "But the fact of the matter was, nobody would care if it was set in any other business.

"So I very consciously set *Swimming with Sharks* in Hollywood, so that everyone would think, 'Because he was an assistant to so-and-so' it would be this dishy, gossipy, kiss-and-tell, when in fact it was really a character study about ambition. But you can't *say* that," says Huang with a trademark laugh. "You've got to have a hook, a gimmick, a story to get yourself noticed."

Because making a film independently today is easier, "it seems like something that you or somebody you know might actually be able to accomplish," says Steven Soderbergh, "because it has a whole do-it-yourself mentality about it. That's why people tend to be, if we're assuming correctly, a little more interested in the backstory of an independent than of a studio film."

The Sundance Institute encouraged the notion of regional filmmaking, drawing on indigenous qualities of filmmakers, which is something Hollywood projects with their "blinders on" approach can't accomplish. Spike Lee didn't come to Los Angeles to make his mark, but stayed in New York and with his $175,000 *She's Gotta Have It* displayed a filmmaking style that in turn led to a prolific output of studio films. John Sayles prefers staying in Hoboken, New Jersey, while John Waters continues making movies in his native Baltimore. Los Angeles product Quentin Tarantino's *Reservoir Dogs* (made in the shadows of Hollywood's studios) showed how a film with financial limitations, featuring minimal characters in a taut situation and filmed in a confined space, could ultimately propel its filmmaker to worldwide recognition.

MIXING THE DOUGH WITH THE ICING

Writing *sex, lies, and videotape* during a cross-country trip back to his hometown in Louisiana, Steven Soderbergh kept cost considerations in the back of his head. "I was writing something that I hoped, at the very least, I could go and make on my own for sixty to seventy grand if I had to. There were built-in limitations. . . . But I think those sort of boundaries are necessary."

Soderbergh's financing for *sex, lies . . .* came first from a video rights deal. This area of the market has since changed radically, primarily due to chain video stores demanding more studio video product and limiting emphasis on independent titles. Money for small indie films now tends to come from limited partnerships of private investors, in addition to preselling foreign territories, either on video or theatrically. Some established indie companies will look at a script, a budget, and an assembled cast to make financing decisions.

"I think it's easier to get an independent film made now," Soderbergh explains. "It's just harder to get it picked up, and that's because of the sheer volume. The second part of that equation is due to the first part of that equation."

Once completed, low-budget films can have much higher returns on investment than most studio fare. The $140,000 spent on Ed Burns's *The Brothers McMullen* brought back $11 million in the United States. Working Title's *Four Weddings and a Funeral* cost $5 million and grossed over $260 million worldwide. For the $6 million *Crocodile Dundee,* backers Paul Hogan and John Cornell took a modest advance from Paramount and earned a bundle of the gross (as well as maintaining sequel rights). 1997's *The Full Monty* cost less than $5 million and has topped $200 million around the world. And the entire *Nightmare on Elm Street* franchise—together with its merchandising and TV series—has accumulated over three quarters of a billion dollars altogether.

Such crowd-pleasers started from humble beginnings. "The key ingredient besides ability, which is going to be evidenced by a screenplay, and ultimately by the direction of the movie, is passion," says Cary Brokaw. "If you look at Park City and the films that get made, these people are incredibly passionate and unrelenting in crafting the material and communicating their vision of it to actors and financiers. That passion has to be all-consuming and really all-powerful. And if you don't have that, it won't happen.

"You can look at all the case studies, but there are no rules," Brokaw says of the independent films that succeed. The process might require rewriting for conflicting financiers or actors with no development money for support. "There are no rules. You simply make it happen and will something into existence. If it's not good—really not good—and enough people say that, you can't will something. But that will, that passion, is what makes those movies what they are."

Chris Moore left a comfortable agent career to raise the money to produce *Glory Daze*. "If you actually have the wherewithal—you're rich, you know people, you have a good script in your head, whatever it is—you're better off going out and just making it. Because Hollywood is not investing in people anymore. They used to do that: the training programs at agencies, the executive ranks at studios, the young writers moving up to being head writers. All that is gone, and it's either immediate," says Moore, snapping his fingers, "or you're gone. You just have to stick with it. And that's so sad, because you learn so much from hanging around with people who've done it before."

When making *Swimming with Sharks,* George Huang's tight budget and limited time forced him to find creative solutions. "The basics are what people respond to. Studios are now hiring independent directors and foreign directors to come and make films to give them an edge. Then you get in the system, and now you have to do it 'this way.' But I don't want to do it that way; I can't do it that way. This is why it will lose its edge, lose its spark . . . and [the studios] hire them, and then they make them try to conform."

HOLLYWOOD'S ALTERNATIVE: INTERNATIONAL MARKETS AND CABLE TV

The cable movie market has broadened the spectrum of the television movie genre, causing networks to adjust their programming slates. As a whole, the business of making movies for the small screen "looks a little bit more and more like the motion picture business," says Broder-Kurland-Webb-Uffner agent Pat Faulstich. "It's a market that's good for at least 250-plus titles a year in production, so if you group together cable and network movie titles, they are at times a very separate market picture business, and at other times seem almost like an adjunctive market."

Home Box Office (HBO), which tends to develop projects that start internally rather than purchase spec scripts, has thrived in part because it broke out during the 1980s when the network movies of the week began to look homogenous. Now scripts can be packaged and produced on a cost-targeted basis for mainstream television, as well as cable outlets such as USA, Turner, Showtime, Arts & Entertainment, and Lifetime.

"I don't think very many writers set out to write spec movies for television," says Faulstich. "They set out to write spec movies that in the course of their self-marketing—or their agent's marketing—may eventually move over to television." Deciding to write the $40 million action movie or $2.5 million drama comes down to a writer's personal decisions and abilities, but today's producers are just as likely to seek out small pictures simply to get projects made.

"There are a lot of producers who may have made a movie every three years—and just are getting tired of the wars when what they really wanted to do was make movies—moving over to the network movie market," says Faulstich. "Turner and HBO have been very solicitous of motion picture producers, I think on the assumption that they are going to invite feature writers to the party, and the feature directors, and the feature actors. So you will see that backpath working more and more.

"Ultimately, it seems as though it's all one industry," says Faulstich, "and that in many cases writers in the movie business who get the most carte blanche—the most power—are the leading stars in the television business. In many cases, they can't afford to work in the movie business."

Independent films allow greater avenues for creativity today, partially due to international distribution and the proliferation of cable networks, such as The Independent Film Channel and The Sundance Channel in the United States, and a wider spectrum abroad. "Comets fly out of Hollywood continually, and either can go out in the heavens and become stars or burn up somewhere," says John McTiernan, reflecting on George Miller's return to his native Australia after disenchantment with the making of Warner Bros.' *Witches of Eastwick.* "He left swearing he's never going to have anything to do with this industry again. Years later, Miller sends back a little tiny itsy-bitsy children's movie [*Babe*] that turns the world on its ear. Imagination and the drive somehow manage to show up again."

Likewise, Stanley Kubrick's frustrations after studio meddling with *Spartacus* caused him to leave Hollywood for England, where he proceeded to make his own brand of film. When Thom Mount ran Universal in the late 1970s, "the independent world wasn't nearly as robust as it is today . . . and the reason it's gotten strong is that the studios have constantly condensed the marketplace and controlled their material internationally, so that buyers outside the United States don't have access to class-A films.

"As a result, independents who are willing to make class-A films and take that risk and make something other than *The Girl That Ate Chicago* are very much in demand," Mount explains. "When we took *Indian Runner* or *Death and the Maiden* into the international market, they were big events. A buyer in Germany can end up owning a Roman Polanski–Sigourney Weaver movie for that market. He has no chance otherwise, because Warners won't let him have their product, Paramount won't let them have theirs. And he relies entirely on quality product in the independent world for his survival."

It's also more common now to structure production deals pairing foreign money with a star a studio desires, therefore making the distributing studio a partner, rather than employer. For instance, with Peter Weir's *Green Card,* which grossed over $75 million worldwide, Disney licensed rights in various territories, collected their distribution fee, and then gave the balance of the profit to Weir.

Cofinancing with international sources allows the provision of full budgets for projects made in the United States, something that wasn't possible in the past and continues to grow more significant. There's an increasing hunger for English language programming in European TV, primarily because, with the exception of Great Britain, there's a lack of indigenous quality source material.

Meanwhile, domestic cable outlets, always conscious of "branding" to build specific profiles, are something akin to the old studios. Movies for Showtime or HBO, made on modest budgets and often showcasing emerging filmmakers, have an advantage over indie filmmaking because of their guaranteed promotion and air date. "Just as in any magazine, the editorial side thinks of the advertising as something that pays for the editorial side," says Jack Lechner, who formerly worked for HBO, "and the advertising side thinks of the editorial as being something to wrap ads around. . . . The whole reason for original programming in pay cable is to have something to promote. You're actually more concerned with the people who *don't* subscribe than the people who do."

THE KILLER BS

Many marvelous Hollywood careers developed from "the Corman School," presided over by Roger Corman, otherwise known as "King of the Bs. Starting in 1955, Corman bagged his job as a 20th Century-Fox messenger boy to direct *Five Guns West* and has since created some 350-plus titles. A patron saint to the independent spirit, Corman spawned such filmmakers as Jim Cameron, Jonathan Demme, Martin Scorsese, Ron Howard, John Sayles, Carl Franklin, Joe Dante, Paul Bartel, Dennis Hopper, Jonathan Kaplan, and Peter Bogdanovich.

Corman's productions provided early roles to actors Jack Nicholson, Charles Bronson, Bruce Dern, Tommy Lee Jones, William Shatner, Kathleen Quinlan (who started as Corman's assistant), Cindy Williams, Peter Fonda, and Robert De Niro, as well as a producing opportunity for Gale Ann Hurd. But apart from Roger Corman's movie factory, the B-movie market has not had such a distinguished training ground.

As a result of the money made from exploitative material, there are plenty of producers making *The Girl That Ate Chicago* or similarly titled trash. As a package-driven outlet for straight-to-video projects (sold on the cash value of certain actors), today's B-movie market remains very distinct from the independent. "They are two entirely different industries," says writer Kurt Wimmer, who toiled in the B-movie market before landing several huge spec sales. "Low-budget B movies are geared toward product and product only. They are geared toward a video box.

"I had at least four movies made—low-budget films—and I was smart enough not to even mention that to people in the industry. It will get you no recognition whatsoever," says Wimmer, who felt their only benefit was that those scripts paid his rent. "In fact, it can hurt you. It's like doing porn, only one step removed, porn being preferable.

"All I really did was sign myself up for four or five years of abject misery," says Wimmer. "It's a very frustrating experience, nothing gratifying about it. I wouldn't recommend it to anybody who really wants to write."

Wes Craven says of his early association with *Friday the 13th* director Sean Cunningham, "In three years of us trying to get other projects, nobody wanted to do anything *besides* another really disgusting horror film, and we were both family men. We wanted to go off and do comedies. So that explains why I didn't make a film from 1972 till 1975, when *The Hills Have Eyes* was released. We were trying to do other films and nobody wanted to hear about it. Finally Sean said to me, 'You have to do another down-and-dirty one, Wes.' It's like the story of my career," Craven laughs.

Producer Ross Hammer, who for years was in the business of buying material from low-budget unknown writers, recommends that writers avoid exploitation flicks just to get a script produced. "First of all, you don't make much money. The *high* end of the low-budget world, you're making $20,000 to $30,000 for a script, and that's a script you may have to do ten rewrites on and spend a year and a half of your life working on, and only to come out with a $1 million straight-to-video movie that doesn't look that great. . . . The best way for a writer to really, really make something happen is to get his *writing* seen—not to get his writing produced in a low-budget format."

While moving toward their ultimate goal, savvy writers often opt for work on movies to hone other skills. Steven Soderbergh worked as an editor while making short films and writing enough material until somebody would give him a directing shot. The financial performance of *sex, lies, and videotape* put Soderbergh into the studio stratosphere, from which he could chart his own course.

"A lot of it was timing," says Soderbergh of his *sex, lies . . .* success. "Something was in the air, and it seemed to be a film people wanted to go and see at that time. I saw a clip of it the other night . . . and it seemed so dated to me. And at the time, that was its strength—that it was so specifically of a certain period—that people locked into it." Yet it was the movie's box office return that was the true secret of success. "If it had made $500,000, I don't think anything really would have happened for a lot of people, including myself."

While today's studio machine isn't prone to nurture talent, filmmakers can turn to short-form alternatives to build a résumé. When Joni Sighvatsson cofounded Propaganda Films in the early 1980s, producing music videos and then commercials provided Propaganda's natural path to its television series, *Twin Peaks,* and motion pictures. "It was born out of a need to make a living while making it into the feature business," says Sighvatsson. "It was the same with the directors at Propaganda. . . . They *all* wanted to make features, but they had to start somewhere as well. So they decided to cut their teeth in other aspects of the medium."

Ultimately, any committed writer or creator of visual art with passion will find some path to create. Between CD-ROM games and Web design, from public access television to micro-budget films to Hollywood extravaganzas, the ease of entry is greater than ever. After all, most independent films begin with a spec script—one that the Hollywood machinery may fail to see realized—but from which a passionate filmmaker builds his or her career. Despite any screenwriter's intention for the big deal, it pays to stay on the path, for any small step along the way beats no step at all.

Major Sales of Unproduced Spec Scripts

Title (Buyer)	Screen-writer(s)	Logline	Purchase Price
AfterLife (Columbia)	Joss Whedon	Scientist's mind is implanted into a younger man to continue a research project. The younger man is serial killer.	$1.5 million against $2 million
Bad Dog (Dream-works)	Dale Launer	Psychologist's patient has dark delusions about a werewolf, which turn out to be real.	$3 million
Blades (Universal/Chuck Gordon)	David Engelbach & John Wolff	News helicopter pilot is deputized by police after the president's helicopter, *Marine One,* is taken over by terrorists. He has to help save the president as terrorists try to manipulate the news media to their advantage.	$1 million
Blaze of Glory (Universal)	Joe Eszterhas	Bio pic of Otis Redding.	$1 million against $2.25 million
Blind Faith (Interscope)	Michael Schiffer & Randall Fried	Set a decade into the future, story centers on invasive new police technologies.	Seven figures
The Cheese Stands Alone (Paramount)	Kathy McWorter	Superstitious Hungarian hunk blames his loss of sex drive on a hex put on him by a jilted girlfriend.	$1 million

Title (Buyer)	Screen-writer(s)	Logline	Purchase Price
The Colony (Sony/ Mandalay)	Don Jackoby	Setting is an island off the coast of Greece that serves as a safe haven for CIA agents whose cover is blown. A man has to escape the island in order to seek revenge on his archenemy.	$1 million against $1.5 million
Dead Reckoning (Warner Bros./ Kopelson)	Christine Roum	Female public defender in Washington gets caught up in a conspiracy to assassinate a prominent senator.	$1 million
Evil Empire (Paramount)	Joe Eszterhas	Based on a true story, plot revolves around a Russian mob's plan to launder money in the United States.	$2 million against $4.5 million
Exit Zero (New Line/ Forge)	Kurt Wimmer	Set in the near future, story of young man and woman who discover that computers have linked up and are plotting to annihilate the human race.	$1 million against $1.5 million
First Comes Love (Westport Films)	Steve Kunes	Sultan makes deposits in sperm bank in case he's assassinated.	$1.2 million
Foreplay (Savoy)	Joe Eszterhas	Plot revolves around a female singer, a former bass player–turned cop, the cop's soon-to-retire partner, and a legendary rock singer.	$1 million against $3.5 million

Title (Buyer)	Screen-writer(s)	Logline	Purchase Price
Gorilla Boy (Walt Disney/ Mandeville)	Dana Olsen	Story of young woman who goes on a safari and creates such problems for her group that she is ostracized, gets lost, and meets a gorilla boy, a sort of Tarzan figure. She brings the boy back to her snotty Boston family where he has to learn to adapt.	$1 million
Ground Zero (Castle Rock)	Sergio Altieri & Martin Zurla	Attempt to take over an American missile silo.	$1.5 million against $2 million
Hell Bent . . . and Back (Hollywood Pictures)	Rick Jaffa & Doug Richardson	Story centers on a squad of WWII GIs who hijack a Berlin-bound Nazi train containing loot taken from Mussolini's Italy. They discover two boxcars filled with Jewish children on their way to a concentration camp.	$1 million
High Roller (Savoy)	J. F. Lawton	*Die-Hard*–type action film set in a casino targeted for an extremely hostile takeover by an over-the-top mobster. The heroes turn out to be the mobster's former hitman and a gambler who reluctantly agrees to be the bodyguard for the daughter of the casino owner.	$1 million against $2.5 million

Title (Buyer)	Screen-writer(s)	Logline	Purchase Price
Kilobytes (Savoy)	Rick Ramage	In the year 2010, retired cop specializing in virtual reality goes back on the job to stop a rogue cop from brainwashing the world with a virtual reality program.	$1.5 million against $3.5 million
Land of the Free (Paramount)	Joe Eszterhas	Focus is on American militia groups and individual rights.	$2 million against $4 million
Male Pattern Baldness (Paramount)	Joe Eszterhas	Nineties relationship movie from a male point of view.	$2 million against $4.5 million
Ocean Boulevard (Columbia)	Greg Taylor & Rowdy Herrington	Actress takes on the mental and physical qualities of an imprisoned woman whose life she's studying for a role.	$1.5 million
Prince of Darkness (Fox/ Schindler-Swerdlow)	Joseph Finder	Female FBI agent finds out that the assassin she's tracking is also her new lover. To make matters worse, he's part of a plan to throw New York's financial district into a tailspin.	$1.5 million
Sea Wolf (Columbia)	Andrew Chapman	Contemporary version of Jack London's classic novel.	$1 million

Title (Buyer)	Screen-writer(s)	Logline	Purchase Price
Sessions (Walt Disney)	Jeremy Lew	Female detective investigating a sex-related murder in New York City becomes involved with a sexy therapist, who is the prime suspect in the case.	Over $1 million
Suspension (Largo/Chuck Gordon)	Joss Whedon	Terrorists seize control of the George Washington Bridge during a traffic jam.	$750,000 against $1 million
Steinbeck's Point of View (Bel Air/Mark Johnson)	Brandon Camp & Michael Thompson	Young man with cancer returns home to reflect on his life.	$8.5 million (2-picture deal)
Texas Lead and Gold (Largo)	Michael Beckner & Jim Gorman	Set in the 1800s, a Texas Ranger and a struggling attorney link up to pursue buried treasure.	$1 million
The Ticking Man (Largo)	Brian Helgeland & Manny Coto	Daredevil guy who defuses bombs for LAPD is called in to defuse a human being rigged to be a walking time bomb.	$1 million
Tracks (Caravan)	Ruth Graham	True Story of Robyn Davidson, who made history in 1978 when she crossed Australian outback alone with three camels and a dog.	$1 million

Title (Buyer)	Screen-writer(s)	Logline	Purchase Price
Ultimatum (Touchstone/ Gale Ann Hurd)	Lawrence Dworet & Robert Roy Pool	Group of terrorists threaten to detonate a bomb unless outlandish terms are met.	$1 million

SOURCE: Courtesy of Spec Screenplay Sales Directory, edited by Howard Meibach.
www.hollywoodlitsales.com   (800) 207-5022

From Titan to Titanic

THE BEACHED WHALE THAT SURFACED AS *WATERWORLD,* FROM A SCREENPLAY BY PETER RADER
Rewritten by David Twohy and a Bunch of Other People
Purchased by Largo; acquired by Universal Pictures
MPAA Rating: PG-13
Director: Kevin Reynolds

In the distant future, after the Earth's polar ice caps have melted, a loner on the water-covered horizon searches for a postage stamp–size vestige of land as humanity's last hope.

CAST OF CHARACTERS

Brad Krevoy, producer for Roger Corman
Andrew Licht and *Jeffrey A. Mueller,* producers at Licht-Mueller Productions
John Davis, producer
Ken Stovitz, agent at ICM
Lawrence Gordon, producer, CEO of Largo
Charles Gordon, producer, Daybreak Productions

"WHAT'S A UNIQUE world?" Peter Rader thought when his idea for *Waterworld,* the first spec script he ever completed, came to mind. "I had always limited my imagination to what I could do as a low-budget movie, what locations did I have access to, what stories took place in one house, or one location," says Rader, who found himself curtailing his creativity by second-guessing the market's demand for what's commercial, or what genres were hot.

As a result, Rader ended up with a half-dozen half-finished screen-plays that just ran out of steam. "They didn't come from a place of truth. They didn't come from a flow. At a certain point, I just kind of took the lid off the whole process and said: 'What's a universe we could go into that will just completely spark my imagination?' "

It didn't take long for Rader to decide that a water-covered world was an idea worth exploring. Rader repeatedly asked, "What would that be like? Can you imagine if we didn't have any land? That seemed to spark so many ideas, and I started walking around boatyards. . . . It was such a rich tableau, it basically wrote itself. When I think back at how that script was written, I can't even really remember it. It just flowed."

TURNING ON THE TAP

Rader's story began as an ecological fable, a dramatic warning of the extreme consequences of destroying the Earth's delicate fabric. Greed and ignorance had led to the melting of polar ice caps, literally causing the globe to drown itself due to its own human excess. By the time of its production and 1995 release, *Waterworld* resulted in what was then filmmaking's biggest-budgeted movie ever, running a tab of over $172 million and watchdogged by a nosy media as an example of Holly-wood's most flagrant excesses.

Its origins were nonetheless unassuming. "I was thinking of Titan, Saturn's moon that's completely covered with water, they think," says Rader, who grew up in Italy and came to Los Angeles after graduating with a visual arts degree from Harvard. The initial inspiration of Titan caused the words to the *Waterworld* script to come easily. "I was so fearless, I was not thinking. I was naive, just writing, blowing my imag-ination wide open."

On the urging of Brad Krevoy, a budding movie producer then working for Roger Corman, Rader sought to try his hand at screen-writing. In 1986, Krevoy met with the hopeful filmmaker, who was then attempting to land a directing assignment at Corman's Venice studios.

"Listen, I got some South African money, and they want to make a *Mad Max* rip-off," Krevoy said. "If you write me a *Mad Max* rip-off,

I'll let you direct it." Peter Rader went home to consider fleshing out a script.

This was the period before Nelson Mandela had been released from prison, and while Rader was concerned that the money seemed tainted, the moral issue wasn't his only concern. "It was more the creative question of whether or not I was willing to do another by-the-numbers *Mad Max* rip-off. And I wasn't." So Rader returned to Corman's company with his pitch: a Western tale taking place on a globe that's covered completely with water.

Krevoy, planning for a feature in the half a million budget range, was aghast. "In two seconds," Rader recalls, "he said, 'That's ridiculous! That's going to cost us $5 million to make.' " Thinking Rader must be crazy, Krevoy sent the would-be writer-director on his way home. Once the bloated *Waterworld* production became a media event, Krevoy's quote quickly became one the funniest sound bites in motion picture history.

Undaunted, Rader sat down to write. He spent the next couple of months scripting his 136-page first draft of *Waterworld*. Futuristic science-fiction fantasies are often statements about current social travails, and Rader developed a story about an amphibious, gilled character, Mariner, searching for a speck of land on an otherwise near uninhabitable globe.

"I felt we'd seen sort of the rusty postapocalyptic darker version, the grittier version of this story, many, many times," says Rader. "I was trying to do something *bold*. Like when *Star Wars* appeared on the scene, it was such a revelation. . . . I was trying to have that mythic level, much more of a fantasy tone than an action-movie tone."

The only working writer Rader knew then was a television scribe his cousin was dating. "So I gave it to him, and he was very discouraging," says Rader, reliving the cold splash of criticism. "I don't know what it was, but I was devastated. He was lukewarm about it . . . so I basically put it on the shelf." *Waterworld* literally sat on that shelf for three years, until late 1989, when it sold in a matter of hours.

During that period, Rader pursued work on crews to acquire "below-the-line," technical filmmaking skills. Still ambitious to direct, he followed the path of the Coen brothers and others by putting together a five-minute excerpt of a movie he could sell at the American Film Market (AFM). "I had a partner who brought me the script and was also the cameraman, a Steadicam operator who wanted a reel." Since

Rader had previously put together a music video, for which he had gathered free equipment and eighty people to work pro bono, his partner was confident of his abilities. "It was a horror movie, set in one house, called *Grandmother's House*. And the two of us funded this five-minute short shot in 16 [millimeter], which had tremendous production value."

Rader's partner brought with him the script, the Steadicam package, and the desire to shoot something, "and I brought the resourcefulness and desire to direct. We kind of worked on the script a little together, but I didn't consider myself the writer of it."

Rader and his cameraman, whom he met on the music video shoot, went out on successive weekends to Redlands, California. "The short was in some ways almost better than the movie," Peter laughs. "Literally, the sequence that we shot in the short, we duplicated exactly in the final movie shot for shot because it was so well conceived. When you're only doing five minutes, you really take the time to storyboard it and really think it through."

The two attended the American Film Market (AFM), sort of a mini-Cannes held yearly on the Santa Monica shore and acquired the half a million dollars to finish *Grandmother's House* from Nico Mastoraukus, known to some as "the Greek Roger Corman." Following that, Mastoraukus offered Rader another movie, but then took over and turned it into an unpleasant experience. "I decided that I didn't want to do any more B movies. Basically, I didn't want to do any more work that I had to apologize for," Rader affirms.

"Okay, what do I have to offer?" Rader asked himself. The thought of making *Waterworld* lurked in his mind, so he brushed the dust off his three-year-old script to reread it, realizing it had a lot more promise than his previous critic had claimed.

"When you have that kind of distance on material, it makes it so much easier to rewrite it," says Rader, who spent the next month polishing and trimming out twenty pages. Then he began giving it to friends and the many connections he had since developed. One of Peter's friends was an assistant for producers Andy Licht and Jeff Mueller (the same duo who brought the *While You Were Sleeping* screenwriters out to Hollywood), who were then under a first-look deal with Davis Entertainment.

"One of my close friends said, 'This is really, really good,' and I'm thinking, 'What does he know?' Then someone else said it was really good, and suddenly there was this *buzz*," Rader recalls. The assistant passed *Waterworld* to Licht and Mueller in hopes of finding the writer an agent. Rader also showed his script to an executive at Walt Disney, who had been a classmate from Harvard.

"We think this is really good, we want to get involved in this," Licht and Mueller phoned up Rader to say. "We want to produce it."

"Help me find an agent," Rader answered, "and I'll let you produce it."

DELIVERING THE PACKAGE

Licht and Mueller went out with *Waterworld* during a spec market upswing following the end of the 1988 WGA strike, a time when everybody saw money, and buyers were looking for marketable ideas. Rader felt having the producer ally was a huge factor in getting his script attention.

"It's very important to not have to sing your own praises," says Rader, "and have someone else say, 'This is the most fantastic script.' It takes the curse off it. So Andy and Jeff did that vis-à-vis the agents, because the agents were now reading it. And it went to the top of the stack."

Licht and Mueller, then based at Davis Entertainment's Century City offices, set up meetings for the *Waterworld* writer with a number of agents; the agents then started the feeding frenzy. "It was quite a surreal period," Rader recalls, "because it was the Hollywood sort of flavor-of-the-month story that we all *dreamed* about, me and my friends. Here it was, happening to me; it was bizarre. I'd get home and would have forty messages on my machine from people I didn't even know. 'I heard about your script, blah-blah-blah,' 'I'm a producer, I heard about this,' or agents calling."

Once the attention reached a crazy point, Rader decided he would sign with the first agent he personally connected with at a large agency to "dispense with the whole circus." Then an agent at International Creative Management, Ken Stovitz, responded to the material, and Rader was satisfied.

"Pretty much at that meeting, we started strategizing," says Rader of his Thursday morning meeting with Stovitz. There were several options regarding Licht and Mueller's role, whether they would be attached at every studio or only select submissions. Both Stovitz and Rader agreed that the young producers, who emerged from the first class at USC's Peter Stark program, were assets and also added cachet because of their deal with Davis Entertainment (run by John Davis, who previously made *Predator* with Larry Gordon).

On Friday, the script went out to 20th Century–Fox to test the waters. Stovitz called over to the exec who had read it at Disney to say, "You have the hottest spec script in town." Suddenly, everyone was reading it. By Monday morning, Stovitz called Disney to discover that six of seven executives liked it, but studio chieftain Jeffrey Katzenberg, who was in Hawaii at the time, was concerned about potential costs. Obviously, his instincts proved correct.

The producers found the week before Christmas to be the ideal time to put the original script for *Waterworld* on the market. "We had big people at the studios sitting there with nothing to do," says Andy Licht. Larry Gordon, who had just started a Japanese-financed company called Largo, phoned up Licht and Mueller.

"I want you guys to come in," the bearded Gordon told the producers.

"That's when they decided to go wide, while they had a nibble," says Rader. "They went everywhere, they just plastered it. And by Tuesday, Larry Gordon had made a preemptive bid to take it off the market. They negotiated it and got it." Stovitz also included a blind-script commitment with a high quote for a firsttime writer.

"I've got good news," Stovitz called Rader from his car phone with the story of the script's sale.

"It was surreal, how quickly it had happened," Rader says.

The revered Larry Gordon, while the forebear of modern action fare, has an avuncular demeanor and holds 1989's sentimental *Field of Dreams* (which he produced with his brother Chuck) closer to his heart than most of his huge action extravaganzas. Having gone from producing Roger Corman flicks and biker movies for American International Pictures to head of 20th Century–Fox (where he would eventually produce *Die Hard*), Gordon bought a couple of high-profile million-dollar specs that never got a green light. Scripts for *The Ticking Man* (a thriller about a man implanted with a ticking bomb) and *Texas Lead and Gold* (a *48 Hours* in the Old West) sat on Gordon's shelf as he looked for another high-profile project. He found it in *Waterworld*.

"I was totally thrilled. Like, what a Christmas present," thought

Rader, whose father and his family happened to be on their way to visit. "It was such a thrill. I literally picked them up in a limo, 'Wow! Let's celebrate.' I was really, really jazzed. Then in January we got down to the reality of development hell. I spent two years [in development] and wrote eight drafts. There was a director who came and went, but mostly it was writing for the studio. And in the course of that, I just totally lost my innocence as a writer. It was baptism by fire."

THE WATERLOGGED WORLD OF DEVELOPMENT

Nothing is free in Waterworld, according to Mariner. Social Darwinism rules the land—or in this case, the water—and Rader found that a Hollywood screenwriter's world isn't much different. "I was really naive," says Rader about the period when he sold his script. "I didn't even realize the distinction between selling a script and making a movie, to be totally honest. Not *that* naive, but I didn't realize the huge gap, the *giant* gap statistically, between studio films and development. What is it, one in thirty?" Yet throughout the development process, the structure and characters of Rader's original script remained intact.

"Another way in which I was naive was not realizing that many, many writers work on scripts," says Rader. "After I handed in my third draft, Andy and Jeff said, 'Hey, it's going well. They seem to really like you. They're keeping you on as the writer.' And I'm thinking, 'Well, of course, it's my script.' I didn't even realize that virtually every movie made has many writers on it . . . it's a very rare movie where there's one writer, or one team. . . . Selling a script with that amount of money, that was just so gigantic, I was not thinking at all about the realities of whether this movie was makable or wouldn't get made. I assumed it would."

Licht-Mueller initially budgeted *Waterworld* at $37 million, devising a number of cost-cutting techniques. Mueller says that his and Andy Licht's vision originally was to make a "Spaghetti Western" on water. "I think Peter's was to do a *Star Wars* on water. The final was a real amalgamation of the visions. . . . This production was so large. I would constantly think back to its simple beginnings of this mythic character in mythic times, with the good cowboys riding this boat in a race."

Reminiscing, Rader can hardly remember how the script was written, since "it just flowed." He didn't begin with an outline, but rather an idea for a first scene to depict a water-covered planet. "Okay, that's the world. Well, what's the coolest way of getting into a world like that? Is there a visual scene that would set up the whole universe in one picture, with no words?"

Rader conjured up the image of Mariner on a raft, purifying his own urine. "Now *that* tells you something about this world," says Rader.

That scene, which remained throughout the entire rewrite process, single-handedly launched Rader's writing of the script. "I knew I was working in a Western type of genre: I certainly thought about *Shane* as a template—the drifter comes into town, hooks up with the peaceful community, and then there's the bad [element] to attack it all. Then into that I layered in this other stuff. In *Shane* there's a little kid too." But in the case of *Waterworld*, Rader decided to make the child "the MacGuffin," carrying sought-after information in the form of a cryptic tattoo on her back.

"The statement about what we do to our planet, I think, is *extremely* important, and it didn't really make it into the movie," according to Rader. "Unfortunately, they decided not to use the most articulate way of stating that, [which is] one of my biggest regrets. I mean, there was some hope, there was wonder, there were classrooms, there were children . . . and more color. It wasn't all drab, so that there was a contrast between these two communities." The good guys' flotilla in Rader's version was not as dreadful as the one in the film.

In the original script, Mariner (played in the film by Kevin Costner) rescues the little girl Elona (Tina Majorino) from the pirate "smokers" and reaches what they think is an empty super-tanker. Reclaimed by nature, the huge rusting ship hosts various trees and a bird colony and, finally, a robed diminutive strange character, who welcomes Mariner, Elona, and Helen (Jeanne Tripplehorn) to his ship. His one requirement is that they remove their shoes, because fuel vapors are so volatile within the ship that friction from a single grain of sand could make the whole thing explode. The pirate smokers then arrive, and the heroes escape in the nick of time using a seaplane.

"At the last moment, they take off from the ship, and the pirate leader says, 'Triumph, the ship is mine!' You see a close-up of his foot, he skids, and there's this one grain of sand. And the whole fucking thing explodes. So the idea being: It's a metaphor inside the movie for what we did to the world to start the movie. In other words, by fighting over the world, we destroyed it. And so too, now we will fight over the ship, as opposed to living together.

"It was just a perfect metaphor," says Rader. "For whatever reason, they made some choices that were better, some choices that were worse. But that's one of the dangers of writing by committee, not honoring the single voice.

"I basically persevered through boundless naive enthusiasm and energy. The thrill of actually being a studio writer carried me, kind of fueled me, for, I would say, certainly the first year and a half of this process," says Rader. "At a certain point, it started catching up to me, and I kind of burnt out. That's what the process does to you; that's the really unfortunate thing. They literally consume writers. And unfortunately I burnt out just when it got exciting, just when Kevin Costner got interested. And I certainly could have kept working on it, but the studio perceived, 'Ahh, this guy's had it, he's done eight drafts, and we need a fresh voice,' and that's it."

THE RETURN OF ROBIN HOOD

"It was a *huge* thrill, the biggest movie star in Hollywood wants to make your movie," Rader recalls of a moment that was just one step below his joy in selling his script. "It was very exciting that Kevin Costner wanted it. But mind you, there were rumors—years' worth of rumors—that Kevin Costner was going to get involved. It was just unfortunate timing. I had a major accident, and I was actually in the hospital when I found out. I got a call from my agent. I wasn't even physically available, even if I'd wanted to be."

Along the path of the development of *Waterworld*, director Kevin Reynolds (a former attorney from Texas who attended USC's film program in 1979) had a look at the script a couple of years before he got involved. After making 1991's *Robin Hood: Prince of Thieves*, Reynolds was seeking out another project and always liked the concept of *Waterworld*. Kevin Costner starred in Reynolds's first picture, 1985's *Fandango*, which emerged from a USC short film by Reynolds that Steven Spielberg saw and then hired Reynolds to direct as a feature.

What was to happen to Reynolds during the making of *Waterworld* was somewhat reminiscent of his experience with 1984's *Red Dawn*.

Originally written under the title *Ten Soldiers,* Reynolds's script (his thesis at USC) was about kids in a small town witnessing Russian and Cuban military invaders round up their elders. It was designed as more of a *Lord of the Flies* than the shoot-'em-up action picture that resulted from United Artists' influence.

At this nascent stage of his career, Kevin Reynolds was bypassed as director. United Artists hired John Milius to direct *Red Dawn,* and every facet of the story began to change. "Yeah, I was not happy with the final outcome," says Reynolds of the passage of *Ten Soldiers.* "But how many writers are?" Even gun-enthusiast Milius, whose script for *Apocalypse Now* and *Jeremiah Johnson* earned him top Hollywood status, wasn't pleased with the studio's meddling on *Red Dawn.* But now with years of experience, and stellar success with *Robin Hood,* Reynolds had a passion to make *Waterworld* a reality.

What grabbed Reynolds's attention most was Rader's final scene, when Helen and the little girl Elona watch Mariner sail away, and Elona stumbles upon a plaque marking Sir Edmund Hillary's 1953 conquest of the summit of Mount Everest, the Earth's highest point. Reynolds felt it carried a *Planet of the Apes* resonance, as when Charlton Heston meets up with the Statue of Liberty, and although the scene was filmed, for reasons never explained to the director it was cut from the finished movie.

"I want to make an eco-fable," Reynolds called Peter Rader to say.

"That's great, that's *exactly* what I want," Rader replied.

Reynolds first contacted Larry Gordon, then developing the property. Unbeknownst to Reynolds, Kevin Costner had simultaneously approached Gordon with an interest in the script. But Reynolds and Costner had run into some clashes during *Robin Hood* and weren't looking to repeat it. So Gordon played mediator, putting "the two Kevins" in a room to work out differences. And they did. By then, Gordon had left Largo and with his projects set up a deal at Universal, through which *Waterworld* would be released.

"I had already gotten a little bit cynical," Rader recalls of the point the two Kevins were going to make the movie, "but it was tempered. Then basically I became an observer. That was kind of odd, that feeling. There were a couple of indignities that I now just accept as part of the business, things like not getting phone calls returned. It was literally *boom,* the next writer, close the door, [or] in reading the next guy and realizing that it was worse, just way, way, way worse. Of course, he was replaced. Then they got another guy. Then they got David Twohy, who did some good work."

As one of the higher-paid Hollywood scribes, David Twohy, screenwriter of *The Fugitive,* now enjoys the perks of success, although it was a long road from his 1979 graduation from Cal State Long Beach's film program. Working as a bartender with ambitions to direct, "I was still trying to auction my scripts through 'friends' and through guys who claimed to be producers, and it just wasn't happening. . . . I didn't get an agent for the first five years because I thought there was another way to break into the industry, trying to find a backdoor. After a while, that wasn't working . . . so then I said, 'Well I guess I'm going to be a screenwriter first, so let's get an agent as a screenwriter and go from there. And I made all the cold calls to agencies. Probably the toughest thing I've ever had to do.

"My first agent really did nothing. She was a one-woman agency, answered her own phones, who breast-fed her child and fed her dog *while* she was taking meetings with you," Twohy laughs. "After about a year of that, and I take *one* meeting with a Columbia story editor, I said, '*maayyy*be there's something better out there . . .' so I finally found an agency with carpet on the floor. And they started getting me work."

In early 1993, Reynolds contacted Twohy, who was then in Mexico researching locations for a feature he wrote called *Shockwave.* Released under the title *The Arrival,* the picture would be Twohy's feature directing debut. When Twohy returned to Los Angeles, he arranged a lunch on the Universal lot with Reynolds.

As Reynolds and Twohy talked about *Waterworld,* the writer was pleasantly surprised to see Costner sit down at the commissary table. After Costner introduced himself, the two Kevins asked Twohy about working on a rewrite; the existing plot line didn't effectively pull the story from one scene to the next. It was what Reynolds termed "a lot of running in place."

"I was interested in rewriting it, but I had obligations to Disney at the time," Twohy explains (*The Arrival* and *Terminal Velocity,* the latter of which was going into production at the time). Wanting to work on *Waterworld,* Twohy asked for a leave from his Disney obligations but the studio wouldn't let him out of his contract. So Reynolds went on to direct *Rapa Nui.*

"They took a shot at it with somebody else, and it wasn't working,"

Twohy recalls. "So they came back to me around September of '93." Reynolds was then posting *Rapa Nui* in Australia, so Twohy, by then freed up from work, spent a couple of weeks working with the director. The writer and Reynolds would confer in the mornings, and Twohy would work on the script in the afternoons while Reynolds edited. "It was a good time. I mean, Sydney, Australia, is a beautiful city. Universal put me up at the Ritz. It was very nice." At this point, Universal was moving forward with a production start date scheduled for eight months away, and an approved $100 million budget.

Universal provided Twohy with two of Rader's scripts, one being the original. "I was quite impressed with the breadth of originality and the level of detail that Peter had viewed this world with," says Twohy. "[But] I don't sit there and bemoan the fact that we're going to lose some rich material when the two guys that are *launching* this said, 'This doesn't work for us'. . . . It was my charge to find something different, and specifically my charge to bring better structure, especially to the middle of the piece.

"You lost sight of the goal of dry land in Peter's scripts, and [Reynolds and Costner] said 'Let's keep that goal as foremost in the audience's mind as we can, because that will make the whole center section feel less flabby and give it some purpose of direction," Twohy recalls, adding that other changes would strengthen the villain's character [played by Dennis Hopper]. Twohy whipped up a synopsis of the revised story, then two drafts of the screenplay. While it's unusual for the rewriter to take two passes, Universal by then was into this project for plenty of money and wanted to have a script they could begin shooting.

Twohy focused on the ecological elements; Reynolds had the idea to make the super-tanker the *Exxon Valdez,* and develop the pirate "smokers" into Neanderthal anti-environmentally concerned types to thus pit the two forces against one another. "By the time I handed in my second draft, this was a cohesive piece," says Twohy, "and I think to the director's satisfaction. . . . Then it went through other rewrites by other writers over his objection.

"Peter's was more of a pirate movie, and ecological movie," Twohy explains. "There was a lot of swashbuckling and knives in mouths and that kind of stuff, which was just scary to the two Kevins. They really didn't want to make a 'pirate movie.' They're more into the ecological thing. So *Mad Max* was bandied around by them a lot, but that wasn't a bad analogy because we all loved the movie."

What Reynolds desired most was to subtly insert analogies for contemporary ecological problems and states of mind, just as Rader initially envisioned. But at that time, Twohy was obligated to begin his preproduction phase on *The Arrival,* and only had minimal input thereafter. Then another writer made changes before the film went into production.

During the shoot, Universal hired Joss Whedon, writer of *Buffy the Vampire Slayer* and who would later write *Toy Story.* Because of Whedon's work on the blockbuster *Speed,* he entered the picture at a reported hundred grand for one week of script doctoring, and read the current script on the airplane. "They needed somebody to go out to the set, 'It'll just be a week, and you can go out to Hawaii, hang out with a big movie star, rewrite the movie, and it'll be fun,'" recalls Whedon of the assignment. "And I spent seven weeks in a tortuous hell.

"I thought it was a wicked, cool concept, or I would have never gone," says Whedon, who knew Chuck and Larry Gordon (from his $1 million spec sale of *Suspension,* about terrorists seizing control of a bridge during a traffic jam) and wanted the opportunity to work with them. "I thought that concept was unrealized, more or less, with what was there, and the last forty pages did not have any water. They ostensibly brought me in to streamline the climax so it was budgetable.

"Costner had done some work on it, Reynolds had done some work on it, so there were a lot of hands in it but no real clear vision about what exactly they wanted," says Whedon, whose assignment was stretched six extra weeks, "and I ended up not really being very useful, I think. I mean, I rewrote the climax, put in some set pieces and dialogue and some jokes, but in the end, I still don't think it was the movie it could've been.

"I've been on other movies where I felt the same thing, like I'm there to comfort people," Whedon concludes. "Because they're not actually using what I write and they're not really interested in making a change. They're just interested in papering over some of the cracks. . . . Quite frankly, at the end of [*Waterworld*] I was taking orders, the world's highest paid stenographer, and that's not useful. I don't want to do that anymore."

MAD MAX ON WATER REVISITED

When Kevin Reynolds first took on *Waterworld,* he disregarded Steven Spielberg's advice about the difficulties of making a movie on water. Spielberg should know; his first major picture, *Jaws,* filmed off the Martha's Vineyard shore, went 100 percent over budget and pushed its schedule from 55 days to 155. Most of *Waterworld* filmed off the shore of Kona, Hawaii.

The production encountered numerous problems, most notably when its flotilla set sunk into the ocean. Press reports flared up about an affair Costner was having during the shoot, which led to the end of his marriage. And Universal executives grew continually concerned about the project's spiraling budget (which escalated to $172 million), fearing they could never recoup their investment.

"You can't even begin to describe to anyone the difficulties you encounter when you're shooting on water until you're there and experiencing it firsthand," says Reynolds. The [production] process takes on an exponentially longer time when staged on water." Thus, the budget continued to rise, just what the water-based productions of Jan de Bont's *Speed 2* and Jim Cameron's *Titanic* would later also encounter. As one of the *Waterworld* crew members said, "It was like filming an avalanche while on an avalanche."

The press christened the project a bomb before anybody saw a frame of the movie, and Reynolds was upset that the media inaccurately reported so many rumors during the shoot. Renewed clashes between Costner and Reynolds further delayed the process as the media made attempts to infiltrate the set. "It just became this gigantic cause célèbre," the director reflects. "We were trying to operate under a microscope, basically."

"This was going to be their 'kiss and make up' picture, and it was going to get made, which always attracts a screenwriter," says David Twohy of his desire to work on *Waterworld.* "I had known Reynolds for some time and he is a rare guy in the industry in that he's a gentleman and thoughtful and always respectful of new ideas. He was a director I wanted to work with and develop stories with. Not all have his good story sense."

Both Twohy and Reynolds have mixed feelings about the final product. "I think there are some of the best action sequences on water that will ever be staged," says Twohy. "And the attack on the atoll was one of the greatest action sequences of all time. Then I think the story loses its focus, especially in the second half. I'm quite fond of the first half; the second half just gets meandering and sort of extraneous. You can just see the give and take, the push and pull between the director and the big star.

"Had Reynolds and I been left to our own devices to shape the story, it would have been a more cohesive thing," Twohy concludes. "But by the time the budget gets up to what it was . . . it was increasingly difficult to carry through a vision of the script. Time and again, you'll be asked to compromise that vision."

Says Joss Whedon, "I think the same of [*Waterworld*] as I think of almost every movie I see: 'Boy that would have made a good movie.' There was a good movie in there." But the natural process of a major studio production tends to dilute or destroy it.

"Being a Hollywood screenwriter is like climbing to the top of a really tall mountain," Whedon continues, "and finding out there's no view. Because the more high-profile the project, the more 'really-more-important' people [surround you]. When you have a giant movie star, a big production, and everybody crowding around you, you really can't see. It's, like, the more successful you are, the more frustrating it gets, to an extent, unless you're making your own movies."

Peter Rader succeeded in moving on to direct, starting with the Disney remake of *Escape to Witch Mountain* for ABC's Saturday Night Movie series. But he looks back with slight regret that *Waterworld* lost sight of its vision and potential. "There were five writers on it," says Peter Rader, "and [with] four of the five writers, a lot of whom are extremely talented writers, they still didn't solve the fundamental script problems. They kind of left them in there. So there are some bizarro tonal things in the final movie, like that Chitty-Chitty Bang-Bang dirigible thing. What the hell is that?

"Now personally, I don't really mind that, per se, as an element," Rader continues, "because in my original draft, I had a lot of fantastical things. There was a lot more of that flamboyant tone: the pirate leader sat on a clam-shell throne, carried a Trident, slept in a waterbed, and there were these visual touches. But in the course of *my* rewrites, of which I did eight, they kept saying, 'Make it grittier, make it more real, make it tougher, make it darker, make it this, make it that, make it more of a Larry Gordon movie, more guns! Guns! Darker! Darker! Grittier! Cyber-punk!' And I kept taking out, stripping all these elements out. I had fish, I had dolphins, just interesting creatures."

In his original script, Rader used birds as navigation devices, since if they did not return, then land must be in the direction they were heading. He also utilized the metaphor of water—the basis of life and what the humans fought over—surrounding everyone, yet there was not a drop to drink. Rader felt undercurrents of his initial story were lost in the reviews and media coverage, which focussed on the feature's excesses and not the film itself.

"I remember reading only one review that I thought was really good—not in the sense of being positive—but just intelligent," says Rader of *The New York Times Literary Supplement* review. "It was just very thoughtful, giving the movie completely the benefit of the doubt type of review. Pretty much every other single review that I read had at least one point reviewing the budget [and] Kevin Costner's marriage. . . . I mean, the film never really got to be just judged as a film. I hope people go back and rent the movie and try to watch it on a different level.

"Even though I think a lot of the themes, and more subtle mythological associations were butchered, there are still some in the movie," says Rader. "*The Times Literary Supplement* reviewer not only got them, but was willing to indulge them and consider the mythic construction and the metaphoric possibilities of such a movie. Even though on the surface, it's a completely commercial, crass action movie, it still has the possibility for metaphor."

By the time *Waterworld* premiered in late 1995, it seemed to have returned to the derivation of *Mad Max* that Corman's Brad Krevoy first suggested, but it happened to cost a lot more than $5 million to produce. *Waterworld* was a turning point in regard to a major studio's concerns for production spending. The ultimate *Waterworld* $172 million budget, plus $60 million in worldwide advertising and about $6 million in interest charges for the five years it remained in development, ran up a studio bill of about $232 million. The movie's worldwide theatrical gross is about $285 million (half of which goes back to the studio).

Yet by the end of the 1990s, studios hardly blink an eye at a $100 million price tag. When *Titanic* topped $200 million (doubling its original budget), it raised eyebrows and its production off Mexico's coast faced similar press-drubbing as *Waterworld*, but Jim Cameron's feature ultimately showed that the billion-dollar-plus box office results could justify such costs. Yet when United Artists made *Heaven's Gate* in 1980, on but a $40 million budget, its resulting lack of box office literally bankrupted the studio.

OPENING UP THE FUTURE FLOODGATE

"At the time I wrote *Waterworld,* basically, that was almost the beginning of my journey," Peter Rader reflects. "Back in 1989, my mother died, it was before *Waterworld* and I started to do a lot of work on myself. [The best training for the writer] is to get some insight into your own personal journey, the mythic paradigm through which you are the vessel.

"I think people still respond to the first draft of *Waterworld* as not just the concept, but because there's an innocence in the language," says Rader. "It was written so quickly and so fearlessly that there's an energy on the page. There's energy in the characters and the words. Some of it is corny and naive and silly, but still, there's something there. And the [studio development] process just homogenizes scripts, it kind of smoothes all the edges. I basically started doing that to my own material, and it *really* affected my writing. . . . I literally lost my craft, because I was so 'second-guessing' what the studios wanted. And it took me two or three years to go back to where I was when I wrote *Waterworld.*

"In the old days, the John Huston era, what a great guy he was," Rader continues. "He had so many careers: He was a boxer, he was a journalist, [and] he had so much life experience by the time he started making movies that he just brought this richness to them. And I love Spielberg, I think he's a great filmmaker. . . . He also was very gifted from the get-go."

But Rader feels the post-Spielberg generation led to a process of churning out filmmakers "where you thought you could go straight from school, sell a script, and basically start writing scripts before you know anything about life. The trouble with that [method] is that the scripts mostly become references to other movies. And Spielberg could get away with that because he's so gifted, he's so talented. But so many writers who followed, in my generation basically, started writing movies that mimic other movies.

"Let's do so-and-so into so-and-so, take this template; let's kind of write this movie, but let's make it a woman or take this and change that. So you're referencing [as] opposed to really getting into that scene on a personal level, which takes a lot more guts. It's a deeper descent, and you have to face a lot more demons, but ultimately, in the long run, anyone who wants to be a serious writer is going to have to face those demons and those battles, which means looking deep into yourself."

Peter Rader's screen-saver carries the floating message: Quantity Not Quality. "Other people have put it in many different ways, but it takes a long time to learn that lesson as a writer. You know, I'm such a perfectionist that I used to labor and labor and labor, write the first ten pages forty times. That's why I had all these half-finished scripts, because I was a perfectionist. It was about the form, it was about what's on the page rather than the content. So discipline is writing, writing, writing, no matter what comes out. And in that process—through that meditation—the [process of perfection] starts to happen. That is also about being in the world. Being real.

"It's mostly about realizing that things aren't accidents," Rader says. "One of the big realizations for me was that it's *not* an accident that I've become a writer. It's not a coincidence. It fell into my lap, yes, but for a reason. . . . I've been blessed, why? What is it that I'm supposed to write? I have an opportunity to get [my ideas] into the world, I've been given this, why? What is it that I need to channel? *That's* the work that writers need to do.

"That's the voice that you need to find. If you find that voice, then you're doing the work, then you are a real writer," Rader concludes. "And you're doing it every day. Discipline is very important, it's the first thing. Because you won't find the voice without the discipline. So that's number one: Write every day, work at it every day. Don't talk about being a writer, be a writer."

Awakening from the 14 *Dream Machine*

THE HOLLYWOOD GAME SPINS LIKE A WHEEL,
AND THE BUSINESS CHANGES DAILY.
AN INSIGHTFUL LOOK BY ITS PLAYERS
INTO WHAT THE FUTURE HOLDS.

The most important part in filmmaking is played by the writers. We must do everything in our power to keep them from finding out.

—IRVING THALBERG,
AS QUOTED BY *CASABLANCA* WRITER
JULIUS EPSTEIN AT A RECENT HEARING
ON WRITERS' RIGHTS

Only a generation of readers will spawn a generation of writers.

—STEVEN SPIELBERG

IN LATE 1926, screenwriter Herman Mankiewicz sent a wire to Ben Hecht asking, "Will you accept $300 per week to work for Paramount Pictures? All expenses paid. The $300 is peanuts. Millions are to be grabbed out here and your only competition is idiots. Don't let this get around." Hecht took his advice, and with Charles MacArthur wrote such features as the classic *The Front Page*. The prolific Mankiewicz, a heavy drinker and problematic gambler who enjoyed one of the most illustrious screenwriting careers in history, subsequently wrote *Citizen*

Kane, which won him and Orson Welles the Best Screenplay Oscar in 1942.

From Ben Hecht to Clifford Odets to Ernest Lehman to William Goldman, screenwriters have held a portion of the celebrity spotlight. Yet the huge spec sales today provide screenwriters a new type of attention. Following the buzz come the buzzards, the studio executives who eagerly hunt down blockbuster-producing writers by throwing big bucks to those with golden pens. "There is a new breed," says Spyglass's Jonathan Glickman, "and I think maybe people are getting known now for the money that they're making more so than the work that they're doing."

Motion pictures are the art of the middle. Neither high- nor lowbrow, they must integrate the desire for creativity with the needs of commerce to deliver a product for an audience almost as large as the population itself. The average cost of a studio motion picture today hovers at around $40 million, up 325 percent since 1980, and marketing costs escalated 386 percent during that period. With the spec market becoming more vital to the initial creation of many projects, it's no wonder that the money associated with the sales gets such a share of media attention.

"Every writer in this town benefits from every big sale," says *Mr. Holland's Opus* writer Patrick Duncan. "Because Joe Eszterhas got more money, I get more money. If Shane Black gets more money, I get some. Some unknown kid who was working at Vendome Liquors goes out and sells a script, that means everyone in town benefits.

"For a while there, before the spec market came up, the writer's piece of the pie was getting smaller as a percentage of the budget," says Duncan. "The directors were getting more money, the actors were getting more money, but the writers were getting less money. Because of that spec market and the big sales, the writers are starting to get parity again, and respect."

Or are they? Only about forty members of the WGA consistently make more than $1 million a year (about 1 percent of the guild's working members), and over half are unemployed. Some contend that the million-dollar-plus sales only raise prices for A-list writers, causing the middle ground to fall behind, making the focus on the big spec deals even more significant. "There will be fewer writers who will be hired on a daily basis, and *more* of them who are willing to sell original material to the studios," says APA agent Justen Dardis. The studios' greater likelihood of throwing $80 to $100 million at an event movie (called an "E-ticket" by Disneyland-raised boomers) means that, despite the million-dollar script sales, screenwriters may again be getting a smaller piece of the overall pie.

"There's going to be a smaller group of writers who the studios look to hire again and again—Paul Attanasio, Ron Bass, people like that," says Dardis. "It's a very select group and I think it will get smaller. But there's always going to be that golden opportunity for someone to come along and sell a great script for a lot of money. That's always going to exist, and I think the prices [in general] will get higher." The studios operate with a finite amount of development money, so that the multimillion-dollar sales ultimately take away from a number of smaller sales.

The singular vision of "classic movies" may have been aided by a particular studio's branding, wherein MGM was known for its musicals, Warner Bros. for its biographies and gangster pictures, Republic for its Westerns, and so on. But the "studio system," just like today, relied on a multitude of writers. Having thirty-two writers for 1994's *The Flintstones* might have been considered overkill, but it took ten of them to lead Dorothy Gale on 1939's journey to Emerald City in *The Wizard of Oz*. The studios tend to treat writers the same now as in Herman Mankiewicz's time. The primary difference today is that the words in his wire transfer have gotten around.

THE AFTERSHOCKS OF THE SPEC BOOM

A drive down L.A.'s Sunset Boulevard displays the empires resulting from the fleeting fortunes of a century of Hollywood moviemaking. From Sunset Boulevard's now dilapidated downtown origins, past Beverly Hills and Bel Air, to its dead end on the world's largest body of water, its serpentine path reminds one of the hapless screenwriter's journey in Billy Wilder's same-named 1950 classic. But there have been a few changes since.

The broken-down palace that belonged to aging screen siren Norma Desmond has probably been retrofitted for earthquakes by now, if not completely regutted by its current occupants. And the pictures that got smaller got bigger again, with wide-screen TV sets. But in Hollywood, a place that changes daily, it seems like the more things change the more they stay the same. While the spec market is cyclical, the screen-writers' talents in generating fresh material will always be the journey's impetus.

The outlook for Southern California's major industry couldn't be better, according to a recent UCLA study: From 1990 to the millennium, jobs in show business will have increased from 143,000 to over 262,000 (not including as many as 50,000 additional employees in related multimedia, theme park, music, and advertising production). It's a modern gold rush that continues to attract its miners, and it all starts with the written word.

"It's a division of the gambling business," says Miramax's Jack Lechner. "We are all gamblers by trade, and making movies is a gamble. Being gamblers, we want systems. We want to have a roulette system that allows us to have some illusion of control over what is in fact pretty close to blind chance. Market research is a roulette system, and having a star . . . and having a presold author or director, or making a sequel, is a roulette system.

"But still it's the ball going around the wheel; it could land in any one of those thirty-six spaces, and you have virtually no control over it," Lechner concludes. "Like what my old boss David Picker says, 'If I had said yes to all the movies I said no to, and no to all I said yes to, it would have worked out about the same.' "

As a risky business, filmmaking continually looks toward multitiered product enhancement, with studio features spinning out into every type of commercial tie-in available. At the dawn of Hollywood's corporatization, when parent companies such as Gulf + Western (taking over Paramount in 1966) and TransAmerica (buying United Artists) entered the game, studio heads "suddenly started going to conferences with the other companies of your conglomerate," says Leonard Goldberg, recalling his days running 20th Century–Fox.

"The truth is, it *isn't* like another business," says Goldberg. "It's different. And yes, there are costs involved, and yes, there should be profits involved. But beyond that it doesn't work like another business, it simply doesn't. I think that was part of the problem.

"Second, I think the level of talent running the studios on the operating level has declined over the years. Declined, because first of all they're not owned by filmmakers, movie business people, they're owned by corporations," Goldberg contends. "Corporations want different kinds of people running their situation, and passion went out of the business. The passion to make a good little movie went out of the business. The media became totally focused on the entertainment business, on the executives that made it work, much more so than in the past. . . . I know that people could argue with me and would probably get very upset with me, but I don't know. In my last round of the studios, I did not see Irving Thalberg, I simply didn't."

MGM's Thalberg, after all, was never subject to the approval of his corporation's financial overlord, Nick Schenck. Yet in today's environment, Goldberg knows of two studio heads who have been told not to make a picture unless they feel that it can make $100 million domestically. "That is their edict from their management. How the hell does anyone know? When I was running Fox, I used to say, 'Don't tell me how much money you think it's going to make, tell me you think it'll make a good movie. That building over there is the accounting building. That's all they do. They keep track of how much it makes. You don't have to. You're a creative person. You come up with something to say, 'I love this script. This will be a wonderful movie. That's your job.' "

It's unlikely that a feature such as *The Conversation* or *Midnight Cowboy* could get made in today's studio setting. So the independent world will likely be drawn upon more and more to provide the new Hollywood vision. As independent filmmakers enter on the riskier level—often after being rejected by the studios—the economic rewards can be tremendous; sometimes their pictures make them multimillionaires from just one success, rewards naturally greater than any studio would initially provide. Since independent filmmaking is driven by original material, just as the spec market is, the two systems will coexist to provide the variety audiences seek out.

"Any of the great screenwriters you can name didn't make their names on a huge commercial sale," says Miramax's Jack Lechner. "They made their names on writing something really good that made people admire them, that made people want to work with them. And if they had huge commercial movies, or even if that first movie was hugely commercial, it was a function of its being good."

Ernie Kovacs once described the entertainment industry's standard formula for success as: If something succeeds, beat it to death. When studios look for safer bets, the audiences sense it. "People can really smell compromise and a committee mentality," says director Steven Soderbergh. "Sometimes they don't care. Certainly there are plenty of successful films out that smell like that. But when it's a certain kind of film, I think they can smell it, and they don't like it; it's when they feel that [a film] was made cynically, that there wasn't somebody at the helm of this movie who really [cared] about what they were doing. People can feel a homogenized piece of 'product' when they watch it."

There will always be room for new companies entering the business, but they will likely depend on ties to larger distribution outlets, namely the studios, for support. "As soon as any company develops any success, in order to keep that success going they want to take *less* risk— usually by protecting the material in some way with stars, with their names, making it safer," producer Jonathan Sanger says. "Things are constantly evolving, things keep moving up and up and up. The larger studios become bigger and bigger and are less interested in material and more interested in making 'amusement parks.'

"*Jurassic Park* is an amusement park. So is *Batman*," says Sanger. "They are rides, they're not really stories anymore. We're not talking about character-driven pieces. The character-driven pieces are the tail, but the dog is really the amusement park. Those are the things that are getting made; they're bigger and bigger and better all the time. But it's a different level of filmmaking."

Because of new money influx into the industry it has become so expensive to make features, and sooner or later competitors have to respond to that, according to Spyglass's Jon Glickman. When companies enter the market with capital, the established players are "obligated to go in and spend $20 million if you want that same [talent], because that's what their price is. I still think writers are the most important aspects to making the movie work, and probably the least valued. It's the strangest paradox.

"Writers are probably the most safe going into the next world because stories are always going to stay the same," says Glickman. "You're always going to need to have a good story. The way it's going to be directed in the future may be different technology, and there may be a new type of director who needs to be able to tell stories. Whoever produces it may be different; the companies may change. But you're always going to need stories, and story construction has been the same since 600 B.C., or whenever. I don't see that aspect of the business changing. There's not going to be some new storytelling, so I think writers are the one constant."

TECHNOLOGICAL HOLLYWOOD

It was the spectacular nature of movies that drew audiences into theaters at the century's beginning. They didn't have dialogue, and their interest came from an ability to scare or excite viewers. Now one hundred years later, the process seems to have recurred with the proliferation of special-effects-driven pictures. Sound, beginning in 1927 with Warner Bros.' *The Jazz Singer,* also brought about substantial changes, as did the advent of color film stock.

The changes in show-business technology provide greater freedom for filmmakers to expand horizons. What became the art form of the twentieth century will become the cyber-playground of the twenty-first century. Silicon Graphics' "virtual set," a cost-cutting production tool, allows instant changes to the backdrop of any news or talk show. With such developments in technology, set decorators as we know them may no longer be needed, replaced by design-oriented computer wizards. With the proliferation of better movie theaters around the world comes a greater desire for the spectacle film. But the greater ease of making features with limited resources also bodes well for independent filmmakers.

"Technology drives *everything,*" says director John McTiernan of the popular use of electronic editing systems such as Avid, rather than traditional film cutting. "I won't call it a revolution, but there's been a change in the style of editing language—literally film language—in the last five years, often coming out of the two particular films that Oliver Stone did, *JFK* and *Natural Born Killers.* You can call it the MTV effect or whatever, but he managed to change what's accepted as film language for a mass-market audience; and that came out of that style. It's an artifact of the machine. I don't want to denigrate what he did, because he was the first one to do it and he did it extraordinarily well, but it was possible because of the machine. The machine eliminated the last vestige of reluctance to cut, the cost of cutting."

In the past, when editors put a slice in the work print or the original negative, making a change was both difficult and expensive. Prior to "nonlinear" editing, the last major change in the cinema language was in the mid-1960s "when Sam Peckinpah suddenly began having guys shot from forty different angles in *The Wild Bunch.* That was a change in the language when suddenly there were so many cut-cut-cuts," says McTiernan, who thought there must have been a similar technological change at the time. "I asked my cutter about it, speculating that maybe it was flatbed editing machines. . . . He said, 'No, it was tape splicers.' Prior to the mid-sixties, when you made an edit you had to physically cut the film with a pair of scissors and then glue it together in the splicer." If the cut didn't work, the editor would lose two frames on either side.

"There was a pressure against cutting when you weren't certain, and all of a sudden you could just slice it up, put a piece of scotch tape over it, and try it. So they did, and it changed the language," says McTiernan. "That something as tiny and insignificant as a tape dispenser hooked to a knife would revolutionize the cinema language is silly, but true. I think the same thing's happening with the computer cutting." While such aspects don't change an intrinsic story, they can have a tremendous effect on how the screenwriter's story is told. Thus, you hear more complaints of features bombarding an audience with visual imagery, while placing less importance on telling a good story.

Alternate visual tracks on digital video disc (DVD) systems have also allowed filmmakers to show portions of the work not available in the theatrical release. Director Joel Schumacher, able to add forty-five minutes to *Batman Forever* in his DVD version, also has a track with *Batman* creator Bob Kane talking about the picture. "That is phenomenal," said Schumacher in *Interview*, "because if you love film, a lot of what you're in love with is the process of it."

Says writer-director Peter Rader, "Now you really can conceive of anything . . . it's both daunting and liberating. Liberating in the sense that you can really be outrageous, but daunting in that you're going to have to work harder and harder to be original."

Those in today's generation take the computer for granted, and the ease of digital recording and manipulation allows greater freedom to create art not only for the masses, but also *by* the masses. Technology opens the writer's mind to worlds unimaginable and may eventually put the screenwriter in control of a process once limited to directors and actors.

THE LONG HAUL UP THE MOUNTAIN

Like the footprints in the courtyard of Mann's Chinese Theater, or the stars along the sidewalk of Hollywood Boulevard, every screenwriter's hope is to leave a permanent mark in shaping future dreams. While four or five years can be the average it takes a producer to bring a script to screen, Marvin Worth, beginning in 1967, pursued *Malcolm X* until it was made into a movie by Spike Lee in 1992.

Harriet the Spy took twenty-two years to reach the screen, *Mrs. Doubtfire* spent nine years in active studio development, and George Miller sat on *Babe* for over a decade until the technology caught up. Likewise, Clint Eastwood hung on to David Webb Peoples's *Unforgiven* for ten years so he would be the right age for the part, and 1998's hit *There's Something About Mary* was also a dormant script, which the Farrelly Brothers punched up and made into a blockbuster.

"As far as spec sales go, the trades feed the mythology that everything goes out and sells in a matter of hours for a large sum," says Debra Hill president Barri Evins. "That's not correct. I think that almost all of us believe it, or buy into that myth, because that's what we read on the front cover of the trades, because those are the dynamic stories."

A filmmaker's patience in nurturing a script (and an executive's or producer's role in acting as a midwife to provide safe birth to a writer's baby) generally results in the best pictures. "Just pick a movie, and you'll find that basically the history of it is that it's been rejected over and over and over and struggled for," says director Tony Bill. "Pick any flop, and you'll probably find, 'Oh, we got to make it right now, we gotta pay seven figures, write a check, hire him up, get into production, rush it out. Be there by Christmas." While the long wait can be discouraging to screenwriters, the rush can be all the more discouraging to audiences, who grow critical of Hollywood formulaic films, but continue to buy into their box office.

Because today's media machinery has so greatly concentrated on weekend opening grosses, audiences are less likely to wait for a feature to prosper, as 1981's *Arthur* did, taking three weeks to find an audience. Today *Arthur* would have been yanked. "The movie [today] has to declare itself a hit opening weekend, or it's gone," says producer Mark Johnson. "With every paper in the country reporting on its grosses, everybody wants to see a hit. They don't want to see a flop."

Likewise, executives are drawn to a spec script's heat and too often might abandon their interest if a sale appears unlikely. Metaphorically speaking, the hype placed on selling scripts is like hot air being blown into a balloon, and the script is the strength of the balloon. The more hot air and the weaker the material, the more likely the sale will explode. The stronger scripts therefore have a resilience to command huge sales if they have the goods. Everyone in Hollywood bemoans the fact that it's difficult finding a good balloon.

"From the time I entered this business, until today, there's always, *always* been a dearth of material," says producer Leonard Goldberg. "That is why there's such pressure on these spec scripts. There are not *nearly* enough scripts, therefore not nearly enough writers who can write a good script. So I think if you're a good writer, and you have an idea, boy, this business is *yearning* for you."

It's an old adage that if you write a great script, you can throw it out your car window on the Hollywood freeway and it will find its way to a filmmaker who will recognize it. "I've never read a wonderful script that hasn't either gotten made," says Tony Bill, "or served its purpose in establishing its writer's credentials." As with the examples this book provides, in today's spec market any script has the potential to become a bona fide motion picture. But the screenwriter generally only acquires a relative power in the industry after a string of successfully produced pictures.

Of the historical emphasis placed on "the filmmaker" as auteur, says writing instructor John Truby, "they build up this incredible mythology about the brilliance that these guys are bringing to shooting a picture when they're going from a script that's already been written. As long as those [filmmakers] get the money and get the power, how can you possibly think that there's going to be an improvement? As long as you have the current development system, you're going to get that level of thinking. Obviously it's the 'art versus money' type of problem, but in any art form, as long as the original creator is not controlling the end product, then you have art by committee. That's the result that you will have."

It's a tremendous help, especially today, to have some experience in the system to know what it takes to write a spec script. Lee and Janet Scott Batchler, who worked as freelance readers before breaking through by writing *Smoke and Mirrors,* contend their prior work "was very formative because we learned right off that most writers don't think through their projects from the point of view of the producer. I recommend to any of my writer friends, if you have the chance, take a job in development. All writers should take a job in development, at some point, just to know what it's like to be on the other side of the desk."

According to Columbia Pictures' Doug Belgrad, the only thing writers need to know is that persistence pays off. "No matter how much talent you have, you've got to stick with it. No matter how little talent you have—if it's a good idea, and you're persistent—it's such a competitive environment that people will find a way to get to the material and buy it.

"Ultimately, it's just hard for writers, from their perspective, to differentiate between what's a great idea worth sticking with, and what's something that's not getting a response for a reason," Belgrad concludes. "You can't tell people when to quit or when to go on, because for the most part, it's just a strange beast."

The beast builds both the blockbusters and the bombs. What ultimately makes a motion picture special and memorable is the degree to which it maintains its vision. Passion always drives the process, but purity is maintained by those individuals who keep the film's integrity in a world more driven by making big bucks.

This book has profiled the play-by-play journeys of five remarkable features, with increased budgets in each successive example. From the $17 million risked on *While You Were Sleeping,* for which its buyers never expected such universal success, to the $83 million *Last Action Hero,* which looked like the sure bet, there's a lesson to be learned: Preserving an initial vision—whether it be because of the script, the director, or the star—results in a feature of which its participants are most proud. The champions of these scripts have fought their way through Hollywood's labyrinth by protecting the writer's (or writers') singular voice, and when the voice was deafened by the beast of the Hollywood system, it resulted in features that not only performed poorly, but left their participants often sorely disappointed.

Success at writing comes from doing, not dreaming. Despite the obstacles the film community imposes on its entrants, the maxim remains: "In Hollywood, it's not who you know, it's who knows you, and it's not what you know, but what you do."

At a recent seminar, an individual planning to embark on a Hollywood screenwriting career asked panel member Clyde Phillips for advice on how to become a successful writer. Phillips, a clever television producer and novelist who taught college-level English before entering the industry, simply replied, "There's one way to become a writer," followed by silence.

for up-to-date information
go to
www.bigdealnews.com

Appendix: Some of the Book's Players

Jeff Apple, producer of *In the Line of Fire*

David Arnott, cowriter of *Last Action Hero*

Paul Attanasio, writer of *Donnie Brasco, Quiz Show;* creator of TV's *Homicide*

Lee and Janet Scott Batchler, cowriters of *Smoke and Mirrors* and *Batman Forever*

Doug Belgrad, senior vice president of production, Columbia Pictures

Bruce Berman, chairman/CEO of Village Roadshow Pictures

Tony Bill, producer of *The Sting, Taxi Driver;* director of *Five Corners, Untamed Heart, My Bodyguard,* and *A Home of Our Own;* works often with first-timers

Roger Birnbaum, chairman of Spyglass Entertainment (formerly Caravan Pictures)

Shane Black, screenwriter of *Lethal Weapon, The Last Boy Scout,* and *The Long Kiss Goodnight*

Bill Block, president of Artisan Entertainment

Les Bohem, screenwriter of *Daylight* and *Dante's Peak*

Pam Bottaro, development executive who first discovered *Smoke and Mirrors*

Cary Brokaw, chairman/CEO of Avenue Pictures responsible for *The Player, Short Cuts,* and *Restoration;* former 20th Century–Fox executive.

Rob Carlson, William Morris agent responsible for selling numerous specs

Phyllis Carlyle, producer of *Seven* and *The Accidental Tourist;* runs a management company repping many international filmmakers

Dennis Cline, attorney at Behr & Abramson; reps many top directors and producers

Robert Cort, producer, The Cort/Madden Company

Jim Crabbe, William Morris agent who sold the spec scripts for *While You Were Sleeping, The Hand That Rocks the Cradle,* and *Tombstone*

Wes Craven, creator, writer-director of *Nightmare on Elm Street;* other movies include the *Scream* series, *The Hills Have Eyes, The Serpent and the Rainbow, Shocker*

Justen Dardis, literary agent at Agency for the Performing Arts; sold the spec scripts for *Only You* and *Cliffhanger*

John Davis, chairman, Davis Entertainment Company

Michael DeLuca, president/COO, New Line Cinema

Patrick Duncan, screenwriter of *Courage Under Fire, Mr. Holland's Opus, Nick of Time;* director of the low-budget films *84 Charlie Mopic, The Pornographer*

Barri Evins, president of Debra Hill Productions

Pat Faulstich, agent at Broder-Kurland-Webb-Uffner

David Fincher, director of *Seven* and *The Game*

David Friendly, head of Friendly Productions

Alex Gartner, senior vice president of Fox 2000; bought *Courage Under Fire*

Alan Gasmer, William Morris Agent responsible for selling numerous major spec sales, including *Smoke and Mirrors*

Jonathan Glickman, president of production for Spyglass Entertainment; produced a number of films at Caravan, including *While You Were Sleeping*

Liz Glotzer, president of production, Castle Rock Films, bought *In the Line of Fire*

Leonard Goldberg, producer (*Sleeping with the Enemy, WarGames*) and former president of production, 20th Century–Fox, under Barry Diller; also produced a number of television series with Aaron Spelling (*Charlie's Angels*)

David Goldman, producer and manager at Spivak Entertainment; former ICM and William Morris agent

Janet Goldstein, union studio reader

Charles Gordon, producer at Daybreak Productions

Lawrence Gordon, Universal-based producer

David Greenblatt, agent and partner at Endeavor

Rima Greer, agent and owner of Above the Line; former head of motion picture literary department at Writers & Artists agency

Peter Guber, chairman of Mandalay Pictures

Jacques Haitkin, cinematographer of *Nightmare on Elm Street, Cherry 2000, Shocker*

Dan Halsted, president of production, Illusion Entertainment Group (Oliver Stone); former senior vice president, Hollywood Pictures, who bought *While You Were Sleeping*

Ross Hammer, producer and former development executive with Sean Cunningham and Addis-Wechsler production and management company

John Lee Hancock, screenwriter of *A Perfect World* and *Midnight in the Garden of Good and Evil;* creator of TV's *L.A. Doctors*

Lynn Harris, senior vice president of New Line Cinema, bought *Seven* and produced *Blade*

Nicholas Hassitt, screenwriter, producer, and former Disney development executive

George Huang, director of *Swimming with Sharks* and *Trojan War*

Scott Immergut, former president of production at Sandollar and Disney exec who shaped much of *In the Line of Fire* before it sold to a competing company

J. J. Jamieson, head of Avenue Pictures Television; former director of development, NBC movies and miniseries

Mark Johnson, producer, *A Little Princess, Donnie Brasco, Diner, A Perfect World, Home Fries, Rain Man*

Barry Josephson, partner at Sonnenfeld/Josephson

Michael Kalesniko, won a screenwriting contest in film school and has made a living on spec and writing assignments since; wrote *Private Parts*

Jeffrey Katzenberg, partner in Dreamworks SKG

David Koepp, screenwriter of *Bad Influence, The Paper* (with brother Stephen), *Jurassic Park, The Shadow, Mission: Impossible, The Lost World,* and *Snake Eyes*

Arnold Kopelson, producer/CEO of Kopelson Entertainment

Robert Kosberg, producer of *Twelve Monkeys, Man's Best Friend;* known as a pitch specialist

Brad Krevoy, copresident, Motion Picture Corporation of America

Sandy Kroopf, screenwriter of *Birdy*

Scott Kroopf, president of production, Interscope Communications, which produced *Mr. Holland's Opus, Bill & Ted's Excellent Adventure,* and *Jumanji*

Fredric Lebow, cowriter of *While You Were Sleeping*

Jack Lechner, executive vice president, production and development, Miramax Films

Adam Leff, cowriter of *Last Action Hero*

Andrew Licht, producer of *Waterworld, The Cable Guy,* and *Idle Hands*

George Litto, producer of *Blow Out, Thieves Like Us;* former agent representing such talents as Robert Altman, Ring Lardner, and Dalton Trumbo

John McTiernan, action-adventure director of *Die Hard (I and III), Last Action Hero, Predator, Medicine Man, Hunt for Red October, The 13th Warrior,* and the remake of *The Thomas Crown Affair*

Jeff Maguire, screenwriter of *In the Line of Fire*

Frank Marshall, producer/director of Kennedy/Marshall Company

Mike Medavoy, chairman of Phoenix Pictures

Ricardo Mestres, producer, Ricardo Mestres Productions

Clark Moffat, former literary agent, producer, and nonunion reader

Chris Moore, agent who sold *Last Action Hero,* produced *Glory Daze,* and coproduced *Good Will Hunting*

Thom Mount, producer of *Bull Durham, Death and the Maiden,* and *Night Falls on Manhattan;* partner at Mount/Kramer Productions

Jeffrey Mueller, producer of *Waterworld, The Cable Guy,* and *Idle Hands*

Michael Nathanson, president of MGM

Michael Nolin, producer of *Mr. Holland's Opus* and *84 Charlie Mopic*

Gianni Nunnari, president of production, Cecchi Gori Films (formerly Penta)

Sanford Panitch, senior vice president, 20th Century–Fox; bought *Seven* while working for Kopelson

Zak Penn, cowriter of *Last Action Hero* and popular script doctor; sold spec script *Suspect Zero* to Universal for $750,000 against $1 million

Wolfgang Petersen, director/producer at Radiant Productions (*Air Force One, Outbreak, In the Line of Fire*)

David Phillips, agent at Innovative Artists; former producer at Davis Entertainment; Willam Morris agent who sold *While You Were Sleeping* and *Jack*

Gavin Polone, agent who sold *Seven;* partner at Hofflund/Polone

Peter Rader, original screenwriter of *Waterworld*

Kevin Reynolds, director of *Waterworld, Fandango, Robin Hood: Prince of Thieves, 187*

Jeff Robinov, Warner Bros. senior vice president; former ICM agent known for selling a number of specs

Stu Robinson, agent/partner at Paradigm Agency; sold the scripts for *E.T.: The Extra-Terrestrial* and *Slap Shot;* represents independent filmmaker John Sayles

Hal Ross, veteran agent turned producer (former partner with the late Evartz Ziegler)

Jonathan Sanger, producer of *The Elephant Man, Frances,* and *Without Limits;* director of network movies; cofounded Chanticleer Discovery Program, giving seasoned writers, editors, and talent a shot at directing short films; now based at C/W Productions

Arthur Sarkissian, producer of *Rush Hour, Last Man Standing;* executive producer of *While You Were Sleeping*

Charles Schlissel, coproducer of *While You Were Sleeping*

Peter Scott, development executive turned literary manager

Walter Shenson, producer of *Hard Day's Night, Help!, Echo Park,* and *Reuben, Reuben*

Ron Shusett, cowriter of *Alien, Total Recall, Freejack,* and *Above the Law*

Tom Sierchio, writer of *Untamed Heart*

Sigurjon "Joni" Sighvattson, former president of Lakeshore Entertainment; cofounder of Propaganda Films; prolific producer of music videos

Joseph Singer, producer of *Courage Under Fire, Dante's Peak, Daylight, Doctor Dolittle*

Steven Soderbergh, director of *sex, lies and videotape* and *Out of Sight*

Jay Stern, senior vice president of New Line Pictures; as an executive for Hollywood Pictures bought *Smoke and Mirrors*

Ken Stovitz, agent at Creative Artists Agency, formerly with ICM

Tom Strickler, agent and partner at Endeavor

Roger Strull, agent and partner at Preferred Artists Agency

Daniel G. Sullivan, cowriter of *While You Were Sleeping*

John Truby, runs a popular Hollywood course on story structure

Jon Turteltaub, director of *While You Were Sleeping, Cool Runnings, Phenomenon*

Andy Vajna, president of Cinergi; partner in new company with Mario Kassar

Christopher Vogler, director of development, Fox 2000

Lew Weitzman, television agent/partner at Preferred Artists

Jonathan Westover, agent at The Gage Group, a talent and literary agency

Joss Whedon, writer-producer, Mutant Enemy (*Buffy the Vampire Slayer*)

Kurt Wimmer, former cabdriver who has a couple of million-dollar spec sales

Janet Yang, partner in Manifest Film Company; former president of Ixtlan (Oliver Stone)

Jeremy Zimmer, agent/partner at United Talent Agency who sold *In the Line of Fire*

Index

and episodic specs, 64
talent arising from, 234
as writer's medium, 234–235
television movies, 235–242
cable networks and, 252–254
as concept driven, 236–237
crossover between features and, 240
development-to-production ratio in, 235
movies of the week (MOWs), 237
prices paid for, 239–240
remade as movies, 241–242
target audiences for, 237, 238
time frame for features vs., 240–241
true-life stories in, 238–239
variety in, 235–236
viewer numbers and, 236
writers of, 235, 238
Temple, Shirley, 51
"tent poles," franchises and, 70
Terminal Velocity, 274
Terminator, The, 60, 76
Terms of Endearment, 88
Tesich, Steve, 47
Texas Lead and Gold, 14, 122, 123, 262, 269
Thalberg, Irving, 282, 286
Theater of Blood, 107
Thelma & Louise 2, 184
There's Something About Mary, 290
Thieves Like Us, 59
13th Warrior, The, 76
Thomas, Diane, 10
Thomas, Kristen Scott, 181
Thomas Crown Affair, The, 51
Thompson, Michael, 8, 262
Thornton, Billy Bob, 119
Thorp, Roderick, 70
Three Days of the Condor, 136
Three Musketeers, The, 40
Three Ninjas, 36
Thurman, Uma, 207
Ticking Man, The, 14, 95, 262, 269
Time-Warner, 1, 159
Titanic, 17, 277, 279–280
Tolkin, Michael, 164, 225
Tombstone, 28
Tomei, Marisa, 29, 33, 66
Tootsie, 29, 81
Total Recall, 9, 19, 75, 90, 125–126
Touchstone, 30, 31, 61, 200
Towering Inferno, The, 59
Tower Records, 93, 94, 96, 106
Towne, Robert, 168
Townsend, Robert, 246
Toxic Avenger, 65
Toy Story, 276

trackers, 55–58, 133
agents and, 57
anticompetitiveness of, 178
as networkers, 55–56, 57–58
secretiveness of, 56–57
TransAmerica, 285
Travolta, John, 234
Triad Artists, 128
Trigger Effect, The, 110
Trimark, 187
Tripplehorn, Jean, 271
Trip to Bountiful, A, 240
TriStar Pictures, 2, 3–4, 39–40, 44, 108, 126, 155, 180, 190, 194, 197, 198, 199, 200–202, 223
Truby, John, 17, 79, 117, 118, 186–187, 291
True Blue, 112
Truffaut, François, 235
Truman, Harry, 183
Truman Show, The, 19
turnaround, 89–91
screenwriters and, 89–90
and studio negotiations, 89–90
Turner, Kathleen, 10
Turner, Ted, 98, 159
Turner companies, 81, 253
Turow, Scott, 228, 230
Turteltaub, Jon, 20, 36–37, 41, 42, 45
TV Guide, 236
Twelve Monkeys, 61
20th–Century Fox, 9, 10, 11, 15, 24, 28, 47, 51, 70, 74, 98, 126–127, 173, 182, 200, 206, 234, 245, 248, 255, 269, 285, 286
subdivisions of, 60, 61
Twenty Bucks, 64
Twilight Zone, The, 234
Twin Peaks, 256
Twister, 136
Twohy, David, 121, 264, 274–276, 277–278

Under Siege, 69
Unforgiven, 130, 131, 290
United Artists, 273, 280, 285
United Talent Agency, 16, 28, 36, 57, 92, 95, 96, 107, 120, 141, 142, 149, 158, 195, 234
Universal Pictures, 23, 25, 46, 52, 59, 68, 85, 89, 92, 93, 95, 96, 224, 228, 237–238, 245, 248, 253
Waterworld and, 264, 275, 277
Untamed Heart, 52, 66
Untouchables, The, 75, 169
USA cable, 240, 253

About the Author

THOM TAYLOR produced television news before moving to Los Angeles to write for such magazines as *Variety, Locations,* and *Millimeter.* He also wrote the first article for *Movieline* and has worked several years in the industry for such filmmakers as Oliver Stone, Thom Mount, and Tim Burton. He currently mines the spec market at an L.A. talent and literary agency.